The Succession Challenge

The Succession Challenge

Building and Sustaining Leadership Capacity through Succession Management

Dean Fink

Los Angeles | London | New Delhi
Singapore | Washington DC

ONTARIO
PRINCIPALS'
COUNCIL
Exemplary Leadership
in Public Education

CORWIN
A SAGE Company

SAGE Publications Ltd
1 Oliver's Yard
55 City Road
London EC1Y 1SP

SAGE Publications Inc.
2455 Teller Road
Thousand Oaks, California 91320

SAGE Publications India Pvt Ltd
B 1/I 1 Mohan Cooperative Industrial Area
Mathura Road
New Delhi 110 044

SAGE Publications Asia-Pacific Pte Ltd
33 Pekin Street #02-01
Far East Square
Singapore 048763

Library of Congress Control Number: 2009936314

British Library Cataloguing in Publication data

A catalogue record for this book is available from
the British Library

ISBN 978-1-84860-695-1
ISBN 978-1-84860-696-8 (pbk)

Typeset by C&M Digitals (P) Ltd., Chennai, India
Printed in Great Britain by TJ International Ltd, Padstow, Cornwall
Printed on paper from sustainable resources

Mixed Sources
Product group from well-managed
forests and other controlled sources
www.fsc.org Cert no. SGS-COC-2482
© 1996 Forest Stewardship Council
FSC

To Ramona, the best is yet to come

Contents

Acknowledgments

This book was a team effort, although the participants didn't know they were even part of a group. The members of this virtual assemblage of expert players live in many parts of the world, perform many different roles in education, and helped me in so many ways that I would need an entire chapter just to document their contributions. When I had questions, they responded promptly and in detail. When I needed second opinions, they were candid and thoughtful. When I was losing the plot, they set me straight; and when I got discouraged, they were encouraging and supportive. I didn't always take their advice, and I suspect I have misinterpreted some of their suggestions, so I can't blame them for any mistakes. They are mine alone. Words cannot express my indebtedness to the following members of my "team".

My thanks to my co-author on many projects and my mentor, Andy Hargreaves, for encouraging me to undertake this project, for writing a foreword to the book, and for being such a great "critical friend." My long-time colleague, writing partner, and friend Louise Stoll was a great help in devising my research strategy. Peter Gronn not only read some of my chapters, but directed me to a great body of important literature with which I was unfamiliar. Dennis Shirley, Alma Harris, Brent Davies, Corrie Giles, Paul Chung, Kathy Lacey, Judy Scotney, Norman McCulla, Tony D'Arbon, Bill Mulford, Gerald MacCruic, Warren Marks, Reynold Macpherson, David Eddy, Graeham Kennedy, Pasi Sahlberg, Paul Duckworth, Larry Sackney, Paul Hatala and Wendy Jackson were all a part of my virtual team who in one way or another responded patiently to my incessant inquiries. I greatly appreciate their advice, critical questions, and scholarship. I also value Dee Romberger's quick and accurate transcriptions of my interviews.

I'm grateful to Linda Massey of the Ontario Principals' Council. Linda was instrumental in gaining the support of OPC for this venture and has been my ongoing liaison. Marianne Lagrange of Sage Publications has been a great support in this undertaking and in *Leadership for Mortals*, and her assistant Monira Begum has deftly and with great tact finessed the difficult task of making sure I did what was required to get the book to print.

While confidentiality prevents my naming them, I'm deeply beholden to the senior leaders in the three school jurisdictions that had the courage and confidence to let me dig into their succession practices. I am especially appreciative of the many principals, school heads, and assistants who filled in my questionnaire and gave up time from very busy schedules to provide me with their insights into leadership succession. They were an impressive lot.

To my daughters, Danielle and Tracy, and my grandsons, Zach and Riley, thanks for making me so obnoxiously proud. To my wife of 47 years, who has put up with my obsessive commitment to this project for the past two years, and my eccentricies for a lot longer than that, words cannot express my appreciation and love. Here's to the next 47 Ramona.

The author and publisher would like to thank the following for permission to use figures in the book:

Hargreaves, A. and Fink, D. (2005) *Sustainable Leadership*. San Francisco, CA: Jossey-Bass. Reprinted by permission of the publisher John Wiley & Sons, Inc.

Foreword

By Andy Hargreaves

We are finally waking up to at least some of the challenges of leadership succession in education. After decades of complacency, when we acted as if our leaders would stay at their posts forever, we now realize that the Boomer generation of leaders is moving on and that about half of our existing leaders (the exact numbers depend on the study) will be retiring very soon.

In state after state and nation upon nation, people are rising to the urgent challenge of preparing the next generation of school leaders. Everywhere I go, across the US, up to Canada, or over to Britain or Australia, there are programs to support and develop young, emerging, or aspiring leaders. The quality varies but the philosophy is the same. Spot those with leadership potential or aspirations early on. Develop their talent, provide intensive support, and push them as fast as possible along the leadership pipeline towards the principalship and beyond.

This is good enough as far as it goes. But in a few years, the crisis will be over. The problem of generational succession will be resolved. There will be a big enough pool of leaders. Hopefully, most of the people in it will be capable and qualified. Everyone will then breathe easy again for another 20 years!

However, solving the problem of generational succession does not solve the enduring issues of leadership succession that impact on individual leaders, on the schools that they lead, and on the systems that hire and fire them and also move them around.

Make no mistake about it. One of the most significant events in the life of a school is when it undergoes a change in leadership. Yet few things in education succeed less than leadership succession. We repeatedly mismanage or overlook it – often with disastrous consequences for students, teachers, and the likelihood of lasting improvement.

Inspiring leaders often lift their schools, only to see the gains disappear when mediocre successors follow them. Heroic leaders may perform miracles in turning schools around, but there is often no broader capacity to maintain the improvements after the leaders have gone. Urban superintendents can keep changing the leader in a desperate effort to revive a struggling school, but teachers just become more cynical and entrenched as they realize their leaders won't last.

Thousands of new charter schools may start spectacularly under their first principals because they can set their own agenda and hand pick their own teachers, but the ensuing leaders then have to take on their predecessor's existing legacy and aging staff, and the improvement curve starts to fall away. Then there are those principals who move to lead a new school and take their best people with them – robbing the capacity of the school they have left behind. These are just some of the challenging succession scenarios I have witnessed and that regularly arise in our schools.

There is a silence about these enduring issues of succession and it is time break it. Among the matters on which we keep quiet are:

- Succession is rarely planned and prepared for in advance; it is usually a reactive, rushed-together process when leaders retire early, get promoted or have to leave in a hurry.
- Many schools and principals do not prepare enough successors behind them. They groom a few who seem to have potential to follow them rather than cultivate the many who can lead together.
- Top-down change and reform strategies deter new candidates; leaders worry they will be implementation managers rather then inspiring leaders; pressures in urban schools make them feel they will be excessively vulnerable; and innovations often promote a few coordinators into the local office rather than spreading leadership opportunities to many teachers who get small amounts of release time to learn to lead together.
- The emotional upsets of succession, of facing the end of work, abandoning a community that has loved you, or even worrying about your mortality, are often borne alone without any legitimate place to discuss them.
- Appointments and reassignments are acts of power. Moving principals is often done with the best interests of the leader, the school, and the system in mind. Like ambassadorial appointments, though, it is also a device to reward loyalty, punish dissent with a distant or unfavorable assignment, and send out warning signals to the rest. Succession decisions are a political privilege that no-one wants to give up.

Not all succession processes and events are this dysfunctional. There are principals and systems that know how to build powerful communities behind them who continue to hold the torch long after their leader has gone. There are others so comfortable in their own skins that they know just when to let go. But without strong systems, increased transparency, and greater emotional honesty and support, many of us handle succession moments badly – in relation to others and also in terms of ourselves.

This is why Dean Fink's book is so powerful and important. In an incomprehensibly barren field, Dean Fink has written the most significant, penetrating, and well-supported account of leadership succession there is. This is not an evaluation of programs or of initiatives, but an analysis of how succession is handled in practice and often in secret, all the time.

There are few more qualified or credible people who could write a book such as this and carry out the work on which it is based. I first met Dean Fink when I was new to Canada in the late 1980s, and, as a district superintendent, he generously opened up access to a cluster of schools in his district that were focusing on collaborative planning. Even then, Dean was no ordinary district administrator. Working energetically to support professional collaboration in his schools, and to develop a systematic but also humanistic approach to school effectiveness and improvement across his district, he promoted continuous inquiry as an impetus for improvement.

Dean Fink connected with some of the most cutting edge expertise in the field, bringing the world's leading experts to international conferences he ran in his district, highlighting its achievements without ever allowing it to rest on its laurels. Among the early founders of the International Congress for School Effectiveness and Improvement, Dean was also a spearhead for connecting research on effectiveness and improvement to the system-wide practice of it. He was a leader of district-level change and systemic reform long before these words became fashionable. One of his staff at this time was Louise Stoll and together, drawing on their research and developmental expertise in the Halton Board of Education, they authored one of the most powerful and practical books on school improvement, *Changing Our Schools*.[1]

One of Dean's other responsibilities was for principal rotation between schools – then an unusual and enlightened strategy to try and move principals every five years or so, in a way that developed their leadership capacities, matched their skills to the needs of particular schools, and developed the overall leadership capacity of the system in doing so. I have met and continue to meet many senior system leaders – men and women – in Canada who were and still are the grateful beneficiaries of the support and mentoring that Dean

Fink offered his upcoming leaders. As Dean has later come to realize and the research in this book shows, principal rotation wasn't a perfect system, but at the time it was introduced, it was undoubtedly a progressive one.

In his mid 50s, as an avid and energetic learner, Dean decided, a little later than most, that he would like to undertake a doctorate. I was fortunate enough to be the supervisor of this unlikely student who was more than a year or two ahead of me. By training and by passion, Dean was and is an accomplished historian, and after scanning around for a topic, he settled on studying – in a way – himself over time.

Dean was connected with, and in some ways was also responsible for, what had been one of Canada's most innovative secondary schools. At different times he had worked there as a teacher, a department head, and a deputy principal, and was later responsible for it under his superintendency. Dean was puzzled about why and how this remarkable school lost its lustre over the years – from being one of the shining lights of the country, to becoming an institution that was almost indistinguishable from others around it. Dean interviewed a substantial sample of former teachers and leaders since the 1970s. His findings pointed to many warning signs of fading innovation, including problems of community support, staff renewal, and so on. But one of the key factors was undoubtedly leadership and, in particular, the issue of leadership succession.

Dean Fink published this thorough and self-reflective historical ethnography as *Good Schools/Real Schools*.[2] Dean's doctorate was one of the sources of inspiration for a project bid I subsequently submitted to the Spencer Foundation, with my professorial colleague, Ivor Goodson, titled *Change Over Time?* This brought together my body of work on educational change with Goodson's historical expertise in school reform, while the entire research design built significantly on and extended Dean Fink's single-school study to eight innovative and traditional high schools in the US and Canada. Dean became a significant part of our project team and a major contributor to the project's findings.

One of the outcomes of the *Change Over Time?* project was a book that Dean Fink and I wrote together, called *Sustainable Leadership*.[3] The book is the product of one of the most significant intellectual and strategic partnerships I have been fortunate to enjoy over a more than 30-year career. It took the leadership aspects of our study – including those involving succession – and brought our findings together within a theoretical framework that was unprecedented in any field of sustainable leadership. This comprised seven principles: depth of purpose, breadth of involvement or distribution, justice in supporting peers and neighbors, complexity in organization, renewal rather than depletion of people's energy, conservation of wisdom from the past as a resource for the future, and effective succession. The book remains one of those wonderfully collaborative products where it becomes almost impossible to recall or identify which sentence was written by whom.

It was never the purpose of the *Change Over Time?* study to investigate leadership succession as such, but succession emerged as one of the most overwhelmingly important influences on the sustainability or unsustainability of educational change. And it turned out that, it was a topic in education at least, that had almost never been investigated before. One of Dean's most distinctive contributions to this large and complex project was to unpack and articulate the issue of succession.[4] The book and his own additional publication highlighted the technical planning aspects, human development issues, emotional dimensions, and sheer timing issues of succession, as well as looking at the kinds of knowledge that leaders carried with them when they came and went.

In the book he has written here, Dean Fink adds to the significant foundation of which he has been a cornerstone. In providing the first book based on detailed data that have been specifically collected for the purpose of understanding succession, Dean deepens the exploration of the planning, management, timing, and emotional intensity of succession, and adds a vital fifth dimension – its politics.

Using his great skill as an oral historian and experienced ethnographer, as well as capitalizing on the rapport he is able to establish with his subjects due to once having been right in their shoes, Dean Fink draws them out magnificently so they speak with candor and clarity about the succession experience.

Among the many strengths of this book is its comparative dimension. Succession processes vary depending on the specific systems that are used for hiring and replacing school leaders. England, for example, is an open national market and school leaders are hired by the governing bodies of individual schools. Many smaller school districts in North America keep leaders in place for many years, as they are grown in the district and tend to stay there, with few options for movement. In a number of larger districts, however, regular rotation of principals, in a way that Dean Fink himself helped pioneer, is employed as a strategy to move schools in the desired direction and keep individual leaders fresh and challenged.

In the end though, despite the differences between one policy system and another, what stands out in Dean Fink's careful study are the universals of succession – an emotionally intense and politically controversial process that carries immense importance but suffers from vast neglect.

There are individual exceptions and examples in this book that point a way forward. But the message of Dean Fink's unique book is clear: improving succession is one of the biggest steps that can and should be taken in securing lasting improvement for our students and our schools. On this compelling subject, *The Succession Challenge* and its author leave an impressive, instructive, and undoubted legacy.

Andy Hargreaves
Boston College
2009

Notes

1   Stoll, L. and Fink, D. (1996). *Changing Our Schools: Linking School Effectiveness and School Improvement.* Buckingham, UK: Open University Press.
2   Fink, D. (2000). *Good Schools/Real Schools: Why School Reform Doesn't Last.* New York: The Teachers' College Press.
3   Hargreaves, A. and Fink, D. (2006). *Sustainable Leadership.* San Francisco CA: Jossey-Bass.
4   Fink, D. and Brayman, C. (2006) 'School leadership succession and the challenges of change', *Educational Administration Quarterly,* 42 (1), 62–89.

Preamble

If there is such a thing as predestination, then I was meant to write this book on leadership succession. Let me explain. I spent the first 34 years of my professional career in educational practice as successively a teacher, a department head, an assistant principal, a principal, an assistant superintendent, and a superintendent. Having reached my level of incompetence, I took early retirement to try my hand as a consultant and an author. During all my years as a practitioner I had authored only one book, a history text entitled *Life in Upper Canada*.[1] The response to it was, to say the least, underwhelming. My second book came 26 years later, which is probably a record for writer's block.

As part of my retirement planning I launched two projects that I hoped would keep me busy during the cold Canadian winters and keep me out of the shopping malls. The first was to write a book with my friend and colleague Louise Stoll on educational change as we had experienced it in our work together for the Halton Board of Education in Ontario, Canada. The resulting book *Changing Our Schools: Linking School Effectiveness and School Improvement*[2], much to my surprise, sold very well and was translated into a number of languages. My working with Louise and looking more deeply into the school effectiveness and school improvement literatures reaffirmed my long-held practitioner's belief in the importance of leadership to school and student success.

My second project was to complete a PhD. Shortly before I announced my retirement I was having lunch with my friend and colleague Andy Hargreaves, who as editor of a change series for the Open University Press had taken a chance on two unknowns, and his gamble resulted in *Changing Our Schools*. Andy asked me if there was anything in my career that I hadn't done that I wanted to. I admitted that I had always wanted to complete a PhD, but personal circumstances, like eating, and providing for my family, had always got in the way. This conversation resulted in my finishing a PhD under Andy's ever vigilant, always supportive, but unrelentingly demanding supervision.[3] My thesis, entitled "The Attrition of Change"[4] was about the failure of change in an innovative school and the influence of this "lighthouse" school on the larger educational system. The inability of the system to appoint an appropriate replacement for the inspirational founding principal was a major reason for the school's "attrition of change". An adapted version of the thesis was later published as *Good Schools/Real Schools: Why School Reform Doesn't Last.*[5] The publishers, I suspect correctly, thought the thesis title was a bit too negative.

Both of my early books coincided with the publications of a number of important books on educational change. Many of these works, including my own, tended to focus on processes and never really addressed in depth the most important questions about educational change; change for what purpose; school effectiveness for what purpose; school improvement for what purpose; reculturing for what purpose? Increasingly, the real goal of many international educational change efforts – when one got past the rhetoric of "raising standards", "world class" education, and "no child left behind" was to raise test scores on tests of questionable efficacy so that this government or that could claim to have improved education. Michael Fullan conveniently connected educational reform to this overtly political motive when he stated that "the new reality is that governments have to show progress in relation to social priorities ... within one election term (typically four years). Our knowledge base is such that there is no excuse for failing to design and implement strategies that get short term results."[6] Such claims ignore the impact of poverty, poor health care, and endemic unemployment as factors in child-care and student achievement. For example, two of the nations often emulated because of their fixation on increased standards through "brute sanity", the United States and the United Kingdom, were ranked 22nd and 23rd in their treatment of children, respectively, out of 23 of the world's wealthiest countries.[7]

In a modest attempt to shift the focus of the discussion on educational purposes beyond the technical debate of how to raise test scores to the truly moral purpose for the existence of schools and education, the enhancement of deep and lasting learning for all students, I co-authored a book with Louise and another friend and long time colleague from the Ontario Institute for Studies in Education, Lorna Earl, entitled *It's about Learning and It's about Time.*[8] In this publication we not only tried to say that it was about "time" we focused on learning, by linking students' learning to teachers' learning to leaders' learning to the idea of professional learning communities, but argued that if students, teachers, leaders, and school communities are to learn, they need the "time" to think, discuss, and in Guy Claxton's words, experience "slow knowing".[9] Sadly, too many promising change efforts that had learning at their core died a premature death from political impatience, under-funding, or lack of sustained leadership. Projects would begin with a great deal of sound and fury, leaders would emerge to move things in very positive directions, and then the priorities of government or school districts or ambitious superintendents would shift, or the initiating leaders would move on for one reason or another, and the entire body of work would disappear or become swallowed up by the next change project *du jour*. As a result, sustainability – and within the idea of sustainability, leadership succession – emerged for me as significant pieces of the larger change puzzle.

In my own career I had succeeded and been succeeded in various leadership jobs over time, and frankly I had not thought much about it. In some cases I found moving in very easy because I was replacing someone who was not particularly popular, while in at least one situation I found it difficult because my predecessor was justifiably admired and mourned. Similarly, some who followed me built on my work and never looked back, while in other cases my efforts were totally undermined within short order. My PhD thesis, which had dealt with an innovative school[10] that over the 30-year period had experienced a number of succession episodes, some successful but many poorly planned and inadequately supported by the system, forced me to examine issues related to succession in depth. As I discovered, unsuccessful leadership transitions went a long way towards extinguishing the light in the "lighthouse" school that resulted in its "attrition of change."

This project became part of a much larger *Change Over Time?* Study funded by the Spencer Foundation and headed up by Andy Hargreaves and Ivor Goodson.[11] Using similar research methods and analytic frames as my thesis, this study looked at eight secondary schools in two countries (Canada and the United States) over 30 years from 1970 to 2000.[12] The importance of leadership development and careful succession planning emerged as an important theme of this extensive project. The *Change Over Time?* work resulted in two books in which I was involved and informs this book as well. In the first, succession became a major topic of *Sustainable Leadership*[13] with Andy Hargreaves in which we proposed seven principles of sustainable leadership and school improvement: depth, length, breadth, social justice, diversity, resourcefulness, and conservation. We described our second principle, length (endurance and succession), in this way: "Sustainable leadership lasts. It preserves and advances the most valuable aspects of learning and life over time, year upon year, from one leader to the next."[14]

The second publication that the *Change Over Time?* Study influenced was *Leadership for Mortals: Developing and Sustaining Leaders of Learning*,[15] which was my attempt to integrate my insights into change, leadership, and learning into a model of leadership development and sustainability. This model looked at those aspects of leadership that shouldn't change over time, like one's commitment to learning, and those values that are the basis of successful leadership, including trust, respect for others, optimism or hope, and intentionality and integrity, which provide a foundation for leadership even in the most turbulent situations. It also suggested that there are aspects of leadership development that should constantly change as we evolve through successive career trajectories, in particular the personal qualities, and the meta-learnings that all educational leaders require regardless of time and space: understanding learning, critical thinking, political acumen, contextual knowledge, futures thinking, emotional understanding, and making connections. In the final chapter of *Leadership for Mortals* I distinguished between succession planning, ensuring that the "right people are in the right place at the right time to do the right things"[16] and succession management, which involves the long-term development of a pool of well-prepared, contextually sensitive, dedicated leaders who are available for promotion whenever the need arises within an organization. I revisit some of these ideas throughout this book.

My purpose in taking this stroll down memory lane, or as I'm sure some might suggest, this exercise in self-indulgent nostalgia, is to position the issue of leadership succession and my own academic odyssey within the larger themes of change, learning, leadership, and sustainability. While a number of articles, an edited book on principals' succession,[17] a scholarly "handbook",[18] and Pat Thomson's very useful recent work on the supply issue[19] are available on the topic, it seems to me the time is right to address this topic in a holistic, comprehensive, and accessible way for those who are engaged in succession management on a daily basis. In addition to synthesizing existing knowledge into a usable format, I have attempted to extend the knowledge base by including the results of a research project that examines leadership succession in three countries: Canada, the United States, and Britain. To this end, with the help of colleagues in each country and the use of a detailed survey, in-depth interviews, and document analysis, I report on the succession practices of a medium-sized school board in Ontario, a small school district in the eastern United States, and a large authority in the north of England. The results of this research – cleverly entitled *Leadership Succession in Three Countries* – informs each chapter but is dealt with in detail in Chapter 5.

As usual with my books I hope the academic community will find this effort suitably scholarly and a contribution to the literature. However, my fondest wish is that superintendents, principals, school heads, inspectors, commissioners, education consultants, school board members, governors, and students of leadership studies will find it helpful in dealing with one of education's greatest challenges in the twenty-first century – developing leadership capacity.

I have organized the book's eight chapters to be read in their entirety, or each chapter as a stand alone to accommodate busy practitioners. Chapter 1, "Warm Bodies or Leaders of Learning", addresses the purpose issue: what kind of leaders do we want to lead our schools in the decades to follow? In this chapter I contend that there are sufficient warm bodies of people who think they can run a school to fill every available position many times over, but the "succession challenge" is to find and assign or hire the right warm body to the right place at the right time for the right reasons. This very notion of leadership succession begs the question: what are the right reasons? I address this question in Chapter 1 by stating that if the educational goal is to mobilize and if necessary coerce teachers and students to comply with top-down mandates to accomplish narrow short-term targets defined in terms of test scores, then a succession challenge doesn't exist. If, however, we are genuinely concerned to ensure that our schools and districts are run by leaders of learning who will prepare young people to participate successfully in a knowledge society, and are ready to treat teachers and other educational workers as trustworthy professionals, and parents and communities as real partners, then we have our work cut out for us.

Chapters 2 and 3 examine the roots of the succession challenge. Chapter 2, "The Succession Challenge: Supply and Demands", addresses the alleged "crisis" in the supply of potential leaders and the changing nature of the demands placed on educational leaders by the standards/standardization agenda that has swept the educational world in the past 10 years. It argues that existing and potential leaders are questioning leadership roles as they are presently defined and asking themselves whether they are worth their time, energy, and commitment. Chapter 3 "The Succession Challenge in Time and Space", looks at the demographic and generational roots of the succession challenge and the contribution of place and location to the inequitable distribution of quality leaders in many countries which makes leadership succession a crisis in some places and a non-issue in others.

Chapter 4 "The Succession Challenge Up Close",[20] reports on the first of two research projects related to leadership succession which I have already mentioned. The first project explores the leadership succession aspects of the comprehensive and widely reported *Change Over Time?* Study that looks at the relationship of succession and school improvement over a 30-year period. The second project described in Chapter 5, The Succession Challenge Up Really Close", describes an original research project *Leadership Succession in Three Countries* on contemporary leadership succession practices which I conducted in a Canadian school board, an American school district, and a British local authority. I examine the influence of the international standards/standardization agenda on school leadership, and how various government-led improvement approaches have affected the quality, quantity, and personal lives of leaders, and by extension how these factors affect the people and schools that they lead.

Chapter 6, "Pipelines, Pools and Reservoirs", attempts to pull together existing efforts to respond to the succession challenge by suggesting that just filling the leadership "pipeline" with qualified people has failed to address the serious problems of leadership succession in some communities and some authorities, and describes the more targeted approaches emerging in some school jurisdictions in which officials identify, recruit, and develop a "pool" of prospective leaders from which schools and districts can choose their new leaders. The idea of a pool, however, depends on the willingness of people to come forward or at least respond to invitations to participate, which in turn suggests that somehow policy makers must address the negative perceptions of educational leadership widely held by younger educators. To this end Chapter 6 discusses distributed leadership as a vehicle for the development of a "reservoir" of potential candidates for a leadership pool, and, perhaps more importantly, as a way to create a "sophisticated vehicle for knowledge transfer and knowledge creation"[21] in a school, district, province, state, or nation.

In Chapter 7, I take the reader on a tour of succession efforts internationally, with a particular focus on the three jurisdictions that I studied in depth. Just as the chapter title "The Good, The Bad, and The Ugly" suggests, we can learn important lessons from the good practices and even the missteps of others.

Finally in Chapter 8, "Succeeding Leaders", I attempt to pull together the various issues involved in succession management into a few key policy options. As I have argued elsewhere,[22] "best practice" is a technocrat's dream in which complex issues are reduced to simplistic formulas. Rather than recycle alleged "best" practices which are almost always context dependent, this chapter presents a series of policy alternatives that system and school officials need to consider if they hope to address the succession challenge successfully.

To begin the process let's move to Chapter 1, which attempts to answer the question: why bother?

Notes

1 Fink, D. (1970). *Life in Upper Canada: An Inquiry Approach.* Toronto: McLelland and Stewart.
2 Stoll, L. and Fink, D. (1996) *Changing Our Schools: Linking School Effectiveness and School Improvement.* Buckingham, UK: Open University Press.
3 I will always be forever grateful to Bob Moon of the Open University in the UK for opening doors for me to complete my PhD.
4 Fink, D. (1997) "The attrition of change", unpublished PhD thesis, Milton Keynes, UK: Open University.
5 Fink, D. (2000) *Good Schools/Real Schools: Why School Reform Doesn't Last.* New York: The Teachers' College Press.
6 Fullan, M (2005) *Leadership and Sustainability: Systems Thinkers in Action.* Thousand Oaks, CA: Corwin, p. 25.
7 UNICEF (2007) Child Poverty in Perspective: An overview of child well-being in rich countries. *Innocenti Report Card* 7 Florence, Italy: UNICEF Innocenti Research Centre, Florence.
8 Stoll, L., Fink, D. and Earl, L. (2003) *It's About Learning and It's About Time.* London: Routledge/Falmer.
9 Claxton. G. (1997) *Hare Brain/ Tortoise Mind: How Intelligence Increases When you Think Less.* London: Fourth Estate.
10 Fink, D. (1999) "Deadwood didn't kill itself: A pathology of an innovative school", *Educational Management & Administration,* 27(2) 131–141; Fink, D. (1999) "The attrition of change", *School Effectiveness and School Improvement.* 10(3): 269–295.
11 Hargreaves, A. and Goodson, I. (2003) Change over time? A study of culture, structure, time and change in secondary schooling. Project #199800214. Chicago: Spencer Foundation of the United States.
12 Much of the detailed evidence from the study is available in a series of articles in a special issue of the journal *Educational Administration Quarterly* (February, 2006, volume XLII, number 1) that is devoted to the project: Hargreaves, A. and Goodson, I. "Educational change over time? The sustainability and non-sustainability of three decades of secondary school change and continuity"; Goodson, I., Moore, S. and Hargreaves, A., "Teacher nostalgia and the sustainability of reform: The generation and degeneration of teachers' missions, memory and meaning"; Fink, D. and Brayman, C. "School leadership succession and the challenges of change"; Baker, M. and Foote, M. "Changing spaces: Urban school interrelationships and the impact of standards-based reform"; Giles, C. and Hargreaves, A., "The sustainability of innovative schools as learning organizations and professional learning communities during standardized reform".
13 Hargreaves, A. and Fink, D. (2006) *Sustainable Leadership.* San Francisco, CA: Jossey-Bass.
14 Ibid, 55.

15 Fink, D. (2006) *Leadership for Mortals: Developing and Sustaining Leaders of Learning*. London/Thousand Oaks, CA: Paul Chapman/Corwin.
16 Rothwell, W.J. (2001) *Effective Succession Planning: Ensuring Leadership Continuity and Building Talent from Within* (2nd edition). New York: AMACOM, p. 7.
17 White, R. E. (in press). *Principles in Succession: Transfer and Rotation in Educational Administration*. Toronto: UWO Press.
18 Lumby, J., Crow, G., and Pashiardis, P. (eds) (2008) *International Handbook on the Preparations and Development of School Leaders*. New York: Routledge.
19 Thomson, P. (2009) *School Leadership: Heads on the Block*. London: Routledge.
20 This chapter draws on the work of Andy Hargreaves, Corrie Giles and Shawn Moore who developed the case studies outlined in the chapter and contributed to many of the insights I have recorded in Chapter 4.
21 Harris, A. (2009) "Future leadership: challenges and implications", *Invitation Seminar '21st Century Schools'* London: Department of Children, Schools and Families.
22 Fink, D (2004). *Best Practice: A Technocrats Dream*. Available at http://www.icponline.org/content/view/81/50/

1

Warm Bodies or Leaders of Learning

The original title for this book was *Succeeding Leaders*, which I felt rather cleverly captured my intent of dealing with the principles of succession management and encouraging schools, school districts, and other educational institutions to develop a coherent and cohesive approach to the ways in which they identify, recruit, develop, and sustain leaders of learning. The publisher's reviewers presciently suggested that I was too clever by half because my title was so enigmatic it sounded like a hundred other leadership books on the market. I then tried to be somewhat apocalyptic by offering *The Leadership Crisis*, but I soon realized that while leadership issues in many countries have created serious problems, they were far from a "crisis". The events of 9/11 were a crisis; the precipitous decline of the economy resulting from the bizarre lending practices of many banks and investment houses internationally was a crisis; the devastation of New Orleans by hurricane Katrina was a crisis; but based on the many impressive leadership programs and leadership networks that seem to be developing exponentially across the world,[1] I concluded that leadership succession is a big challenge but hardly a crisis. This led to the title *The Succession Challenge: Building and Sustaining Leadership Capacity through Succession Management* – not terribly sexy I admit, but it does describe exactly what this book is about. My title begs the question, succession management for what purpose? Had there been room on the cover, the second subheading would have been *By Developing and Sustaining Leaders of Learning*.

It's about Learning and It's about Time

From one point of view succession is not a challenge; it is easy for school jurisdictions and other governing bodies to find warm bodies to fill leadership positions. There are lots of people out there willing to run a school. The challenge of course is to find and assign or hire the the right warm body to the right place at the right time for the right reasons. Successful leadership succession therefore really depends on the purposes of educational jurisdictions and how well their prospective leaders can meet organizational goals. If all that counts in education is good accounting, paper management, and political score keeping, then anyone with a managerial background will probably do.[2] Some school jurisdictions that have defined their purposes in terms that valorize only improved test scores have done just that. For example, a report by PricewaterhouseCoopers has urged the British government to address its succession challenge by recruiting non-teachers to lead its schools.[3] Such a policy[4] would, as Helen Gunter and Gill Forrester have pointed out, downgrade the status of teaching "in comparison to generic leadership skills and attributes."[5] Stein and Nelson's examination of the interaction of instructional leaders supporting the teaching of mathematics suggests that leading learning is a complex process that requires learning content knowledge that they define as "the kind of knowledge that will equip administrators to be strong instructional leaders."[6] They indicate that instructional leadership requires four "layers" of knowledge:

- An innermost layer – knowledge of the substance and subject matter: what the work is about.
- A second layer – knowledge of how to facilitate the learning: the how of the work.
- A third layer – knowledge of how teachers learn to teach and how others can assist their learning: the how of learning for the previous two layers.
- A fourth layer – knowledge of how to guide the learning of other adult professionals: the how of learning for the previous three layers.

This is a level of sophisticated knowledge that requires an in-depth understanding of the teaching–learning process gained through experience, study, and reflection which non-educators and prematurely promoted educators would not normally possess or easily acquire in a short course or an immersion program. For example, a Canadian school leader described how her "sophisticated knowledge" contributed to her work with children and their parents:

> There's no way in five years of teaching experience that a person can know and understand all three divisions,[7] and that worries me because, number one, I don't know how you can support your staff, and number two, I don't know how you can be believable to parents that you really

have a clue on what's going on for their children. Whereas I pulled on my experience so often, especially working with parents of special needs kids, but also parents whose children were struggling in whatever way, or even parents whose kids were gifted and didn't understand why we might not want to identify that particular thing until later in their life.

If the educational goal of an organization or school jurisdiction is to mobilize teachers and students to achieve narrow short-term targets and they're not too choosy about how to get there, then a succession challenge really doesn't exist. They can manage by hiring people from outside education or just rushing young educators through preparatory courses in educational management. If, however, the concern is to recruit, select, and develop leaders of learning who possess the "learning content knowledge" to contribute to the preparation of young people for successful participation in a knowledge society, and are ready to treat teachers and other educational workers as professionals, and parents and communities as partners, then all those responsible for leadership succession have a real challenge in front of them.

There is no question that leadership is a crucial variable in determining whether students and schools succeed. It is second only to the in-school effects of classroom teachers in determining student success. As Ken Leithwood and his colleagues explain: "While leadership explains only five to seven per cent of the difference in pupil learning and achievement across schools (not to be confused with the typically very large differences among pupils within schools), this difference is actually about one-quarter of the total difference across schools (12 to 20 per cent) explained by all school-level variables, after controlling for pupil intake or background factors."[8] They continue:

> Our conclusion … is that leadership has very significant effects on the quality of school organisation[9] and on pupil learning. As far as we are aware, there is not a single documented case of a school successfully turning around its pupil achievement trajectory in the absence of talented leadership. One explanation for this is that leadership serves as a catalyst for unleashing the potential capacities that already exist in the organisation.[10]

In a similar vein, well-known Australian researchers Halia Silins and Bill Mulford's comprehensive study of leadership effects on student learning reported that:

- School-level factors have a stronger influence on students' academic achievement than do students' socioeconomic status or home background.

- Leadership characteristics of a school are important factors in promoting systems and structures that enable it to operate as a learning organization. In recent years, it has become a well-accepted principle that school leadership makes a difference to student achievement.[11]

If leadership is such a significant factor in determining student success, then successful leadership succession becomes crucial. Leithwood and his colleagues make the connection when they state that:

> The leadership succession research indicates that unplanned headteacher[12] succession[13] is one of the most common sources of schools' failure to progress,[13] in spite of what teachers might do. These studies demonstrate the devastating effects of unplanned headteacher succession, especially on initiatives intended to increase pupil achievement. The appointment and retention of a new headteacher[14] is emerging from the evidence as one of the most important strategies for turning around struggling schools or schools in special measures.[15]

This last statement is accurate if the purposes of education are narrowed to increasing test scores and achieving short-term targets like "adequate yearly progress". With this quite limited definition of improvement, there are innumerable examples of school and system "turnarounds". But if sustained improvement over extended periods of time in deep learning for all children is the goal, then there are very few documented cases. While education as part of a national transformation in Finland provides a well-documented exception,[16] some of the most publicized "turnarounds" such as the so-called "Texas miracle"[17] and the recently abandoned British literacy strategy[18] have proven illusory.[19]

Our best information, therefore, on the long-term effects of leadership succession comes from the fields of business and professional sports where the goals are well and easily defined: to win and to make a profit in both cases. Glenn Rowe and his associates' examination of sports teams, and especially the National Hockey League teams over a 60-year period, provides insight into how leadership succession impacts on performance.[20] The authors use three theories of succession. The first, the "vicious circle theory", portrays leadership succession as "a naturally disruptive and destabilizing force in organizations"[21] because it leads to new policies and challenges the prevailing organizational culture and practices. While succession can add new ideas, this theory holds that lowered morale and reduced efficiency leading to further succession usually offset any gains. The second theory, "ritual scapegoating", suggests that the major factor in team performance in sports like baseball, hockey, and North American football is the quality of the players provided by the team owner or the general manager. This is little different from the situation new principals or heads face when they assume the leadership of a teaching staff assembled by previous principals or heads, school districts, local authorities, or governors. When the team or school fails to improve quickly, it is easier to unload the coach, manager, principal, or head, and blame the organization's futility on the departed leader, than to admit that the governing policies, personnel, or conditions that the leader inherited were at fault. England, with its intrusive inspectoral system, provides an unfortunate educational example of ritual scapegoating.[22] Third, successful teams such as the Pittsburgh Steelers of the National Football League and Manchester United of the British Premier Football League have followed a "common-sense theory" of succession, ensuring stability and continuity by limiting disruptive succession episodes. While tending to short-term goals, they address long-term success. Their purpose is to win today but, more importantly, to keep on winning season after season. They have avoided the pathologies of both vicious circle succession and scapegoating – theories that describe the mindset of the terminally impatient. The need for stability appears to be also true in schools. John Howson's research in the United Kingdom shows a strong positive relationship between a school's performance and the stability of its leadership.[23]

Rowe and his colleagues argue that successful teams and businesses have followed a common-sense theory of succession that posits that leadership succession does improve organizational performance under certain conditions. As they explain: "the often-observed negative correlation between firm performance and leaders' succession is usually assumed to be the result of organizations striving for strategic renewal by changing their leaders."[24] Organizational learning is the key ingredient in strategic renewal and leaders need time for their own learning and that of their colleagues to occur. According to Mary Crossan and her associates, organizational learning involves 4 mental processes: intuiting, interpreting, integrating, and institutionalizing.[25] Intuiting is the preconscious recognition of the possibilities or patterns inherent in one's personal experience; interpreting is the explanation of an idea or insight; integrating occurs when a shared understanding develops; and institutionalizing is turning these understandings into routine actions. These processes take time to transfer knowledge from individuals to groups and from groups to entire organizations. Even the addition of money, such as has occurred in Ontario's literacy initiative in elementary schools, the British literacy and numeracy strategies, or the American "No Child Left Behind", is not going to speed up the ability of the members of an organization to jointly make sense of new ideas and practices, especially with a newly appointed unfamiliar leader.

Intuition is a key skill for leaders and is often unavailable to freshly minted leaders. It may take as long as 10 years and the acquisition of 50,000 chunks of knowledge to become expert based on intuiting historical patterns.[26] As Rowe and his colleagues state, the intent is not to suggest "new leaders need time to learn 'how to do things here'. Indeed our intent is to argue that new leaders need time to lead the organization to reconstruct (learn) new ways to 'do things here'."[27] This would be particularly challenging for leaders without a background in education. It is a mistake to assume that competence in one field is always transferable. Even in business there are many examples of leaders who failed to transfer their learning from one business to another. Carly Fiorina, deposed CEO of Hewlett Packard, is one of the most egregious casualties.[28] Not only does it take time for staff members to learn new ways, it takes time for leaders to recruit new people, and in light of union contracts, to dismiss the unproductive or dysfunctional. One of the keys to successful "turnarounds", according to Collins and Porras, is to get "the right people on the bus":[29] that's much easier to do in business and on professional sports teams than in schools and school districts. Attempts to force any of these processes "will lead to diseconomies – that is worsening performance."[30]

To begin the process of organizational turnaround or renewal, the first question the late management expert Peter Drucker used to ask business executives was, "what business do you think you are in?" For Drucker, a clearly articulated sense of purpose and direction was the first step to renewal. The same is true in education: if you don't know where you are going, any place will do. What differentiates business and education, however, is that business purposes may not always be moral. Some businesses produce products that cure cancer and some produce products that cause cancer. Some businesses produce products that support the environment and others produce products that degrade the environment. What matters in a business is pretty straightforward: make a profit and a good return for the investors.

If school leadership matters, and leadership succession matters, then the moral purposes that motivate leadership matter more. Paul Begley, a Canadian scholar respected for his research and writing on ethical issues, contends that people working in professional roles require purposes and goals every bit as much as they do in their personal lives. Without purposes educational leaders are, at minimum, vulnerable to directing energy to inappropriate or wasteful tasks, and at worst, subject to manipulation and exploitation by individuals, organizations and special interest groups bent on pursuing their self interests.[31]

He suggests that educational purposes relate to leadership in three ways:

1   They help leaders to understand the cognitive processes of individuals and groups of individuals that affect their values, motivations, and attitudes.
2   They provide a guide to action in solving educational problems or resolving ethical dilemmas.
3   Educational purposes become tools to "support actions taken, model ideal practice, and/or promote particular kinds of organizational or societal activity."[32]

It seems logical, therefore, in a book about leadership succession to ask the question: leadership succession for what purpose? In the remainder of this chapter I lay out a perspective on the purposes of education that is ethical and sustainable, and a view of leadership that provides the rationale for my subsequent discussion of leadership succession that not only provides warm bodies, but provides the right warm bodies for the right reasons.

Schools as Living Systems

Let's begin with a really wide lens – Fritjof Capra's *The Hidden Connections: A Science for Sustainable Living*[33] – and then narrow down to some specifics. In *The Hidden Connections*, Capra links the laws of nature to human organizations. From his perspective, schools, states, or nations are "living systems" interconnected in spheres of mutual influence; each is a network of strong cells organized through cohesive diversity rather then mechanical alignment, and with permeable membranes of influence between the spheres. Schools, districts, and other educational jurisdictions are ecosystems within ecosystems: classrooms connected to schools, connected to school districts or authorities, connected to communities and their agencies, and so on. Like a web, each has an essential skeletal structure of rules and regulations that frame relationships among people and tasks, distribute political power, and guide daily practice. In education these formal arrangements appear in seating plans for the children in a classroom, policy documents, organizational charts, written contracts, and budgets. These are the structures, forms, and functions designed by policy makers, leaders, and teachers to provide stability, order, and direction to organizations and classrooms. This ability to design is solely a human function.

In nature all change occurs through emergence, evolution, and the survival of the fittest. All living systems, both natural and human, possess two qualities:

- They are self-organizing networks of communication. "Wherever we see life, we see networks."[34] Schools, districts, and indeed nations are organized into a myriad of communities of practice[35] that can interconnect to move society forward, such as the civil rights or the environmental movements, or conversely join together to inhibit changes or block new directions, like the coalition to stop health care reform in the United States.
- Creativity, learning, and growth are inherent in all living systems and the appearance of a qualitatively new order of things emerges with the creation of meaningful novelty in the environment. This novelty may be as small as an insightful remark or as large as a new government policy. It can be spontaneous or by design.

It is human design that keeps society from becoming a jungle, and provides purpose, meaning, cohesion, and stability. Human design taken too far, however, can overwhelm and stifle emergence within the various ecosystems. It is the informal interconnections and inter-relationships among people that cut across formal structures and intersect with an organization's informal structures, "the fluid and fluctuating networks of communications" that give the web its "aliveness".[36]

Most policy arguments in education and other fields evolve around the relationships of human design, usually defined in terms of government policies, plans, and structures, and the innate human urge for emergence – to be free, to be creative, to be liberated. For example, if society allowed everyone to drive on our roads any way they wished – to be as free, creative, or as liberated as they wanted – then anarchy would result. Emergence taken too far, therefore, can become chaotic, and in the extreme, anarchic. As a result, govern-ments over time have designed rules of the road, developed licensing procedures and the like, to bring some order to our daily drive to work or play. To continue the driving analogy further, if the rules of the road become too restrictive, licensing becomes too limiting, and tolls are enforced on most roads, then driving would become restricted to a select few who can conform, and above all pay. Design taken too far can result in inequities, autocracy, or oligarchy, and the stifling of human creativity, ingenuity, and opportunities. It is this interplay between design and emergence that fuels our economic, political, and educational debates. The challenge at all levels is to find a balance that ensures excellence of results, fairness for all, within a paradigm that is affordable in terms of human, environmental, and material resources. The cross-currents created by conflicting views of what should be designed and what should be left to emerge lead to policy conflicts over the rights of individuals versus the needs of society, the requirements of a globalized economy versus the preservation of indigenous cultures, and the demands of international corporatism versus the democratic rights of citizens. All these themes, among many others, have infused the debate over educational purposes and policies that affect school leaders on a daily basis.

Andy Hargreaves and Dennis Shirley's recent book *The Fourth Way: The Inspiring Future of Educational Change* describes four eras of educational change.[37] They provide a convenient historical context and organizer to help us understand how these forces have influenced education and particularly educational leadership over time, and some idea as to where they might be taking us. In the "First Way" in most developed nations, the state supported everything in the public domain. It created conditions for opportunity and social mobility, set out an inspirational vision of social change and common good, and allowed professionals to get on with the job. The spirit of the times drew many inspired and innovative teachers into the profession but it also tolerated incompetence and eccentricity. School leaders were remembered as larger-than-life figures (in good and bad ways) who were emotionally attached to their schools, stayed with them and placed their stamp on them. The First Way brought innovation, but unacceptable variation in student performance and a perceived lack of accountability to taxpayers. Many critics have argued that state supported education was monopolistic and monolithic. In other words, there was too much design and not enough opportunity for emergence.

The Perfect Storm

During the Thatcher years in the United Kingdom and the Reagan years in the United States, a "Second Way" of markets and competition emerged in most western countries, particularly the United Kingdom and the United States, where schools competed for clients, performance results were published, and services were increasingly privatized and outsourced. Market norms of competition and self-reliance replaced the cooperative, high-trust social norms of the First Way. An entrepreneurial-managerial model of leadership, usually described as site-based management, that decentralized budgetary and staffing decisions to schools, gradually replaced the bureaucratic-professional model of leadership of the First Way. Initially, these neoliberal approaches generated energy and initiative, especially in secondary education. But they became increasingly mixed with neoconservative policies intended to return to some mythical age of accountability, discipline, and traditional knowledge. These strategies, which reserved to the state the power to design a standardized curriculum for all children, standardized tests to ensure accountability, standardized inspectoral regimens, and increasingly standardized teaching methods, euphemistically called "best" practices, compromised emergence through genuinely free educational markets and short-circuited any potential for creativity and innovativeness in the Second Way. The Second Way for school leaders resulted in shifting "geographies of power"[38] that gave them considerable control over managerial issues such as budgets, staffing, and maintenance of buildings but little influence over older autonomies such as curriculum, teaching, and testing.[39]

Michael Apple argues that a "perfect storm" has connected the neoliberals' privatization agenda, the neoconservatives' nostalgia, and the religious fundamentalists' and evangelicals' desire to "return to (their) God in all our institutions"[40] with a growing cadre of middle class technocrats who are more interested in forms, functions, and efficiency than human beings, to drive the forces of the Second Way in directions that have produced a confused and contradictory educational agenda. This agenda calls for personalized learning programs for children within a policy framework of standardization; requires principals and school heads to be leaders of learning while being excellent managers and creative entrepreneurs; exhorts teachers and schools to cooperate but at the same time to compete with their colleagues and other schools; and advocates for schools that are responsive to the needs and abilities of everyone's child but encourages selective schools for some and exclusive religious schools for others, all paid for by the state.

How did this happen? In the *The Shock Doctrine*, Canadian writer Naomi Klein describes how the radical right has taken advantage of international disasters such as the 2004 tsunami, the Iraq War, and the devastation of New Orleans to surreptitiously implement its privatization agenda in what previously had been the public sphere.[41] She provides vivid and sometimes tragic examples of how the influence of the prophet of unfettered markets, Milton Friedman, extends far beyond his grave, and intentionally or unintentionally influences public policies including educational policies that in turn determine how our school systems operate. As she explains, if one were to venture into the economics department of the University of Chicago in the heyday of Friedman and his followers in the 1960s you would have read a sign that said "Science is Measurement". By reducing economics to that which was measurable, and ignoring the human costs of an ideology that asserted that government has a very limited role to play in the economy except to create a climate for investment, and that everything else, including education, health care, and social security, can best be handled by the private sector, they gave an intellectual veneer to hyper-individualism and a rationale for ignoring social needs and economic inequities.[42] Although the recent economic slump has challenged these assumptions, Friedman's followers still are providing leadership to countries like the United States, Canada, and until very recently Australia, and to international organizations such as the International Monetary Fund and the World Bank. Even though the applications of their economic theories in Pinochet's Chile and Suharto's Indonesia failed miserably, and caused untold horror for vast numbers of people,[43] Friedman's true believers and their supporters remain convinced that where society has a choice, private interests always trump public interests. For example, when Katrina wiped out many of the poorest neighborhoods in New Orleans and destroyed most of its schools, the aged Friedman wrote, "Most New Orleans schools are in ruins as are the homes of the children who have attended them. The children are now scattered all over the country. This is a tragedy. It is also an opportunity to radically reform the education system."[44] Before Katrina the public school system ran 123 public schools, and they now operate four; before Katrina there were seven charter schools run by private operators, and there are now 31. A total of 4,700 members of the New Orleans teachers union were fired and replaced by younger and cheaper teachers.[45]

The Chicago school of economics not only influences the educational policy environment in New Orleans, to say nothing of the scandalous privatization of the disaster cleanup;[46] we see it in the educational policies of many educational jurisdictions around the world. The dramatic increase in voucher programs and charter schools in the US, the "for-sale" signs on UK academies, where for the bargain price of £2 million wealthy people or organizations can buy into state schools, the P3 program of private–public partnerships to build and influence schools in Alberta,[47] and the increasing need for schools to turn to private funding sources to remain viable, all point to the work of Friedman and his supporters. Similarly, the measurement sign on the University of Chicago door has been given a life of its own through a plethora of testing and inspectoral schemes that in many situations determine the success or failure of students, teachers, principals, and schools on very narrow measures of human potential. The strategy of the Friedman acolytes is always the same: find a crisis like Katrina, or create one; use it as an excuse to undermine the public services; and, while people are otherwise engaged, begin the process of privatizing education, health care, and other social functions by turning these services into commodities to be bought and sold. In this model of how the world should work, citizens become customers of these formerly public commodities, rather than citizens who share these services with their neighbors and pay for them with their taxes.[48]

In Ontario in 1995, the then Minister of Education unintentionally articulated this approach when he was surreptitiously videotaped telling his subordinates that, "Creating a useful crisis is part of what this will be about. So the first bunch of communications that the public might hear might be more negative than I would be inclined to talk about [otherwise] … Yeah, we need to invent a crisis, and that's not just an act of courage; there's some skill involved."[49] In the United States the language of "crisis" permeated educational discourse as early as 1983 with the publication of *A Nation at Risk*, which declared that "Our nation is at risk … The educational foundations of our society are presently being eroded by a rising tide of mediocrity that threatens our very future as a nation and a people."[50] David Berliner and Bruce Biddle in *The Manufactured Crisis* document how data, particularly from international comparisons, have been twisted by successive American administrations to ratchet up the sense of education in crisis.[51] In Australia the Minister of Education under the Howard government pushed the crisis theme by downplaying educational successes such as Australia's high standing on various international comparisons and actively fostering the view that teachers and schools in the public sector were failing. He implied that parents who do not do everything possible to get their children into private education are failing them. Gene Glass captures this "crisis" rhetoric when he states that the old adage "if it ain't broke don't fix it" has been replaced by a new corollary, "if you want to fix it, declare it broken."[52]

Glass, a renowned American researcher and statistician, argues that shifting demographics and political manipulation fuel the Second Way in the US. He contends that medical and technological advances such as the birth control pill have affected the numbers of children (especially white children) who attend school, extended lifespans which has significantly increased the number of adults without school age children, and contributed to a "hyper consuming middle class culture producing growing debt and eradicating savings" that "quickly loses sympathy for public institutions that attempt to serve the common good" and "find it more and more unappealing to support the institutions that are 'stewards' of other people's children."[53] He sees the push for privatization of social institutions such as schools, and related to this the reduction of taxes, as the result of the desire of "White voters to preserve wealth, consume material goods, and provide a quasi-private education for their children at public expense."[54] While difficult to prove, this theory is worth investigating in countries with ever increasing numbers of recent immigrants like the UK, Australia, and Canada. In the balance between design and emergence, the Second Way seeks to reduce the "design" structures that inhibit the emergence of commercial and market operations. Governments exist to protect the market and it is up to individuals to look after themselves. As Margaret Thatcher so famously said:

> I think we've been through a period where too many people have been given to understand that if they have a problem, it's the government's job to cope with it. "I have a problem, I'll get a grant." "I'm homeless, the government must house me." They're casting their problem on society. And, you know, there is no such thing as society. There are individual men and women, and there are families. And no government can do anything except through people, and people must look to themselves first. It's our duty to look after ourselves and then, also to look after our neighbour. People have got the entitlements too much in mind, without the obligations. There's no such thing as entitlement, unless someone has first met an obligation.[55]

Targets, Tests, and Tunnel Vision

The excesses and unpopularity of the Second Way policies in the UK led Tony Blair and his New Labour government to articulate and act on a "Third Way". Like Bill Clinton's administration in the US, Blair's "New" Labour promised a Third Way between and beyond the market and the state – a rather inventive blend of design and emergence. As opposed to the Second Way approaches of the Thatcher and Major governments in the UK, the Howard government in Australia, and the Bush government's under-funded "No Child Left Behind" in the US, the Blair government provided substantially more support by restoring educators' salaries, improving working conditions, providing a focus on literacy and numeracy, investing in a massive regeneration program, establishing networks of schools helping schools, and creating policies and programs to attend to growing shortages of school leaders, particularly principals. At the same time it kept the Second Way strategies of competition, and significantly ratcheted up the pressure on schools and educators by widening and tightening targets and prescription. Moreover, its all-consuming motivation for change was unapologetically and narrowly economic. In the words of the government's education ministry, "We are talking about investing in human capital in an age of knowledge – to compete in the global economy."[56] Schools and the public sector as a whole had to become more business-like, target-driven, and responsive to their customers, the parents, and more productive as measured by standardized tests. Policy became centralized and designed and driven from Whitehall, the British government in London. Curriculum, testing, teaching, and school organization became standardized and enforced by government inspectors. The emphasis on accountability, oversight, and conformity to government policies has stifled creativity and innovation in many schools, especially those in less affluent areas. Stephen Ball in his *The Education Debate* traces the evolution of Third Way policies in the UK and concludes that the Third Way has profoundly changed the role of government and the direction of education: "The state is increasingly dispersed and in some respects smaller, as it moves from public sector provisions to outsourcing, contracting and monitoring roles, from rowing to steering, but also at the same time more extensive, intrusive, surveillant and centred."[57] Ironically, the driving purpose behind the Third Way is "to make the most of ourselves – to be creative, innovative, and entrepreneurial … this is driven by the subordination of social policy to the demands of the labour market flexibility and/or employability and the perceived imperatives of international competitiveness in the name of which the individual and 'its' society become ever more interwoven."[58] While the UK, particularly England, provides the best (or worst) example of the Third Way, we see manifestations of it in plans for performance pay in Victoria, Australia,[59] literacy targets in Ontario, Canada, and the introduction of standardized tests to replace an extensive and widely accepted system of local student assessments in Nebraska, US. But Ball asks the pertinent question of whether the standardized outcomes determined by external (to schools) testing

> actually stand for and thus represent valid, worthwhile or meaningful outputs. Does increased emphasis on preparation for the tests and the adaptation of pedagogy and curriculum to the requirements of test performance constitute worthwhile effects of 'improvement'? In terms of economic competitiveness, is what is measured here what is needed?[60]

Increasingly, evidence is mounting that this change strategy based on standardized tests, short-term targets, and teaching aligned to tests is not working in improving student and school performance. Peter Tymms and his colleagues at Durham University have concluded:

> Evidence from the UK, US and elsewhere suggests that within educational systems, hugely expensive policy initiatives have often failed to lead to significant positive improvements. For instance the National Literacy Strategy in England cost £500 million but appears to have had almost no impact on literacy levels of 11-year-olds in English primary schools despite widespread claims to the contrary. Indeed it has been questioned whether it has ever been shown that educational standards have in fact risen by any significant amount over any time period anywhere as a result of policy.[61]

In spite of this compelling evidence, many governments persist in pursuing untested and empirically unsupported change strategies based on short-term curricula aligned to targets,[62] and an array of accountability measures that have led to such "collateral damage"[63] as guilt and hopelessness for teachers, superficial, narrow, mind-numbing curriculum and teaching for students, and high stress and low morale for school leaders. In England the government has expanded target setting into a series of increasingly complex and hierarchical expectations with very much of a top-down thrust. For example, the British government, in a complex directive on target setting to education authorities and schools, declared: "We have announced an aspiration that 85% of young people will achieve level 2 at 19 by 2013."[64] This and similar top-down targets take micro-management to new highs (or is it lows?). There is little evidence that this kind of target setting gains support or even compliance, or justifies the time and energy of the people who have to implement the targets. Ontario, which has also hitched its policy horse to the short-term targets wagon, continues to focus on literacy and numeracy in spite of the fact that the achievement of Ontario's students in literacy and numeracy is among the highest in both Canada and the world.[65] This myopia has resulted in little serious attention to the arts and other important areas of the curriculum, as well as only modest efforts to attend to the province's burgeoning multicultural population. Most evidence of successful target setting as a change strategy comes from very small-scale studies of relatively simple tasks, primarily in the United States. There is no compelling evidence to support target setting as a long-term change strategy in organizations as complex as an educational institution.[66] This is not to say that short-term targets have no use. Short-term gains can provide "quick wins" for teachers and others to demonstrate that change is possible and it is worth their time and effort to invest in more difficult long-term change strategies.[67] David Hopkins supports the quick wins notion and convincingly argues that short-term "changes to the school environment, attendance and uniform can result in tangible gains"[68] that lift morale. Similarly, community activists know that when disempowered groups such as ethnic minority parents agitate for change, concrete early victories demonstrate that their investments of energy can indeed get results.[69] But perseverating on a series of short-term targets or arbitrary politically inspired targets creates the feeling among the people involved of being in an ongoing series of sprints to the finish, only to be faced with another and another sprint to achieve targets in which they have little personal investment. The target becomes *the* purpose rather than the learning involved in achieving the target. Curriculum begins to narrow and become focused on approaches to raising test scores rather than long-term sustainable learning strategies for students.[70] The human cost of this tunnel vision shows up in failed students, cynical teachers, harried school leaders, and disenchanted communities.

As previously mentioned, the all-purpose argument for this systemic, radical, and frenetic change over the past 20 years has been narrowly based on the instrumental imperatives of the corporate world for increased productivity and profitability. I have had the opportunity of hearing presidents, prime ministers, secretaries of state for education, ministers of education, corporate leaders, and senior political and bureaucratic leaders from around the world, and they all give essentially the same speech: "we must improve our educational system so that our country (province, state) can compete in the globalized marketplace." Improvement is usually defined in terms of test scores although there is little correlation between test scores and national productivity. For example, my country of Canada ranks highly on most international comparisons of student achievement such as PISA, but is 13th in national productivity.[71] The most productive economy is still that of the United States, yet on international educational comparisons the US is at or below the median on many measures. The pundits of profitability declare that "we need more math, more science, more engineers, more university graduates" to meet the competition of a knowledge economy. Where's the evidence? In Ontario for example the Ontario Society of Professional Engineers state that:

> Growing evidence suggests that Canada, and specifically Ontario, is not keeping up with the creation of jobs specific to the skills of available

engineers. As a result engineers are either becoming unemployed, or working in non-engineering related areas. In addition, graduating engineers are finding it more and more difficult to find employment that would fulfill their licensure requirements. Finally, many internationally educated engineering graduates still have a great deal of difficulty getting their one year of Canadian work experience.[72]

The US has more engineers now than it can use.[73] Moreover, why the big panic to push more and more young people through university, when it is estimated that only 30 per cent of the jobs in the United States available in 2010 will require university or college graduation?[74] The American Bureau of Labor Statistics indicates that, by 2015, 13 million new jobs will be created that do not require post-secondary education, and the number of new jobs that will require at least a bachelor degree is 6 million.[75] I doubt the ratio is higher elsewhere. As Michael Crawford explains in the *New York Times Magazine*:

> The current downturn is likely to pass eventually. But there are also systemic changes in the economy, arising from information technology, that have the surprising effect of making the manual trades – plumbing, electrical work, car repair – more attractive as careers. The Princeton economist Alan Blinder argues that the crucial distinction in the emerging labor market is not between those with more or less education, but between those whose services can be delivered over a wire and those who must do their work in person or on site. The latter will find their livelihoods more secure against outsourcing to distant countries. As Blinder puts it, "You can't hammer a nail over the Internet." Nor can the Indians fix your car. Because they are in India.[76]

If this is the case, how can policy makers justify "one size fits all" curriculum and testing programs, unless there is another motive? A cynic might suggest that the corporate demand for more highly educated engineers, software developers, and the like is more of a market-driven strategy to increase the numbers of these high-paid professionals as a way to drive down their wages than a national approach to international competitiveness and economic wellbeing. Perhaps this is just one more way for those social elements that already control the levers of political and economic power to perpetuate their dominance; or it could be social snobbery towards people who work with their hands; or then again, maybe the whole knowledge economy thing has been oversold. Regardless of motive, there has to be more to education than preparing our students to make a living sitting in front of a computer as a drone in the knowledge economy. There is a better way.

The Moral Purpose for Educational Leadership

This better way begins with the question: what is the moral purpose of education in the twenty-first century?[77] History provides some guidance. David McCullough's superb Pulitzer Prize winning biography *John Adams* stimulated my interest in the second and sixth presidents of the United States, John Adams and his son John Quincy Adams, two of the most maligned yet brilliant American presidents, both of whom faced incredible adversity but remained dedicated to larger moral principles.[78] Only in recent years have they received the historical recognition they deserve. At a time when the United States was fighting for its independence from the British Empire, the emergent nation sent John Adams and his son, who acted as his father's secretary, to Paris to try to gain French support for their new nation. To explain to his lonely wife Abigail why he was prepared to give up everything he loved for the cause of American independence, John Adams described his vision of the future:

> I must study politics and war, that our sons may have liberty to study mathematics and philosophy. Our sons ought to study mathematics and philosophy, geography, natural history and naval architecture, navigation, commerce and agriculture in order to give their children a right to study painting, poetry, music, architecture, statuary, tapestry and porcelain.[79]

In these few words John Adams captured the essence of why educational leaders must continue to struggle against the attempts to privatize and commodify education. Adams believed that the role of government was to protect and empower all of its citizens so that they could pursue their goals; that the purpose of education was not for purely utilitarian purposes, but to enrich the lives of all citizens and to help them achieve their potential. This is a broad liberal education that includes not only mathematics and the sciences, but also the humanities and the arts. It is deep and engaging and not for just an elite but for everyone. As Adams stated in another letter to Abigail in 1776, the year of the Declaration of Independence: "Laws for the liberal education of youth, especially for the lower classes of people, are so extremely wise and useful, that, to a humane and generous mind, no expense for this purpose would be thought extravagant."[80] Later, in 1786, he wrote: "The education of a nation instead of being confined to a few schools and universities for the instruction of the few must become the national care and expense for the formation of the many."[81]

While the foregoing could be easily relegated to the dustbin of irrelevant history, consider this very recently published long-term study of secondary education in England and Wales by leading scholars from four major British institutions. The Nuffield Report makes five overarching demands of British policy makers:

- *The reassertion of a broader vision of education* in which there is a profound respect for the whole person (not just the narrowly conceived "intellectual excellence" or "skills for economic prosperity"), irrespective of ability or cultural and social background, in which there is a broader vision of learning and in which the learning contributes to a more just and cohesive society.
- *System performance indicators fit for purpose* in which the "measures of success" reflect this range of educational aims, not simply those which are easy to measure or which please certain stakeholders only.
- *The redistribution of power and decision-making* such that there can be greater room for the voice of the learner, for the expertise of the teacher, and for the concerns of other stakeholders in the response to the learning needs of all young people in their different economic and social settings.
- *The creation of strongly collaborative local learning systems* in which schools, colleges, higher education institutions, the youth service, independent training providers, employers, and voluntary bodies can work together for the common good – in curriculum development, in provision of opportunities for all learners in a locality, and in ensuring appropriate progression into further education, training, and employment.
- *The development of a more unified system of qualifications* which meets the diverse talents of young people, the different levels and styles of learning, and the varied needs of the wider community, but which avoids the fragmentation, divisiveness, and inequalities to which the present system is prone.[82]

Whether we are talking about founding an educational system over 300 years ago or critiquing an existing system, the moral purpose for educators remains the same, and involves "convictions about, and unwavering commitments to, enhancing deep and broad learning, not merely tested achievement, for *all* students."[83] To explain the meaning of "deep and broad" learning, Andy Hargreaves and I borrowed from the UNESCO Commission that proposed "four fundamental types of learning which, throughout a person's life, will be the pillars of knowledge:"[84]

- *Learning to know* includes the acquisition of a broad general knowledge, intellectual curiosity, the instruments of understanding, independence of judgment, and the impetus and foundation for being able to continue learning throughout life. Additionally, learning to know "presupposes learning to learn, calling upon the power of concentration, memory and thought."[85] To do this Guy Claxton explains that students and all other learners need to acquire *resilience*, the ability to "stay intelligently engaged with learning challenges" despite difficulties and setbacks;[86] *resourcefulness*, the capacity to use a range of intellectual tools including imagination and intuition to address learning challenges; and *reflection*, the facility to "monitor one's own learning and take a strategic overview."[87]

- *Learning to do* involves the competence to put what one has learned into practice (even when it is unclear how future work will evolve), to deal with many situations, and to act creatively in and on one's environment. It includes teamwork, initiative, readiness to take risks, being able to process information and communicate with others, and also to manage and resolve conflicts. In *A Whole New Mind*, Daniel Pink argues that the technology that has allowed low-paid Asian workers to replace high-paid western workers in manufacturing has now spread to "white-collar" work. He states, "Any job that depends on routines – that can be reduced to a set of rules, or broken down into a set of repeatable steps – is at risk."[88] Paid tasks that have primarily required left brain thinking, that are logical, linear, and rational – like writing a will, completing tax forms, writing up an insurance policy, or even diagnosing illnesses – will either move offshore to low-pay environments, or be done by people at home on their computers. The future, therefore, belongs to those who engage the right side of the brain, with its abilities to think holistically and long term, recognize patterns, and interpret emotions and non-verbal communications, in partnership with the left side of the brain. In addition to doing mathematics and science, students will need to engage in such right brain dominated activities as designing buildings and works of art, telling stories, composing music, and volunteering in hospitals, schools, and old age homes. The top jobs of the future are in the helping professions, designing new or modifying old products, and creating new technologies. At the same time we will still need people who can build houses, repair the plumbing, put in sewers, and attend to all the services that make modern life livable.

- *Learning to be* addresses who we are, and how we are with people. It incorporates our aspects of the self – mind and body, emotion and intellect, aesthetic sensitivity and spiritual values. People who have "learned to be" can understand themselves and their world, and solve their own problems. Learning to be means giving people the freedom of thought, judgment, feeling, and imagination they need in order to develop their talents and take control of their lives as much as possible.[89] The Body Shop, in one of its many publications, captured the need for such learning goals when it declared:

Let's help our children to develop the habit of freedom. To encourage them to celebrate who and what they are.

Let's stop teaching children to fear change and protect the status quo. Let's teach them to enquire and debate. To ask questions until they hear answers. And the way to do it is to change the way of our traditional schooling.

Our educational system does its best to ignore and suppress the creative spirit of children. It teaches them to listen unquestioningly to authority. It insists that education is just knowledge contained in subjects and the purpose of education is to get a job. What's left out is sensitivity to others, non-violent behavior, respect, intuition, imagination, and a sense of awe and wonderment.[90]

Education is more than preparing students to make a living, although that is important; it is also about preparing them to make a life.

- *Learning to live together* calls upon students and others to develop understanding of, respect for, and engagement with other people's cultures and spiritual values. It calls for empathy for others' points of view, understanding of diversity and similarities among people, appreciation of interdependence, and ability to engage in dialogue and debate, in order to improve relationships, cooperate with others, and reduce violence and conflict. Learning to live together is an essential element of deep and broad learning in an increasingly multicultural world where millions of families and their children have been mired in decades or even centuries of racial hatred, religious bigotry, or totalitarian control. It is truly amazing how many ways policy makers find to separate students from each other – socioeconomically, racially, religiously, by gender, and so on. How can we learn to live together if we never get to know "the other"?

To these four pillars, we added a fifth:

- *Learning to live sustainably* is about learning to respect and protect the earth which gives us life; to work with diverse others to secure the long-term benefits of economic and ecological life in all communities; to adopt behaviors and practices that restrain and minimize our ecological footprint on the world around us without depriving us of opportunities for development and fulfillment; and to coexist and cooperate with nature and natural design, whenever possible, rather than always seeking to conquer and control them.[91]

The title of the book my colleagues Louise Stoll and Lorna Earl wrote a few years ago, *It's About Learning and It's About Time,* Goes to the very heart of what I believe education in the twenty-first century should be about, and therefore what educational leadership and leadership succession should be about.[92] It is "about time" we focused on learning and not on all the artifacts of learning that tend to dehumanize children by reducing them to aggregated and disaggregated numbers; and "about time" we gave students, teachers, and school leaders the time to focus on what the job is all about; and "about time" we began to actively seek, develop, select, and sustain "leaders of learning" rather than just "managers of things" in all of our schools and school districts. At the heart of the succession challenge is the reluctance on the part of many dedicated educators to risk their personal security and professional ethics in the pursuit of policies that are at odds with the reasons they became teachers in the first place.

Notes

1   See Huber, S. (2008) "School development and school leadership development: new learning opportunities for school leaders and their schools", in J. Lumby, G. Crow and P. Pashiardis (eds), *International Handbook on the Preparation and Development of School Leaders*. New York: Routledge, pp. 163–75; Huber, S. and Pashiardis, P. (2008) "The recruitment and selection of school leaders", in Lumby et al., op. cit., pp. 203–31. This handbook also describes leadership training in North America, Australia, Latin America, Europe, Africa, the Middle East, China, and small island states such as Cyprus.

2   Morrison, N. (2009) "Heads who can't teach: does putting non teachers in charge of classrooms harm teaching?", *Times Educational Supplement*, 9 March. Available at http://www.tes.co.uk/article.aspx?storycode=6009814, 11 March 2009.

3   PricewaterhouseCoopers (2007) *Independent Study into School Leadership: Main Report*. London: Department of Education and Skills.

4   BBC News (2007) "Top Heads for toughest schools". Available at http://news.bbc.co.uk/1/hi/education/6256175.st

5   Gunter, H. and Forrester, G. (2007) "New Labour education policy and the rise of school leadership in England", presented at *AERA*, Chicago, unpublished, p. 6.

6   Stein, M.K. and Nelson, B.S. (2003) "Leadership content knowledge", *Educational Evaluation and Policy Analysis*, 25 (4): 423–48, p. 424.

7   This refers to primary, age 4 to 8; junior, age 9 to 11; and intermediate, 12 to 15 or 16.

8   Leithwood, K., Day, C., Sammons, P., Harris, A. and Hopkins, D. (2008) *Seven Strong Claims about Successful School Leadership*. Nottingham: National College for School Leadership, p. 4.

9   I have used the original spelling, in this case from a British source.

10   Leithwood et al., op. cit., p. 5.

11   Silins, H. and Mulford, B. (2002) "Leadership and school results", in K. Leithwood, P. Hallinger, K.S. Louis, P. Furman-Brown, P. Gronn, W. Mulford and K. Riley

(eds), *Second International Handbook of Educational Leadership and Administration.* Dordrecht: Kluwer, pp. 561–612.

12 The person in charge of a school in the UK is the head or headteacher, and the same job in the US and Canada is the principal. I use both terms somewhat interchangeably.

13 Matthews, P. and Sammons, P. (2005) "Survival of the weakest: the differential improvement of schools causing concern in England", *London Review of Education*, 3 (2): 15–76.

14 Principal: see note 12.

15 See also Murphy, J. and Meyer, C.V. (2008) *Turning Around Faliling Schools: Leadership Lessons from the Organizational Sciences.* Thousand Oaks, CA: Corwin.

16 Hargreaves, A., Halász, G. and Pont, B. (2007) *Finland: A Systemic Approach to School Leadership.* Case Study Report for the OECD Activity "Improving School Leadership".

17 McNeil, L. (2000) "Creating new inequalities: contradictions of reform", *Phi Delta Kappan*, 81 (10): 729–34.

18 British Broadcasting Corporation (2009) "Key schools policy to be amended". Available at http://news.bbc.co.uk/2/hi/uk_news/8120152.stm, 26 June 2009.

19 Tymms, P. (2004) "Are standards rising in English primary schools?", *British Educational Research Journal*, 30: 477–94; Tymms, P. and Merrell, C. (2007) *Standards and Quality in English Primary Schools Over Time: The National Evidence. Primary Review Research Survey* 4/1. Cambridge: University of Cambridge Faculty of Education.

20 Rowe, G., Cannella, A., Rankin, D. and Gorman, D. (2005) "Leader succession and organizational performance: integrating the common-sense, ritual scapegoating, and vicious circle succession theories", *The Leadership Quarterly*, 16: 197–219.

21 Ibid., p. 199.

22 Marley, D. (2009) "Fivefold leap in the number of heads sacked", *Times Educational Supplement.* Available at http://www.tes.co.uk/article. aspx? storycode=6009746, 9 March 2009; Barker, I. (2009) "From hero to zero and back again", *Times Educational Supplement.* Available at http://www. tes.co.uk/article. aspx?storycode=6009749, 9 March 2009.

23 Howson, J. (2003) *The Relationship Between Headteachers' Length of Service in Primary and Secondary Schools and Selected PANDA Grades.* London: National College for School Leadership.

24 Rowe et al., op. cit., p. 210.

25 Crossan, M.M., Lane, H.W. and White, R.E. (1999) "An organizational learning framework: from intuition to institution", *Academy of Management Review*, 3: 522–37.

26 Prietula, M.J. and Simon, H.A. (1989) "The experts in your midst", *Harvard Business Review*, 61: 120–4.

27 Rowe et al., op. cit., p. 202.

28 Bethal Murray, S. (2009) *A New Breed of Leader: 8 Leadership Qualities That Matter Most in the Real World.* New York: Berkley.

29 Collins, J. and Porras, G. (2002) *Built To Last: Successful Habits of Visionary Companies,* rev. edn. New York: Harper Business Essentials.

30   Dierickx, I. and Cool, K. (1989) "Asset stock accumulation and sustainability of competitive advantage", *Management Science*, 12: 1504–11.
31   Begley, P. (2008) "The nature and specialized purposes of educational leadership", in Lumby et al., op. cit., p. 23.
32   Ibid., p. 25.
33   Capra, F. (2002) *The Hidden Connections: A Science for Sustainable Living.* New York: Anchor.
34   Ibid., p. 9.
35   Wenger, E. (1998) *Communities of Practice: Learning, Meaning and Identity.* Cambridge: Cambridge University Press.
36   Capra, op. cit., p. 111.
37   Hargreaves, A. and Shirley, D. (2009) *The Fourth Way: The Inspiring Future for Educational Change.* Thousand Oaks, CA: Corwin
38   Robertson, S. and Dale, R. (2003) "New geographies of power in education: the politics of rescaling and contradictions", in British Association for International and Comparative Education and British Educational Association (eds), *Globalisation, Culture and Education.* Bristol: University of Bristol.
39   Ball, S.J. (2008) *The Education Debate.* Bristol: Policy Press/University of Bristol.
40   Apple, M. (2006) *Educating the Right Way: Markets, Standards, God and Inequality.* New York: Routledge, p. 9.
41   Klein, N. (2007) *The Shock Doctrine: The Rise of Disaster Capitalism.* Toronto: Knopf.
42   MacLaggan, C. (2009) Texas "a battleground" over privatization of health and human services, child protective services, Medicaid, food stamps on the block to lowest bidder. *American Statesman.* Available at http://www. publicvalues. ca/ViewArticle.cfm?Ref= 00293, 15 February 2009.
43   Klein, op. cit., pp. 99–110, 78–81.
44   *Wall Street Journal* (2005) "The promise of vouchers", 5 December; quoted in Klein, op. cit., p. 5.
45   Klein, op. cit., pp. 5–6.
46   Ibid., pp. 5–6; Giroux, H. (2006) *Stormy Weathers: Katrina and the Politics of Disposability.* London: Paradigm.
47   Pratt, S. (2007) "School-board gag order flew in face of democratic representation", *Edmonton Journal*, 9 December. Available at http://www.canada.com/ edmontonjournal/columnists/story.html?id=bfec8c66-3c75-43f5-8e2a-591b 357f8361, 11 December 2007.
48   Saltman, K.J. (2007) *Capitalizing on Disaster: Taking and Breaking Public Schools.* Boulder: Paradigm.
49   Brennan, R. (1995) "Minister plotted 'to invent a crisis'", *Toronto Star,* 13 September: A3.
50   National Commission on Excellence in Education (1983) *A Nation at Risk: The Imperative for Educational Reform.* Washington, DC: US Government Printing Office.
51   Berliner, D. and Biddle, B. (1995) *The Manufactured Crisis: Myths, Fraud and the Attack on American Public Schools.* Reading, MA: Addison-Wesley.
52   Glass, G. (2008) *Fertilizers, Pills and Magnetic Strip: the Fate of Public Education in America.* Charlotte, NC: Information Age, p. 21.
53   Ibid., pp. 15–16.

54 Ibid., p. 16.
55 *Woman's Day Magazine* (31 October 1987) "Epitaph for the eighties? There is no such thing as society". Available at http://briandeer.com/social/thatcher-society.htm.
56 Department for Education and Employment (1997) *Excellence in Schools: White Paper*. London: DfEE, p. 3.
57 Ball, op. cit., p. 202.
58 Tuschling, A. and Engemann, C. (2006) "From education to lifelong earning: the emerging regime of learning in the European Union", *Educational Philosophy and Theory*, V (38): 452.
59 Tomazin, F. (2008) "Schools to trial merit-based pay", *The Age*. Available at www.theage.com.au/education/schools-to-trial-meritbased-pay-20080708-3bwO.html, 10 August 2009.
60 Ball, op. cit., p. 150.
61 Tymms, P.B., Merrell, C. and Coe, R.J. (2008) "Educational policies and randomized controlled trials", *The Psychology of Education Review*, 32 (2): 3–7, 26–9; Tymms, op. cit. See also Tymms and Merrell, op. cit.; Coalition for Evidence Based Policy (2002) "Bringing evidence-driven progress to education: a recommended strategy for the US Department of Education". Available at http://www. excelgov.org/admin/Form Manager/filesuploading/coalitionFinRpt.pdf; Hattie, J. (2005) "What is the nature of evidence that makes a difference to learning?", presented at the 2005 Acer Research Conference, Melbourne, Australia, 7–9 August. Available at http://www.acer.edu.au/enews/0508_Hattie.html, 7 March 2006.
62 Coe, R. (2000) "Target setting and feedback: can they raise standards in schools?", presented at the British Educational Research Association Annual Conference, Cardiff, September 2000.
63 Nichols, S. and Berliner, D. (2007) *Collateral Damage: How High-Stakes Testing Corrupts American Schools*. Cambridge: Harvard University Press.
64 Department for Children, Schools and Families (2007) *Guidance for Local Authorities on Setting Education Performance Targets. Part 1: LA Statutory Targets for Key Stages 2, 3, 4, Early Years Outcomes. Children in Care, Blacks, Minorities, Ethnic Groups, Attendance*. London: DCSF.
65 Council of Ministers of Canada (2008) *Pan-Canadian Assessment Program-13, 2007*. Available at www.cmec.ca/pcap, 2 May 2008; Mullis, I., Martin, M., Kennedy, A. and Foy, P. (2007) *Pirls 2006 International Reading Report: IEA's Progress in International Reading Literacy Study in Primary Schools in 40 Countries*. Boston: International Study Center, Boston College; OECD (2004) *Learning for Tomorrow's World: First Results from PISA 2003*. Paris: OECD.
66 Coe, op. cit.
67 Schmoker, M. (2006) *Results Now: How We Can Achieve Unprecedented Improvements in Teaching and Learning*. Alexandria: Association for Supervision and Curriculum Development.
68 Hopkins, D. (2001) *School Improvement for Real*. London: Routledge/Falmer, p. 167.
69 Shirley, D. (2002) *Valley Interfaith and School Reform: Organizing for Power in South Texas*. Austin, TX: University of Texas Press.
70 Nichols and Berliner, op. cit.
71 Porter, M., Schwab, K., Sala-i-Martin, X. and Lopez-Claros, A. (eds) (2004) *The Global Competitiveness Report*. New York: Oxford University Press.

72   Ontario Society of Professional Engineers (2005) "OSPE Meets with Minister of Labour and Housing to discuss oversupply of engineers in Ontario". Available at http://www.ospe.on.ca/gr_connections_meetings_MPP_Fontana_Aug_05.html, 11 December 2007, p. 1.

73   Freeman, R. (2007) "The market for scientists and engineers", National Bureau of Economic Research. Available at http://www.nber.org/reporter/2007 number 3/freeman. html, 12 December 2007.

74   Cuban, L. (2004) *The Blackboard and the Bottom Line: Why Schools Can't Be Businesses*. Cambridge, MA: Harvard University Press, p. 169.

75   Glass, op. cit., p. 25.

76   Crawford, M. (2009) "The case for working with your hands", *New York Times Magazine*. Available at http://www.nytimes.com/2009/05/24/magazine/24labor-t.html?em, 28 May 2009.

77   This discussion is influenced, but not limited by, Hargreaves and Shirley's (2009) discussion of the Fourth Way.

78   McCullough, D. (2001) *John Adams*. New York: Simon & Schuster.

79   Ibid., pp. 236–7.

80   Ibid., p. 103.

81   Ibid., p. 364.

82   Pring, R., Hayward, G., Hodgson, A., Spours, K., Johnson, J., Keep, E. and Rees, G. (2009) *Nuffield Review: Education for All: the Future of Education and Training for 14–19 Year Olds: Executive Summary*. http://www.nuffield1419review.org.uk/cgi/documents/documents.cgi?t=template.htm&a=206, 9 June 2009.

83   Hargreaves, A. and Fink, D. (2006) *Sustainable Leadership*. San Francisco, CA: Jossey-Bass, p. 28.

84   Delors, J., Al Mufti, I., Amagi, A., Carneiro, R., Chung, F., Geremek, B., Gorham, W., Kornhauser, A., Manley, M., Padrón Quero, M., Savané, M.A., Singh, K., Stavenhagen, R., Suhr, M.W. and Nanzhao, Z. (1996) *Learning: The Treasure Within. Report to UNESCO of the International Commission on Education for the Twenty-First Century*. Paris: UNESCO, p. 85.

85   Ibid., p. 86.

86   Claxton. G. (1997) *Hare Brain/Tortoise Mind: How Intelligence Increases When You Think Less*. London: Fourth Estate, p. 55.

87   Ibid., p. 4.

88   Pink, D. (2006) *A Whole New Mind: Why Right-Brained Will Rule the Future*. New York: Riverhead.

89   Ibid., p. 38.

90   This is from a publication by The Body Shop which is at least 20 years old and speaks eloquently to the present situation and to a business that was certainly ahead of its time. My efforts to contact The Body Shop have been unsuccessful, so I no longer have the exact reference.

91   Hargreaves and Fink, op. cit., p. 38.

92   Stoll, L., Fink, D. and Earl, L. (2003) *It's About Learning and It's About Time*. London: Routledge/Falmer.

2

The Succession Challenge: Supply and Demands

At first glance, the succession challenge that faces most jurisdictions in the western world[1] may be viewed as strictly a problem of mathematical misalignment: too many jobs and not enough qualified people to fill them. But the problem has more to do with politics and educational philosophy than with issues of supply and demand. As this chapter will argue, it has more to do with the increasing *demands* (thus the chapter title) placed on school and district leaders as a result of innovation overload and change related chaos,[2] the unwillingness of many educators to conform to policies that they view as unproductive or even destructive to their schools and students, and the pressure to support activities that they believe have more to do with good politics than good education.

The Supply Issue

In the early part of this decade, when we were in the midst of the *Change Over Time?* study, many alarmist reports focused policy makers' attention on the supply of qualified leaders. In 2001, the American National Association of Secondary School Principals reported that the average age of principals in the US in 1993–94 was 47.7 years, with 37.0 per cent over age 50, 53.6 per cent between ages 40 and 49, and 9.5 per cent age 39 or under. Half of the school districts surveyed in 2000 reported that there was a shortage of qualified candidates. "This shortage occurred among rural schools (52 per cent), suburban schools (45 per cent), and urban schools (47 per cent). These shortages of qualified secondary school principal candidates also occurred at all levels: elementary (47 per cent), junior high/middle (55 per cent), and senior high (55 per cent)." NASSP attributed this failure to attract quality leaders to:

> increased job stress, inadequate school funding, balancing school management with instructional leadership, new curriculum standards, educating an increasingly diverse student population, shouldering responsibility that once belonged at home or in the community, and then facing possible termination if their schools don't show instant results.[3]

Some reports at the time from the US indicated that sufficient qualified people did exist to meet that nation's needs, but some states and districts faced serious recruitment and retention problems.[4] For example, Kentucky and Texas reported a low applicant pool; temporary principals led many schools in New York City and Los Angeles;[5] and 48 per cent of surveyed principals in New York State intended to retire by 2006.[6] Diane Pounder and Randall Merrill[7] suggested that high mobility rates among school and district leaders in the US created the perception of a supply problem even though there were sufficient numbers of qualified people in the US to fill available jobs. The trends and forecasts were similar in Australia[8] and New Zealand.[9]

In England, John Howson's study of leadership demographics in 2005 found that severe shortages existed in some regions for some types of schools. A study of the frequency of newspaper advertisements for heads (principals) and deputies (assistant principals) concluded that the number of advertisements for headteachers was above the average for the past 10 years at 2,688 and the highest recorded for four years; and that too many schools still failed to appoint a new headteacher after the first advertisement.[10]

Similarly a study commissioned by the Ontario Principals' Council (OPC) reported in 2001 that close to 60 per cent of principals and 30 per cent of assistant principals in elementary and secondary schools in public school boards would retire by 2005. By 2010, more than 80 per cent of principals and about 50 per cent of vice principals will retire. The study forecast that 1,900 Ontario schools out of about 3,200 in the English component of the public system would have a new principal by 2004. Moreover, the study reported that close to 8,000 teachers with principals' and assistant principals' qualifications were likely to retire by 2005, while only 715 teachers have acquired the principals' qualifications each year on average between 1997 and 2000.[11]

As a result of real or imagined shortages of leadership candidates, and projections of massive future retirements, nations, states, provinces, and school districts around the world have invested in leadership programs to ensure that they fill their leadership pipeline.[12]

Yet as early as 2003, doubt emerged about leadership succession as strictly a supply side issue. For example, the Wallace Foundation commissioned three studies to investigate the widespread reports of a principal shortage in the US. Its synthesis of the studies concluded that since "there is no shortage of qualified candidates for the principalship, it makes little sense to rely on strategies aimed solely at adding more candidates to the pipeline."[13] The report argued that:

> It's time to move beyond the pipeline, away from policies aimed solely at increasing the number of certified candidates, and focus far more attention and resources on reforming policies and practices to:
>
> - Adjust incentives and working conditions to enable non-competitive schools and districts to attract qualified candidates;
> - Bring local hiring practices into line with heightened expectations for principals' performance; and
> - Redefine the job itself in ways that allow principals to concentrate on student learning above all else.[14]

Also from the US, a study by Aimee Howley and her associates, summarized in an article appropriately entitled "The pain outweighs the gain: why teachers don't want to become principals", shows that many teacher leaders are qualified to go forward, but they just don't want to make the big step to principalship.[15] In a similar vein, a study at the University of Arkansas reported that a survey of superintendents concluded that while there was a sufficient number of qualified applicants for leadership roles, fewer than 40 per cent met the interview criteria.[16] In yet another study involving 200 interviews of American principals from across the United States, Sheryl Boris-Schacter concluded:

> The principals in our study were remarkably consistent in their assertion that they entered the principalship in order to be instructional leaders, and lamented that they spent the vast majority of their time dousing fires, fixing school facilities, attending meetings, and completing paperwork driven by state and federal mandates. Although they wanted to be reflective and planful, they found themselves being primarily reactive to non-instructional activities. This is precisely what prevents many credentialed and experienced teachers from transitioning from the classroom to the office and has, I think, contributed to the principal shortage.[17]

The Demands Side of the Equation

In England, the National College for School Leadership[18] indicated that 55 per cent of school leaders are eligible to retire by 2012. As disturbing as this may seem, the source of the problem doesn't appear to be the number of qualified people available for promotion to replace the potential retirees. Howson's 2008 assessment of the state of the leadership supply in England based on applications for headships indicates an improving situation and only pockets of difficulty in recruitment.[19] In fact, the UK government plans to halve the number of candidates taking the NPQH[20] headship qualification program over the next few years because "too many don't bother applying for the top job."[21] Rather than a supply problem in England, the real dilemma seems to be the unwillingness of deputy heads, middle leaders, and teacher leaders to aspire to and seek headships.[22] A PricewaterhouseCoopers study of the state of British headship found that "43 per cent of deputy heads and 70 per cent of middle managers say they do not aspire to headships ... Only 10 per cent of all middle level leaders go on to become headteachers."[23] Anecdotal accounts in the popular press in England and in Scotland reinforce these findings.[24] A head in my *Three Countries study* succinctly captured the deputy's dilemma:

> There are many deputies and potential deputies who have leadership potential who are put off from being a head because there are too many time constraints on heads. Most heads and deputies are interested and passionate about teaching and learning but end up dealing with unrelated issues. This gives rise in some cases to a public relations nightmare – who would want to take a job that many of the current post-holders do not enjoy? This then means that people become career deputies which holds up the process for other younger staff to take deputy positions and so on.

An Ontario study conducted by The Learning Partnership that builds on Tom Williams's influential 2001 work,[25] both sponsored by the Ontario Principals' Council (OPC), shows that the pipeline has filled up; there are plenty of people with principals' qualifications in the province. The Ontario Teachers' Council reported that the number of its members with principal qualifications has increased each year from 16,357 in 2003 to 17,335 in 2007, and approximately 44 per cent of the 2007 figure was under 44 years of age.[26] That's the good news. The bad news is that the motivation for potential candidates to apply for school and system leadership positions also appears to be diminishing. Salary differences between teaching and administrative roles are becoming less of a motivator. For example, in the *Three Countries* study, 60 per cent in Ontario saw inadequate salary as an inhibitor. Respondents in the same study indicated that potential leaders considered the salary differential between a senior teacher or especially a department head in a secondary school and a vice principal in Ontario was insufficient to compensate for the increased pressure and accountability, and the loss of holiday time, evenings, and family time, that would come with a promotion. This pattern was evident in both the British and the American school districts that were part of the study. In the UK particularly, 60 per cent of the respondents considered that salaries were insufficiently attractive to interest new applicants in leadership roles.

Perceptions of the nature of administrative positions in Ontario are also becoming more negative. As one of the Ontario secondary principals in my *Three Countries* study explained,

> there is a perception that we are working all the time and they are looking at life–work balance and asking why should I do that? The problem is partially our responsibility, sometimes we look busier than we need to be; there are some things we don't need to do. They also see we are under increased pressure around liability and legalities, and staff say why would I put myself in that position?

In his six years as principal, this respondent has been named in two lawsuits. While both were never acted on, he admitted that the increasingly litigious nature of Canadian society has become very worrying.

Interestingly over 70 per cent of vice principals[27] in Ontario aspire to principalship, according to the 2008 OPC study, which suggests a different dynamic in Ontario. Ever since the Ontario government forced principals and vice principals out of the teachers' unions in the late 1990s, the unions have made it difficult for a principal or vice principal to return to the teaching ranks in most school boards in Ontario. The key decision point in Ontario, therefore, is to leave the teaching ranks and security of union membership and become a vice (assistant) principal, rather than the decision to go on to become a principal. For this reason, 25 per cent of principals in the Ontario school board identified this decision as a sticking point for some potential school leaders. This statistic compares to only 2 per cent from the survey of British school leaders. The fact that there are fewer principals' jobs in Ontario than vice principals' jobs could mean that the leadership pipeline may well become plugged with unfulfilled career vice principals. In addition, in Ontario, the conventional route to gain leadership experience at the secondary level, the department headship, has fallen on hard times. As a result of reduced funds for leadership roles from the government, these preparatory roles have become increasingly unattractive to potential school leaders. The job of department head has broadened beyond leadership in a subject area in many districts to include cross-school leadership while providing very little, if any, time for heads to provide this leadership.

This theme of diminishing interest in formal leadership roles in education is widespread. In Australia, Karen Barty and her colleagues reported that based on the best available data there is no shortage of qualified potential leaders in Australia, but "consistent evidence that significant numbers of teachers are deterred by the modern principalship with its emphasis on management rather than educational leadership, does … point strongly to the need for coherent and robust efforts to redesign this critical educational work."[28] Similarly, a recent OECD look at education in New Zealand identified:

> a shortage of suitably qualified teachers applying for such positions. Typically, the reason cited for not applying is that the requirements of the job have grown to the point where they seem unmanageable. As workload increases, there is no corresponding reduction in ancillary functions which are unrelated to the professional role. There are issues around the relative remuneration and/or the "do-ability" of the job.[29]

It would appear then that in most educational jurisdictions there are sufficient qualified and capable people to assume future leadership jobs, but the demands placed on incumbent leaders have made the jobs so unattractive to future prospects that the pipeline has stopped flowing.

It is instructive to survey a few of the many reports that attempt to come to grips with this "demands" issue. In the previously mentioned Arkansas report, the authors summarize the deterrents to advancement under five headings:

- The pressures of testing and accountability are considerable.
- The job is generally too stressful.
- The job is too big and requires too much time.
- Societal problems make it difficult to be an instructional leader.
- It is difficult to satisfy the demands of parents and the community.[30]

In the OPC's Ontario study in 2008,[31] the researchers asked vice principals, principals, and superintendents to review a list of reasons that some people have given for not applying for vice (assistant) principal or principal positions and to select the reasons most descriptive of the situation in their boards. Among the reasons provided included:

- The job is viewed as very stressful.
- The time required to fulfill job responsibilities has increased substantially, making it difficult to balance family and school demands.
- It is difficult to satisfy the many demands of parents and the community.

- The issues related to poverty, lack of family supports, and other societal problems take time away from focusing on instructional issues.
- The funding and resources available are insufficient to do the job.
- The salary and compensation are inadequate.
- There is not enough autonomy in the role.
- There is an increase in violence in schools.
- The recruitment, training, and induction processes are inadequate.
- The role of the principal is primarily managerial and not educational.
- There is potential for not being able to return to the teaching ranks if required.
- The costs associated with acquiring the qualifications necessary for administrative positions are substantial.
- Management–union relationships are of concern.

Pat Thomson, in her thorough dissection of the frustrating nature of the British headship, captures the underlying contradiction in modern leadership between the requirement for leaders to be visionary, creative, and entrepreneurial, and the policy realities they live with, when she asks: "[how is it] actually possible for school leaders to develop a vision for education in situations where much of what they do is prescribed and delimited, and where there can be harsh consequences for going against policy, or simply failing to live up to it?"[32]

An additional factor that came up often in my interviews in the *Three Countries* study was the sheer weight of information overload produced by the use, and perhaps more importantly the misuse, of modern communications technology. As one experienced Ontario principal explained: "we get more and more information. A few years ago I would check my e-mail once or twice a day and have only a few messages; now I have 30 or 40. We must process lots of information, but not all of it is useful or helpful and this has made my workload greater." He particularly mentioned people who seem to think everyone should know what they are doing and copy their every utterance to the principal. Information of course goes two ways and virtually every principal or head in each of the three countries mentioned the paper blizzard required by the accountability agenda. There was a feeling that people above them were covering their backsides by expecting the schools to provide this piece of data or that report or to submit to various inspectoral regimens. An American principal captured this frustration:

> And the paper, I didn't even talk about that. I mean – I was already drowning in paper. Now I'm really drowning in it, as well as the vice principal because I had to share it, and also the secretary. We're drowning in the sheer number of documents that we have to bubble in, check off, send to the state.

A well-respected British head of a large primary school responded to the question on what was the biggest change for heads:

> Obviously more paperwork – I'm now an office manager. I used to believe the people that said the business people could run the schools were "barking" and that would never happen. The longer time goes on and the job changes, I could have anyone who knows about business and organizations and running businesses [and they] could run the school.
>
> I now shuffle paperwork. That's what I do. I shuffle paper. I answer e-mails and answer phone calls. I still do see a lot of the children, and I still do observe teachers, and I still do monitor, and I still see parents, but I have to work three hours virtually every night to enable me to do that because if I did all my paperwork at school I would never see a teacher or a child.

Similarly, in my interviews in Ontario the word "compliance" came up time and again when I asked principals the same question about what has changed over time in the role of the principal. A second-year principal in Ontario admitted that the "whole compliance thing is huge." A long-serving principal who had been principal of three different schools in the district stated that:

> when I first got the job it was much more of an entrepreneurial job – now it is much more structured – now you have to fit school interests within a certain framework of provincial and board requirements. While some of these are based on solid work, I see my role as much less entrepreneurial and a great deal more pressured to comply. But after 13 years I'm more conscious of what is going to cost me my pension and what is going to send me to jail, so after I consider those factors, I am confident of what my school needs and proceed ahead, so I guess I become passively subversive to those things that are imposed.

For an experienced and well-regarded elementary principal in the same jurisdiction, her response to external pressures is more overt:

> I don't think I've ever met a guideline or a timeline. I know if it is really important somebody will tell me. I mean, some of the stuff that is asked of me, I mean, I have just said to my superintendent, well I don't believe in that and that's not a good use of my time so I'm not going to do that. I'm up front about it. I'm not trying to hide it. But, you know, school effectiveness plans and following a simple template from the board, that's a waste of my time to write it like that. If you want to know what I'm doing in my school, I have a portfolio, I've collected the data, come in and see it. Don't ask me to put it on paper. Other people would spend hours making it look pretty. That doesn't really work. So I think some of that stuff comes with a bit of confidence.

Overburdened, Overworked, and Overwhelmed

To survive, leading has become a subversive activity in all three jurisdictions and elsewhere, a game which most experienced school leaders know how to play. They have learned how to gatekeep in the interests of their students, teachers, and schools. Over time they have acquired the skills necessary to choose what to endorse, what to block, and what to subvert. In England, some heads have become quite proficient at "target gaming" through strategies such as "ratchet effects" (negotiating undemanding targets) or "threshold effects" (concentrating on children on the bubble and boosting their scores above the desired threshold).[33]

Newer recruits who have never learned these tactics feel they must respond to every requirement and end up feeling overwhelmed or burned out. As Phil, a 38-year-old second-year Ontario primary principal stated, "it has become a role that has become unmanageable. That is what is perceived by staff and by the community." His vice (assistant) principal, described by her principal as "incredible", has decided to revert to a teaching position to try to return to a more balanced lifestyle. Potential leaders seeing the travails of leaders like Phil, whom the system considers "very successful" but who face multiple and often conflicting requirements, have decided in increasing numbers that their life involves more than work and that the disadvantages of leadership outweigh any advantages such as higher pay and the increased influence that a leadership role would bring.

Similarly, in the US increasing accountability demands on principals appear to be undermining the morale of existing leaders and deterring potential leaders from aspiring to lead.[34] In the Eastern School District in the US, a mid-career female principal, described by her supervisor as "wonderful", commented that she was "miserable" and "frustrated" by:

> this whole thing with No Child Left Behind, accountability, data, the amount of paper and less time for the work I love to do which is coaching teachers, creating a vision for the school, being passionate in getting to know the kids. Doing this kind of work I think has made my school very special … It is in many ways the school I had envisaged. The piece I am frustrated about is how do we get better if we are so busy spending time with the paper things we are doing, and we are losing the passion and the creativity. I feel that so much of what we do is about aligning documents, making up paper plans, but for me, the job is creating the story, somehow the passion is lost.

One of her equally experienced colleagues claimed that he still enjoyed the job but at times had the feeling that he was "overwhelmed, drowning, and buried alive." Those above him were always "adding, never subtracting." Interestingly, a British head used similar words to explain his context: "Nothing ever seems to be taken away, just added. That's the difficulty." An experienced female principal of a large diverse primary school in the US, recently identified for not making adequate yearly progress after a number of successful years, declared that this is a "terrible way for a principal to end up." The process was all pressure and little support, and it "feels punitive" and "short-sighted" and promotes "divisiveness" in the district between schools that supposedly meet their targets and those that don't. She explained that the process was plagued with unfairness. If a school has 40 or more of a racial subgroup that fails to make expected progress then that school experiences pressure to improve test results, whereas a school with 39 of the same type of students is ignored. Interestingly, the schools in this district that failed to meet targets just happen to serve the publicly supported housing area of the district. The attitude of policy makers, she suggested, seems to be "not how can we help you but how can we punish you." Fortunately, the Eastern District is an example of the benefits enjoyed by certain places, as I outline in the next chapter. It is a very desirable place to live and work, so it has little trouble drawing principal candidates from other less attractive school districts and feels little pressure to "grow its own." For example, the system had 40 applicants to replace a recently retired principal. The vast majority of these applicants were from surrounding less advantaged school districts.

The theme of unfairness plays out in England as well. A successful school head, who works with a less successful school in another authority, stated:

> They're [inspections] not equal. That's the thing that is so unfair. I could tell you about the schools near [a large neighboring city] where schools that have got worse results than others have got better grades, because they have an inspector that's understood where they're coming from. Everyone would recognize the most difficult school in [the neighboring city], I mean, only somebody who is mentally deranged would want to be the headteacher at that school, and the head is phenomenal. The woman that runs that school had to fight for two days to get a satisfactory rating. That school should be given outstanding because of what they achieve. If they can get the children into school ready to learn each day that is an outstanding achievement but they had to fight to get satisfactory.

A secondary head of a very successful, middle-class school from the same authority, who is a school improvement partner[35] for a school in a large industrial city in the British midlands, commented:

I think that too many times simplistic notions of effectiveness are thrown into the system by the central government which makes the accountability agenda very difficult to deal with. Life's not as simple as that. The obvious example is the decision by the national government 12 months ago that schools that had not got 30 per cent of the students to achieve five A* to C grades [GCSEs][36] were nationally challenged schools[37] purely on the basis that they hadn't achieved the 30 per cent. I work as a school improvement partner, which is part of the government's accountability agenda. I work in [name of city] which is an interesting contrast to the [Midlands Authority]. One of my schools was below 30 per cent but in every other aspect it was an excellent school and OFSTED[38] said it was an excellent school. And it was in one of the most deprived areas of England, let alone in [name of city]. It was a purely arbitrary benchmark. It was a simplistic response to what is actually a very complex issue.

British heads, perhaps more than leaders in the other settings that I looked at in the *Three Countries* study, felt disrespected by government and society in general. As one head wrote:

I love being a headteacher. I find it a most rewarding role as well as a privilege. It is not without its challenges. I feel that it is becoming a role without respect from parents and society. It seems to be acceptable that we are berated by the media for every aspect of childhood where in actual fact we spend our days trying to make the lives of our pupils rewarding and fulfilled. Perception and reality are wide apart. Teachers see this and wonder why we do the job as the buck always stops with us!

Another wrote on my questionnaire:

There are too many government initiatives brought out in one school year. My staff looks at me and says no thanks. Being a head is actually not worth aspiring to in a small school with small salary and HUGE[39] responsibilities as there are not enough staff members to carry them out. Salaries should be addressed; new initiatives; heads given time to research and look at their school instead of throwing a cold cup a soup down your neck in 3 minutes at lunchtime whilst being asked to make life changing decisions! Give heads some respect back – who is in charge?

School heads in England face the twin pressures of ensuring ever improving examination results and satisfying government officials who keep moving the "expectations goalposts". Peter Gronn has described the British approach to educational change as a "war on schools". He argues that while schools and schooling have always been "battlegrounds" among various interest groups, education has now become a media "blood sport" with government collusion:

The ante is upped considerably when the state's strategy hardens into one of rounding on its own schools, especially the people in charge of them, not merely by means of the compliance afforded by a vast regime of audit and surveillance, but … [by] resort to public humiliation and demonisation … [which] has now become a weapon of first resort in this war. Indeed so far have their rules of engagement shifted that government spokespersons often combine forces with media to chase down instances of feral leadership in order to publicly purge them. Is it any wonder that such experiences spawn a culture of complaint and lament among heads and principals' associations?[40]

A study by Alan Smithers and Pamela Robinson of the Centre for Education and Employment at Buckingham University concluded that there

is evidence of an impending shortfall in the recruitment of headteachers in the maintained sector[41] … three quarters of the [primary] schools reported having teachers with the qualities to become a headteacher but who did not want to move up. Nearly two thirds of the primary headteachers thought that this was because the pay differential was not sufficient incentive … Overall, workload was the reason the heads thought there were recruitment difficulties, with accountability a close second, particularly with the vulnerability of heads to sacking in light of a bad OFSTED report.[42]

Elsewhere, Smithers commented that the reluctance of classroom teachers to become heads was an important factor in the rise in the number of failing British primary schools. He contended that "heads are being held responsible for their schools in the way football managers are being held responsible for their team's performance.[43] The aspiring head is likely to go for a top performing school in the same way as football managers want a high-flying club rather than the Macclesfields[44] of this world."[45] Like the manager of a sports team, principals can often feel very lonely, especially in a crisis. "Schools are not shut off from what happens outside the school gates and they must often work through highly complex and emotive issues. The loneliness of leadership is palpable when heads talk about what this actually means in practice."[46] While it is difficult to quantify, British heads seem far more vulnerable and pressured than their Canadian and American counterparts. A crucial difference would seem to be the role of OFSTED.[47] A recent study of attitudes of existing headteachers and deputies in England, sponsored by the National Association of Headteachers, stated: "Almost 9 out of 10 (86.2 per cent) said current inspection arrangements make it 'somewhat' or 'very much' less likely that potential candidates will be willing to apply for Headships. Around 6 in 10 (62.5 per cent) of deputies said current inspection arrangements made them 'less willing' to apply for Headships."[48]

Even in Scotland with a less intrusive inspectoral regimen than England, a survey of 119 headteachers by University of Edinburgh researchers found that almost half of them work 60 hours a week or more – the equivalent of working from 8 a.m. to 6 p.m. every day, except Sunday, without a lunch break. Only a few of the 100 deputies, who also took part, said they were keen for the top job. More than two-thirds (68) agreed with the proposition that going for a headship was not "an attractive proposition." According to the researchers, "Since this corps of people is where the next generation of headteachers will come from, it must be a matter of some concern that the headteacher post is perceived in this way by so many deputy heads." In an echo of warnings already sounded by headteacher organizations over problems with succession planning, the researchers concluded that "recruitment to these senior posts in future may be problematic."[49]

In fairness, some jurisdictions have made serious efforts to reduce the pressure on school leaders. For example, the British government added resources to schools to reduce the workload produced by its rigorous accountability agenda through its "workload remodelling programme"[50] which provides resources to add teachers' assistants, and support staff to reduce the non-teaching jobs historically executed by qualified teachers. On the surface this appears to be an enlightened policy. However, as Helen Gunter explains, behind the rhetoric and spin the policy views teachers as the problem in education, so it is

> based on shifting the work from teachers to other adults rather than a conceptualization of who teachers are and what teaching is about, and it does not give recognition to the moral dimensions of teaching and teachers' work, and how their identity is located in curriculum innovation, designing learning, enabling progress and praxis.[51]

Heads (principals) feel pressured to ensure that all the pieces fit together and the policy works as intended. For school heads, the additional resources have only added to their workload and the pressure of the job, particularly from teachers' unions that demand compliance with the "letter" of the law when local circumstances often make conformity difficult.[52] Site-based management[53] is far more prevalent in England than in Canada and most US states. When one looks at the responsibilities of British heads compared to American and Canadian principals in my study, site-based management adds to school leaders' managerial and administrative workload and limits involvement with teaching and learning. With notable exceptions, school boards in Canada and school districts in the US play a much more active role in making sure the buses run on time, the toilets flush, and the roofs of schools don't leak. A study by

Michael Bristow and his colleagues for the British National College for School Leadership determined that the heads spent 39 per cent of their time on management and administration, 17 per cent dealing with external stakeholders, and only 7 per cent on strategic leadership activities such as classroom observations, leadership development, and school improvement planning.[54] In this same study, 41 per cent targeted accountability, bureaucracy, and external demands as major ingredients in making the job so time consuming.[55] As Pat Thomson has pointed out with reference to British school heads, their dissatisfaction arises from the disconnection between the job, defined in terms of the moral purposes of the profession, and the work, the reality of what they had to do on a day-to-day basis.[56]

In addition to augmenting resources, some school jurisdictions have responded to concerns about the demands placed on school leaders by experimenting with alternative ways to organize school leadership. For example, the American Eastern School District that I report on in Chapter 5 describes itself as having 10 schools: one secondary school, eight pre-kindergarten to grade eight elementary schools, and one early education school. As the principal explained:

> I am the principal of ages three to six. Once the children go to kindergarten I'm partnered with each elementary principal to supervise the kindergarten teachers, support professional development and to consult around children and curriculum. I evaluate every kindergarten teacher in Eastern, which is a daunting task.

This example is a type of what David Hopkins has called "executive leadership"[57] and reflects the system's recognition of the importance of early years education and the unique qualifications and talents of the principal of the early years school. It requires considerable liaison between the early years principals and the in-school principals and a negotiated distribution of tasks. There is some doubt whether this plan actually reduces the workload, but all principals agreed that it does help the system to focus on its early years priority.

In what appears to be the last gasp of a dying government, the British "New" Labour Party has gone even further in creating executive headships by opening the door for heads in government certified excellent schools to assume overall supervision of less successful schools.[58] Marion Court summarizes similar shared arrangements internationally, and she describes five distinct patterns:[59]

- Full-time task specialized co-principals in which two people working together divide up the various leadership jobs based on their strengths and interests and the workload. This approach assumes that tasks can be easily divided and overlooks the fact that most aspects of school are integrated holistically and not easily separated into job descriptions.

- Full-time supported dual leadership in which two people working side by side in a supportive and collaborative way attend to the leadership needs of the school based on the premise that "two heads are better than one." Court reports that schools that have tried it find that this can be a powerful approach to school leadership, but requires extraordinary harmony and mutual support between the co-leaders.
- Part-time job sharing in which time is divided between two people so that one for example might work mornings and the other afternoons or on alternate days. Once again this system can work well if the partners are collaborative, mutually supportive, and organized.
- Integrative co-headships in which co-leaders and other staff leaders collaborate to create leadership by committee.
- Teacher leadership collectives, in which a committee of teachers acting in concert completely replaces the principal's or head's position.

Norton Grubb and Joseph Flessa contend that the impossibility of traditional one-person principalships in the present policy context, and the need to address so many diverse issues, necessitate looking at joint or collaborative structures. They suggest that such arrangements employ the strengths of two or more leaders, ensure that someone is always on site, always provide someone teachers can go to with difficulties, distribute the emergent problems and annoying administrative tasks, free up leaders to work directly in classrooms, and give leaders themselves someone they trust with whom they can work through issues.[60] The challenges for such arrangements are considerable. Ronald McQuaid's[61] survey of leadership partnerships in the UK public sector lists a few of the more common difficulties: unclear goals, resource costs, unequal power, cliques usurping power, impacts upon other mainstream services, differences in philosophy between partners, organizational problems.[62] After surveying the field of alternative leadership structures, Ron Glatter and Janet Harvey, in their report to the National College for School Leadership, urged caution before leaping into such arrangements and concluded that:

- There is not sufficient evidence to suggest that any of the models of shared headship we explored could work in all schools.
- There is no one model to suit all circumstances.
- Job redesign should be part of a larger educational vision, not simply an expedient to deal with a current problem.

- With unconventional models of headship, it is particularly important to secure the maximum support of all stakeholder groups including staff, students, families and the wider local community.
- Research into introducing new models of headship should focus as much on governance – including local authorities – as on school leaders and should look closely at the interaction between them.[63]

There is a burgeoning literature on alternative leadership structures and some modest attempts internationally to create different leadership patterns to help leaders cope with the demands placed on schools. But few authors have had the temerity to question current educational policies and argue for the change in the very nature of school and district leadership that would make the jobs doable. Few jurisdictions have seriously addressed the question of restructuring leadership roles so that the requirements on individuals and schools can be reduced while enabling leaders to provide the kind of leadership necessary to respond to the educational issues of a knowledge society. Second Way and Third Way policies and practices have placed schools, school districts, and their leaders under intense pressure to implement numerous, often conflicting and shifting reform policies, some supported by resources, others requiring more for less.[64] "As a consequence efforts to implement and integrate different initiatives face a basic paradox – creating new incentives for improvement and aligning some policies may motivate or smooth the way for some school reform effort, but it takes capacity to build capacity at the school level."[64] New initiatives, regardless of purpose and degree of support, require schools and districts to weigh the possible benefits of the program, the availability of resources, and the positive publicity that may result against the costs in terms of people's time, energy, and commitment. A principal in a study by Tom Hatch put it very simply: "It reaches a point where it doesn't make any difference how much money there is. You don't have the time and energy."[65] Hatch's work adds an important dimension to understanding capacity building in leadership. Many systemic change theorists in education stress that sustainable improvement needs to invest not only in exerting pressure on educators but also in providing support or capacity building for them in terms of money, materials, training, and time to think and plan.[66] For Hatch, though, human capacity has some parallels with water capacity. You can increase capacity by increasing supply – providing more water in the first case, or resources and training in the second. But you can and should also increase capacity by reducing unnecessary demand – washing the car or watering the lawn less often, or, in educational terms, limiting the number and pace of external initiatives. This is the demands side of leadership capacity. When leadership turns into management of innumerable imposed initiatives, exposure to endless and unwanted interventions, and evaluation according to unfair and inappropriate forms of accountability, the demands on leaders become unreasonable and few people are called to lead anymore. There is an underlying current throughout the change literature that human energy, motivation, and initiative are infinitely exploitable, but like all resources this too has its limits.

In the balance between design and emergence, incumbent and potential leaders in most western countries sense that the pendulum has swung too far towards design and compliance to "Second and Third Way"[67] mandates and left little room for emergence, creativity, innovation, and entrepreneurialism. For example, in virtually every interview in my *Three Countries* research, mid- and late-career principals continued to express enthusiasm for the job and a commitment to making a difference for all children, and welcomed the increased policy emphasis on instructional leadership. However, they also commented on how the seemingly unending imposition of time-consuming managerial requirements from building issues, to health and safety mandates, to signing off on all expenditures, large or small, frustrated their efforts to focus on supporting teaching and learning. With younger principals, the phrase "overwhelming" recurred and, while they declared their enthusiasm for the job, they admitted that they coped by working harder and harder to meet all the varied expectations. They leaned heavily on mentors such as former colleagues for advice. A number of newer principals and heads indicated that their initial instinct was to clear their desks every day and sort out any problems before they went home. As a result they acted precipitously on some issues and felt that their biggest learning was to determine what had to be acted on immediately and what could go on the "back burner". When asked why younger people seemed reticent to step forward, three first- or second-year principals indicated that they had tried to encourage new applicants but admitted that "we're bad examples" because they survived by overworking. Many principals and heads, old and new, quoted a staff member as saying "I wouldn't want your job". This overwork is what Peter Gronn has called "greedy work." These leaders "are addicted to what they do and are unwilling to manage or incapable of managing their time and energy. The more they complain the harder they work, just to try to prove to themselves and others that they are super or exceptional."[68] This was particularly true at the elementary (primary) level where principals have limited leadership support when compared to most secondary schools in the regions in which I conducted my research. Secondary schools are larger and more complex: most have department heads, and some have business managers or bursars.

As this chapter has indicated, the role of school leaders and particularly principals and school headteachers is changing, and well it should to meet the issues of a knowledge society. However, Second Way and Third Way changes have leaned more heavily on centralized mandates, micro-management, educational frameworks more suited to an industrial age, and "designer leadership"[69] – all strategies that have proven to be unsustainable.[70] A recent OECD study of education in five OECD countries conducted by renowned international researchers[71] succinctly summarizes the leadership supply and demands challenge this way:

> there are concerns across countries that the role of principal as conceived for needs of the past is no longer appropriate. In many countries, principals have heavy workloads; many are reaching retirement, and it is getting harder to replace them. Potential candidates often hesitate to apply, because of overburdened roles, insufficient preparation and training, limited career prospects and inadequate support.

To this end they recommend that policy makers need to:

- *Provide higher degrees of autonomy with appropriate support.* School leaders need time, capacity and support to focus on the practices most likely to improve learning. Greater degrees of autonomy should be coupled with new models of distributed leadership, new types of accountability, and training and development for school leadership.
- *Redefine school leadership responsibilities for improved student learning.* Policy makers and practitioners need to ensure that the roles and responsibilities associated with improved learning outcomes are at the core of school leadership practice.
- *Develop school leadership frameworks for improved policy and practice.* School leadership frameworks can help provide guidance on the main characteristics, tasks and responsibilities of effective school leaders and signal the essential character of school leadership as leadership for learning.[72]

Ironically, while offering these solutions, the OECD is part of the problem. It has contributed to the succession challenge by turning education into a global rat-race through PISA[73] and similar international competitive league tables in which a nation's position becomes a matter of national pride or disgrace, and a source of government pressure for ever improving results on heads and principals.

In subsequent chapters I attempt to suggest solutions to the succession challenge, but before doing so there are two aspects of this issue that most studies ignore. These are issues of time and space: the need to address conflicting generational views of life, work, and leadership; and the need to come to grips with the fact that the world is not flat and not equitable, and place or location plays a large role in determining educational outcomes and leadership succession.

Notes

1 Pont, B., Nusche, D. and Moorman, H. (2008) *Improving School Leadership – Vol. 1: Policy and Practice*, Pont, B., Nusche, D. and Hopkins, D. (2008) *Improving School Leadership.Vol 2: Case Studies on System Leadership*. Paris: OECD. www.oecd.org/document/62/0,3343,en_2649_39263231_37125310_1_1_1_1,0 0.html, 10 April 2009.

2 Abrahamson, E. (2004) *Change Without Pain: How Managers Can Overcome Initiative Overload, Organizational Chaos, and Employee Burnout*. Boston: Harvard Business School.

3 National Association of Secondary School Principals (2001) *The Shortage of Principals*. Reson, VA: NASSP.

4 Roz, M., Celio, M., Harvey, J. and Wishon, S. (2003) *A Matter of Definition: Is There Truly a Shortage of School Principals*. Report to the Wallace Foundation. Seattle: Center on the Reinvention of Education, University of Washington.

5 Steinberg, J. (2000) "Nation's schools struggling to find enough principals", *New York Times*, 3 September: A1A4.

6 National Association of Elementary School Principals 1997, "NAESP Fact Sheet on Principal Shortage". www.naesp.org.

7 Pounder, D. and Merril, R. (2001) "Job desirability of the high school prinicipalship: a job choice perspective", *Educational Administration Quarterly*, 37 (1): 27–57.

8 Gronn, P. and Rawlings-Sanaei (2003) "Principal recruitment in an age of leadership disengagement", *Australian Journal of Education*, 47 (2): 172–85.

9 Brookings, K., Collins, G., Cour, M. and O'Neill, J. (2003) "Getting below the surface of the principal recruitment 'crisis' in New Zealand primary schools", *Australian Journal of Education*, 47 (2): 146–58.

10 Howson, J. (2005) *20th Annual Survey of Senior Staff Appointments in Schools in England and Wales*. Oxford: Education Data Surveys.

11 Williams, T. (2001) *Unrecognized Exodus, Unaccepted Accountability: The Looming Shortage of Principals and Vice Principals in Ontario Public School Boards*. Toronto: Ontario Principals' Council.

12 See the section entitled "International Reflections" in Lumby, J., Crow, G. and Pashiardis, P. (eds) (2008) *International Handbook on the Preparations and Development of School Leaders*. New York: Routledge, pp. 300–467.

13 The Wallace Foundation (2003) *Beyond the Pipeline: Getting the Principals We Need Where They Are Needed Most*. Center on Reinventing Education. www.crpe.org, 15 February 2009, p. 4.

14 Ibid., p. 12.

15   Howley, A., Andrianaivo, S. and Perry, J. (2005) "The pain outweighs the gain: why teachers don't want to become principals", *Teachers' College Record*, 30 May. www.tcrecord.org, 10 March 2007.
16   Hewitt, P., Pijanowski, J., Carnine, L. and Denney, G. (2008) "The status of school leadership in Arkansas". http://dailyheadlines.uark.edu/13184.htm, 14 September 2008.
17   Boris-Schapter, Sheryl (2007) "Got a minute? Can instructional leadership exit despite the reactive nature of the principalship?". www.acre.edu.au/documents/RC2007_Boris-Schater-GotAMinute.pdf, 3 August 2009, p. 25.
18   The National College for School Leadership has recently changed its name, to reflect government policies, to the National College for School Leadership and Children's Services. For simplicity I have chosen to use old name throughout.
19   Howson, J. (2008) 23rd *Annual Report of Senior Staff Appointments in Schools for England and Wales*. Oxford: Education Data Surveys. www.educationsurvey.org.uk_q=suystem_files-23rd+Annual+report.pdf-Adobe Reader, 9 January 2009.
20   National Professional Qualification for Headship.
21   Barker, I. (2008) "Headship trainees to be halved", *Times Educational Supplement*, 4 April. www.tes.co.uk./article.aspx?storycode_2602456, 6 April 2008, p. 1.
22   Curtis, P. (2008) "Schools 'timebomb' as 55 per cent of heads near retirement", *The Guardian*, 19 June. http://education.guardian.co.uk/print/o,,335121902,00 html, 19 June 2008.
23   PricewaterhouseCoopers (2007) *Independent Study into School Leadership: Main Report*. London: Department of Education and Skills, p. 2.
24   Moggach, Tom (2006) "Too happy being number two", *Education Guardian*, 21 March, p. 3; Hepburn, H. (2008) "Teachers shun top job", *Times Education Supplement*. www.tes.co.uk/?story_id=2651002 & window_ type= print, 8 January 2008; Smith, E. (2009) "Going for headship not an 'attractive proposition'", *Times Educational Supplement*, 9 January. www.tes.co.uk, 6 February 2009.
25   The Learning Partnership (2008) *Final Report. Succession planning: Schools and School Boards*. Toronto: Institute for Education Leadership, p. 90. www.thelearningpartnership.ca., 61–2; Williams, op. cit.
26   The Learning Partnership, op. cit., p. 75.
27   This is a similar role to an assistant principal in the US or deputy head in the UK.
28   Barty, K., Thompson, P., Blackmore, J. and Sachs, J. (2005) "Unpacking the issues: researching the shortage of school principals in two states of Australia", *The Australian Educational Researcher*, 32 (3): 1–18.
29   OECD (2008) *Improving School Leadership: Country Report for New Zealand*. www.oecd.org/edu/schoolleadership, December 2008.
30   Hewitt et al., op. cit.
31   The Learning Partnership, op.cit., p. 86.
32   Thomson, P. (2009) *School Leadership: Heads on the Block*. London: Routledge, p. 59.
33   Hood, C. (2007) "Gaming in targetworld: the targets approach to managing British public services", *Public Administration Review*, 66 (4), 517–18.
34   Recent research in the US suggests that the premature departure of principals from their school because of the accountability agenda make recruitment

of new leaders increasingly difficult. See Vladero, D. (2009) 'Turnover in principalship focus of research', *Education Week*. www.edweek.org/ ew/articles/2009/10/28/09principal_ep.h29.html?tkn=QNPFB OuK6m8Awy TzgPTBq5QCnCdM9ysCq%2BXc, 26 October 2009. See also, Fuller, E. and Young, M. (2009) 'Tenure and retention of newly hired principals in Texas', University Council for Educational Administration-Department of Educational Administration, The University of Texas at Austin. http://docs.google. com/gview?a=v&q=cache:04Ux09hokP4J:www.ucea.org/storage/pdf 26 October 2009.

35 See Chapter 5 for a detailed discussion of this role.

36 General Certificate of Secondary Education.

37 The National Challenge was launched by the Secretary of State on 10 June 2008. It is a program of support to secure higher standards in all secondary schools so that, by 2011, at least 30 per cent of pupils in every school will gain five or more GCSEs at grades A* to C, including both English and mathematics.

38 The British inspection agency.

39 The emphasis is the respondent's.

40 Gronn, P. (2008) "The state of Denmark", *Journal of Educational Administration and History*. 40 (2): 173–85, p. 174.

41 Government funded schools.

42 Smithers, A. and Robinson, P. (2007) "School headship: present and future". www.teachers.org.uk/story.php?id=3897, 4 December 2008.

43 Barker, I. (2008) "Are heads really as vulnerable as football managers?" *Times Educational Supplement*. www.tes.co.uk/article.aspx?storycode=2580493, 9 March 2009.

44 Macclesfield is a British soccer team noted for its futility.

45 Quoted in Garner, R. (2007) "Number of failing primary schools rises by a quarter", *The Independent, 1 February*. www.independent.co.uk, 23 January 2008.

46 Thomson, op. cit.

47 In Britain, accountability is determined centrally through standardized tests and a large and intrusive inspections agency.

48 Goss, P. (2009) *Final Report. An Investigation into the Possible Pressures on Headteachers – Particularly the Current School Inspection Arrangements in England and Wales – and the Potential Impact on Recruitment.* Preston: University of Central Lancashire, p. 45.

49 Smith, op. cit.

50 www.ofsted.gov.uk/Ofsted-home/Publications-and-research/Browse-all-by/Documents-by-type/Thematic-reports/Remodelling-the-school-workforce.

51 Gunter, H. and Rayner, S. (2007) "Modernizing the school workforce in England: challenging transformation and leadership", *Leadership*, 3 (1): 47–64, p. 48.

52 Marley, D. (2009) "Non-compliance could trigger industrial action", *Times Educational Supplement*. www.tes.co.uk/article.aspx?storycode=6011931, 25 April 2009.

53 In the UK this is called local managment of schools (LMS).

54 Bristow, M., Ireson, G. and Coleman, A. (2007) "A life in the day of a headteacher". Nottingham: National College for School Leadership. www.ncsl.org.uk/ media-4ed-3e-a-life-in-the-day-of-a-headteacher.pdf, 2 March 2009, p. 50.

55 Ibid., p. 55.

56   Thomson, op.cit.
57   Hopkins, D. (2007) *Every School a Great School: Realizing the Potential of System Leadership*. Maidenhead: Open University Press.
58   BBC News (2009) "Best heads 'to run school chains'". http://news.bbc.co.uk/1/hi/education/8125331.stm, 30 June 2009.
59   Court, M. (2003) "Different approaches to sharing school leadership". Nottingham: Natioanl College for School Leadership. http://forms.ncsl.org.uk/mediastore/image2/court-sharing-school-leadership-full.pdf, 23 May 2008.
60   Grubb, N. and Flessa, J. (2006) "A job too big for one: multiple principals and other non traditional approaches to school leadership", *Education Administration Quarterly*, 42 (4): 518–50.
61   McQuaid, R. (2000) "The theory of partnership: why have partnerships?", in S.P. Osborne (ed.), *Public–Private Partnerships: Theory and Practice in International Perspective*. London: Routledge, pp. 9–35, p. 22.
62   See also Thomson, P. and Blackmore, J. (2006) "Beyond the power of one: redesigning the work of school principals", *Journal of Educational Change*, 7: 166–77.
63   Glatter R. and Harvey, J. (2006) "Varieties of shared headship: a preliminary exploration", report prepared for the National College for School Leadership. www.bedfordshire.gov.uk/Resources/PDF/EducationAndLearning/Governors/GovernorsPDFS/New%20models%20of%20headship.pdf, 30 May 2009.
64   Hatch, T. (2002) "When improvement programs collide", *Phi Delta Kappan*, 83 (8): 626–34, p. 623.
65   Ibid., p. 623.
66   Elmore, R. (2002) *Bridging the Gap between Standards and Achievement*. Washington, DC: Albert Shanker Institute; Fullan, M. (2007) *Turnaround Leadership*. San Francisco, CA: Jossey-Bass; Lambert, L. (1998) *Building Capacity in Schools*. Alexandria, VA: Association for Supervision and Curriculum Development.
67   Hargreaves and Shirley (2009), op. cit.
68   Gronn, P. (2009) personal communication.
69   Gronn, P. (2003) *The New Work of Educational Leader: Changing Leadership Practice in an Era of School Reform*. London: Chapman.
70   Hargreaves and Fink (2006), op. cit.
71   Pont, B., Nusche, D. and Moorman, H. (2008) *Improving School Leadership: Policy and Practice: Executive Summaries*. Paris: OECD. www.oecd.org/edu/schoolleadership, 1 December 2008.
72   Ibid., pp. 1–2.
73   Programme for International Student Assessment. www.pisa.oecd.org/pages/0,2987,en_32252351_32235731_1_1_1_1_1,00.html.

3

The Succession
Challenge in Time
and Space

I never realized how easy I had it when I was growing up until I began to look at the burgeoning literature on generations, and how the date of a person's birth affects a person's values, outlook, and life chances.[1] At the same time, the work of Richard Florida has also made me appreciate that living within a short driving distance of one of the creative centers of the world, the Toronto corridor, has enriched my life and created opportunities for me and my family.[2] In other words, where we are in both time and space has a great bearing on our opportunities and success in life. This in turn suggests that these two dimensions have an important impact upon education and the leadership needs of schools and school districts. In this chapter, I first look at how our birth date affects our attitudes and views on life and leadership and how generational similarities and differences bear upon the succession challenge. Second, I examine the concept of the "flat" world of Thomas Friedman and argue that his notion of anyone being able to participate in the knowledge society is only partly true, because the world is also "spiky" so that economic and creative activities are centered in specific geographical areas in the world and people living in those areas have better opportunities than people in less advantaged ones.[3] This creates not only economic and social advantages and disadvantages, but also geographical disparities that have a bearing on education, and on the nature of educational leadership and the succession challenge.

While governments and school districts have responded to the impending supply problems of school leadership in varying degrees, and a few have tried to address the demands placed on leaders, there appears to be little discussion of the fact that four generations of teachers and school leaders with different experiences, values, and goals work side by side in schools all over the world, and these generational attitudes often create conflicting views on leadership and learning. A recent study in Ontario recommended that a

> study be undertaken to examine the attitudes and views of potential leaders. The new generation of leaders is different in many ways from previous or current generations and we need to ensure that we understand their values and aspirations and how to meet their needs. They are our future and we need to invest in them appropriately.[4]

An important part of an understanding of the succession challenge, therefore, is first to recognize that approaches to leadership as practiced and advocated by older generations may have only limited appeal to younger generations; and second, in the event that they do go forward, to find ways to respond accordingly. The succession challenge is to reconcile the reality that the "silent generation" and particularly "baby boomers" who dominate most of the positions of power in governments, school districts, and even schools have defined educational leadership in their own image, and expect and often demand that younger generations, "generation X" and the "millennials," or as some have called them "generation Y," must follow their lead. I would suggest that an old Hebrew proverb with a slight modification should guide our efforts to address the succession challenge: "Do not confine your future leaders to your own learning, for they were born of another time." It isn't sufficient to dress up age-old approaches to leadership and expect that they are appropriate for a new age and for new generations. Rather, it is necessary to redefine and redraft leadership philosophy and practices to correspond more closely to the values, outlook, and lifestyles of succeeding generations, and to respond to the emerging issues of a knowledge society.[5] For example Kenneth Johnson, an American demographer, indicates that in the US the millennials, born after 1978, will be less white, because the young white population in the US has declined 5.3 per cent and the non-white has increased 15.5 per cent, and more socially liberal, advocating for policies to combat global warming, support public health care, allow gay marriage, and liberalize immigration policies. There are at present 17 million more millennials in the US than baby boomers and, whether older generations like it or not, they will control governments and ultimately educational policy.[6] They have already elected a president.

The Generations

Although the term "generations" is often used in social and statistical studies, there is no scientifically agreed definition of the term, and its use is often rather arbitrary. William Strauss and Neil Howe, two of the most prolific writers on the topic, define a generation as "the aggregate of all the people born over roughly the span of a phase of life who share a common location in history and hence a common collective persona."[7] Like each person, a generation is mortal; in time it must perish and leave the world to a younger generation, and as a result "the composite life cycle becomes altogether new and fundamentally changing the entire society's mood and behavior."[8] It usually refers to periods of 20 or 30 years that are framed by significant world events like World War II or the new millennium.[9] While birth dates that delimit each generation are somewhat fluid, experts on the topic tend to agree that:

- The "veteran" generation predates 1928, the year before the great Wall Street Crash, making the youngest in 2010 therefore 82 years of age: think of Margaret Thatcher, Queen Elizabeth II, George H. W. Bush, and Jimmy Carter.
- The "silent" generation was born after 1928 and before the end of World War II in 1945, making the oldest in 2010 therefore 81 and the youngest 65: think of Sir David Frost, Gloria Steinem, Woody Allen, Colin Powell, John Major, and John McCain, and John Howard (former Australian prime minister).
- The first-stage "boomers" were born between 1946 and 1953, making the oldest in 2010 therefore 64 and the youngest 57: think of Tony Blair, Gordon Brown, Bill and Hillary Clinton, George W. Bush, Bill Gates, Prince Charles, and Helen Clark (former New Zealand prime minister). Late-stage "boomers" were born between 1954 and 1963, making them 56 to 47 in 2010: think of Barack Obama, Sarah Duchess of York, Steve Jobs (Apple Corporation), and Steven Harper (Canadian prime minister).
- "Generation Xers" were born between 1963 and 1978. The year 1963 is usually denoted as the end of the baby boom because the birth control pill became readily available. When this was combined with more liberal abortion laws and increasing numbers of women in the workplace, birth rates began to decline precipitously in most western nations for the next 15 years. In the UK for example the birth rate per woman in 1963 was almost 3.3 children and within the next 10 years declined to 1.7.[10] By 1978 when fertility rates began to gradually increase again, in the United States there were 89 million boomers and 59 million generation Xers. In 2010, generation Xers are between the

ages of 47 and 33: think of David Cameron (British Conservative leader), Michelle Obama, Tiger Woods, Michael Jordan, Michael Dell (computers), and Wayne Gretzky (hockey player). It is from this much smaller demographic that schools and school districts must replace retiring first-wave boomers. Over the next 10 to 15 years the discrepancy in leadership availability will have to be augmented by younger people born after 1978 – the millennials.

- "Millennials" were born between 1978 and 2000. As of 2010, they are between the ages of 32 and 10: think of Prince William, Prince Harry, Lebron James (basketball star), Daniel Radcliffe (Harry Potter films), Sidney Crosby (hockey player), Britney Spears, Avril Lavigne, Ronaldinho, Wayne Rooney (soccer players), and Zachary and Riley Harrop (my grandsons).[11] This is a much larger demographic, and potentially larger than the boomers if you include immigrants to western countries.[12] In time this larger generation will solve any supply problems in educational leadership, assuming we can get the demands side right and redefine leadership to make it more attractive to this emerging generation.

Some individuals such as President Obama have been called "cuspers"[13] because they are between generations and tend to imbibe attitudes from both generations. While life history research[14] suggests that within generations there are life cycles that tend to follow predictable patterns from youth through old age, each of these five generations sees itself as unique, and has difficulty placing itself in the larger course of history, or understanding the experiences and outlook of the other generations. They all have "unique work ethics, different perspectives on work, distinct and preferred ways of managing and being managed, idiosyncratic styles, and unique ways of viewing such work-world issues as quality, service, and well – just showing up for work."[15]

The Vets and the Silents

I am a member of the silent generation, born between 1928 and 1945. Why silent? We didn't make waves, we did what we were told, we played the game, we paid our dues; and now, in our declining years, we expect and insist on the rewards our conformity has earned us. Our world was pretty much designed for us by previous generations, and opportunities for emergence were circumscribed. In fact, non-conformists either stayed in the closet or were ostracized. We were too young to directly experience the Depression and World War II, events that made a profound impression on our parents – the veteran generation. Shaped by these experiences, my parents and other veterans, or as Tom Brokaw the American author called them "the greatest generation,"[16] were thrifty; my father refused to ever get a credit card, was loyal to country and company, and believed in the corporate structure and chain of command. They married young, often because they had to; they stayed married because they were expected to; and they seldom divorced because churches and governments didn't allow them to. When the men came back from the war in 1945 and 1946, this veteran generation produced on average 3.3 children per couple, and the baby boom generation was literally born.

In spite of their involvement in war work, their wives and girlfriends returned to traditional female roles after the war. Society expected women to marry and stay at home and raise children. For a woman to be unmarried was considered somewhat of an aberration, and many women tolerated dysfunctional marriages rather than face social disapprobation, and an inhospitable work environment for which many had limited employable skills. If women did go to university, it was often assumed that they went to find a suitable mate. They were said to be looking for an MRS. Women's job opportunities were limited to sales clerk, teaching, nursing, and secretarial work. Women rarely assumed executive roles, and certainly were not considered suitable to run a school, especially a secondary school. A former male colleague admitted to me, with some embarrassment, that he got his first principal's appointment at age 26 in the 1950s because he was the only male teacher on a primary school teaching staff of quite mature and capable women. Minorities, especially in the US, were relegated to menial jobs that did not compete with white males. Like women, many of whom had contributed magnificently to the war effort, they were pushed out of higher-paying jobs when the vets returned from overseas. After quick introductory teacher training courses, the vets joined the teaching profession and brought with them their military experience and its emphasis on discipline, order, and structure. This is the school system that most of us silents experienced.

We, the comparatively few silents, born between the larger veteran demographic and the boomers, were in a "demographic trough". The Depression had made child bearing an expensive proposition that few could afford, and the war made it physically impossible. Our coming of age was more uncomplicated than subsequent generations because we had fewer people to compete against. Entry to university, summer jobs, and post-graduation employment seemed to come relatively easily in the booming 1950s. We inherited our parents' concern for financial security, and the belief that by suppressing our individual needs and desires and working with others we could achieve common goals. The pursuit of these beliefs and values whether in school or the workplace would ensure our personal safety, security, and in time, if we were patient, promotion to more senior positions and the resulting rewards. It is no accident that many of the corporate leaders who rewarded themselves generously in the 1990s at others' expense, such as in the Enron scandal, were of the silent generation and believed they were merely receiving justified compensation for years of loyalty and self-sacrifice on behalf of the organization – although boomers at AIG and other large firms have recently shown they are not behind in pillaging investors.

We silents had our hang-ups. Sex was something young people thought about, talked about, but didn't do much about. It has been said that the silents were the most sexually repressed generation of the twentieth century. Most of us silents came from intact families: fathers worked outside the home at a time when jobs were available, and mothers stayed at home to look after the children. In many ways we imbibed our views on organization and leadership from our veteran parents and valued loyalty, hard work, and paying your dues. For those of us who became teachers, we did so just as the first wave of baby boomers was hitting the schools. New schools went up, promotions accelerated, and teaching jobs became more plentiful. Governments allowed many of us to rush through teacher training, and school jurisdictions faced the prospect of hiring and hoping that their new recruits would succeed. The spirit of the times drew many inspired and innovative teachers into the profession, but it also tolerated incompetence and eccentricity. There was little or no support for young teachers; it was either sink or swim. The vets were running the schools and school districts and government education departments, so they tended to replicate military structures dedicated to obedience, order and conformity. The first criterion of a good teacher and a good principal was the ability to maintain order: were you a good disciplinarian? In my experience, many truly appalling teachers survived because they could maintain discipline. By the late 1960s and early 1970s late-stage boomers poured into school systems and particularly secondary schools and early-stage boomers began to join the teaching ranks.

The Boomers

The boomer generation was the first television generation. By the early 1950s most homes had one quite expensive (for the times) television in the living room and families shared their favorite shows together. Television brought events like the Korean War, the assassinations of the Kennedys and Martin Luther King, Vietnam, Watergate, Woodstock, personalities like the Beatles, the Stones, and Elvis, movements such as civil rights in the US, separatism in Quebec in Canada, and feminism in most western societies into every virtually living room and helped to shape boomers values and outlook.

Inspired by their veteran parents who returned from the war effort determined to create a better world for their children, the first-stage boomers fashioned the consciousness revolution of the 1960s and 1970s. After years of looking outward to fight wars and depression, young people now looked inward on their society and found the values and mores of previous generations wanting and determined that change was necessary. Boomers came of age when times were good, the economy was growing, expansion was everywhere, and change was possible. If the defining quality of the silent generation was loyalty, the defining quality of the boomers was optimism: "all things are possible if we just work hard enough."[17] They were also very competitive – they had to be with so many fighting for places in good schools, good jobs, and teaching positions – and they learned to share and work as teams because crowded schools only had so many books to go around and so many desks to work on.

As they have matured they have changed the world around them. They revolutionized sexual mores and transformed attitudes towards reproductive rights; and, for the first time, a generation demonstrated a genuine interest in ecology. As one first-stage boomer expressed it, "we were eaten up by intensity."[18] Raised for the most part within intact families, often indulged by parents influenced by the more liberal child-rearing philosophies of such experts as Benjamin Spock, encouraged by their veteran and early silent parents who had sublimated individual goals for larger purposes like fighting a war, boomers have often been called the "me" generation for their self-absorption and pursuit of self-gratification. If a marriage didn't work, they moved on; divorce rates skyrocketed in most western countries in the 1960s and 1970s. If caught in a shady enterprise, like Bill Clinton the prototypical boomer, they apologized and kept moving; if the job didn't work out, they quit and found another.

As they have aged, boomers have grown more conservative; they elected Reagan in the US, Mulroney in Canada, Thatcher in the UK, and Howard in Australia. Boomers who found ways to avoid serving in Vietnam in their youth, like George W. Bush and Dick Cheney in the United States, joined hands with youthful rocker Tony Blair and student rebel Jack Straw in the UK to take their respective nations into the Iraqi quagmire. Boomers who had worked against the establishment in their younger days now became the arbitrators of what was right, and good, and moral. At the highest political levels they have been the architects of the standards/standardization movement in education in the 1990s. As a generation, boomers have successfully created the spin that this ideological and corporatist agenda is the only way to ensure "world class" educational systems and that "no child will be left behind". And in spite of great resistance, especially from early boomers who nostalgically remember the heady days of the 1960s and 1970s when all things seemed possible, other boomers have ensured compliance through a technocratic managerial leadership model driven by accountability systems.

Now, as the first wave of boomers approaches retirement, many have decided not to retire but to refocus.[19] Some have simply refused to retire altogether and continue on, much to the frustration of younger generations, while others have moved on to second careers. The boomer attitude seems to be that "aging is mandatory, growing old is optional."[20] I meet periodically with seven former principals from my old school district – three late silents and four early boomers, all of whom are in their sixties or seventies. None has really retired: four of them are deeply involved in teacher education, one is an award-winning real estate agent,[21] one is a successful mortgage broker, and the last is a celebrated volunteer director of the food-bank[22] in his community. And here I am, writing another book.

Boomers have profoundly changed the educational landscape. In the 1950s and 1960s, their sheer numbers forced an explosion of new school construction, teacher hiring, and promotions to leadership positions. By the late 1960s and throughout the 1970s as they moved into teaching positions, this ambitious generation quickly became restive with the traditional structures and the paternalistic leadership of older generations. Anxious to move up the ranks, they promoted more open approaches to schooling such as non-graded schools, open classrooms, destreaming,[23] and more collegial approaches to leadership. Innovative, progressive, and experimental schools sprang up in every western nation, staffed by idealistic late silents and early boomers determined to change the very nature of schooling. By the early 1980s, as the boomers moved into leadership positions, these experiments either died or experienced what I have called the "attrition of change"[24] as declining enrollments, economic slowdown, and a conservative backlash forced them to "regress to the mean": for example, schools such as Countesthorpe in Leicestershire, England, William Tyndale in London,[25] Lord Elgin and Thornlea in Ontario, and John Adams High School in Portland, Oregon, among hundreds of others.[26]

Beginning in 1983 in the US with *A Nation at Risk*, which expressed concern for "a rising tide of mediocrity," and the 1988 Education Reform Act in the United Kingdom, the maturing boomers now locked into major leadership positions responded to the economic, political, and demographic social forces of the day, pushed their values of competition, hard work, innovation, and accountability, and orchestrated many of the changes in education over the past 15 years. They replaced traditional educational structures that protected out-of-date leaders and their practices by designing policies such as local management of schools in England and charter schools and voucher programs in Alberta and most states in the United States, eliminating local school boards in New Brunswick and New Zealand, and drastically reducing the powers of local school districts in the UK and Ontario.

Frustrated by dated organizational structures and leadership practices that failed to respond in a timely fashion to the perceived needs of a globalized economy, boomers revved up the educational change process by adopting market forces of competition and survival of the fittest among schools and school districts, and by driving improvement through competitive standardized tests that not only ranked all students, rewarding the successful and penalizing the unsuccessful, but also forced their teachers, principals, and schools to compete to improve test scores as a way to increase[27] enrollments or in some cases to keep jobs.[28]

The cost to human energy was never considered because boomers think everyone should work as hard as they do, and be as committed to their careers as they are.[29] "Workaholism" is endemic among boomers. Since boomers tend to dominate regulatory bodies such as OFSTED in England and accreditation teams in many states in the United States, they not only determine the educational agenda but ensure that other boomers and younger generations, like generation X, comply.

Generation X

Squeezed in a demographic trough between the huge boomer generation and the potentially larger millennial generation is generation X, popularized by the author Douglas Coupland.[30] To boomers they are slackers, entitled whiners, socially inept, and pushy. Xers see themselves quite differently: as generation Xer Corrie Stone-Johnson states, "What others see as slack, we see as flexible. What others see as entitled, we see as balanced."[31] This is the generation of latchkey kids who during their formative years came home from school to an empty house, flat, or apartment, as more and more of their mothers joined the workforce either as a matter of values and choice or to compensate for shifting economic realities that made two incomes a necessity. In addition, spiraling divorce rates obliged many single parents, usually women, to work outside the home. For example, in the period between 1961 and 1971 in the United States, divorce rates increased 165 per cent.[32] With parents often out of the home, and increasingly mobile, Xers learned to rely on themselves and build friendship networks as a way to survive. The long-running television program 'Friends' is about a group of Xers in which their circle of friends acts as a surrogate family.

Xers have often been described as skeptical or even cynical. Their skepticism is well founded. In contrast to boomers who grew up in times of economic growth, Xers matured during the 1980s and early 1990s during times of economic hardship and dislocation. When they left school, jobs were hard to come by, even in teaching. As they matured, they witnessed their parents' and older siblings' loyalty to corporations and public institutions rewarded with dismissal and redundancy as corporations and public services sought to further enhance productivity by downsizing, outsourcing, restructuring, or reengineering to allegedly meet the demands of the global marketplace. Xers witnessed the trauma of their elders, who defined themselves by their work, losing their jobs, and they decided that for them a job was a job, no more, no less. Rather than living to work, they would work to live. Rather than job security, they would look for security in a well-developed résumé. Xers sought positions with a variety of challenging opportunities that would look good for their next job application. Since organizational loyalty was a thing of the past, they wanted to be prepared for the next downsizing or redundancy. To many Xers, however, teaching is just a good job with good holidays and reasonable pay – certainly not a calling or mission as some boomers might insist.[33] Lusting after and competing for leadership roles like their boomer older brothers and sisters is just not in their makeup.[34] For Xers, the need for balance in life is a vital driving force and motivator. They value their family time, and treasure their leisure time for sports and activities away from the job. This is particularly true of women who still bear the greatest share of child-care in our societies. Interestingly, many of generation X sports, like the X games, are individual but done in groups.

After growing up observing the very public ethical and moral failures of too many public officials, the egregious behavior of some predatory priests and other clerics, and the greed of more than a few corporate executives, generation Xers tend to trust only themselves and their small network of friends, and at work their community of practice.[35] They often resent external agencies that limit their autonomy, and particularly agencies that police their efforts such as OFSTED[36] in the UK. This inspectoral system, designed to ensure predictability of outcomes, control over teachers' and leaders' practices, and compliance by school and local authorities with government policies, would be anathema to most generation Xers, and there is some evidence that it is an important deterrent to the recruiting, development, and retention of high-quality leadership in England.[37]

While this generation may not be about to put in the hours that its predecessors did, it is the first truly "wired" generation, so it tends to work smarter if not harder, and has brought the phrase "multi-tasking" into our lexicon. Raised on the Walkman, multiple radio stations, and early electronic games, generation X was also the first computer generation. By the early 1980s, early Apple products like the Mac SE and the ubiquitous Commodore 64 began to appear in schools. Parents in more affluent communities scrambled to raise funds so that their children could get a head start on the new technology. Since only one person could interact with these early technologies at a time, they intensified the Xers' sense of isolation and independence. As a result, Xers thrive in situations where they have challenging, meaningful work and are given the freedom to pursue results independently or in self-selected groups. For Xers, time is a variable, not a constant; results are what count. Why adhere to traditional time slots, timelines, and time-consuming meetings when the job can be done just as well, if not better, electronically, and with more flexible use of time? They don't do well with the stress of supervisors hanging over their shoulders, or threats of dire consequences for failure. They would rather walk than conform, or at least avoid pressured situations by steering clear of positions of formal leadership. Some authors have suggested that "management by objectives" is on its way back as a useful way to balance this generation's requirement for challenge and independence with the organizational need for accountability.[38] Xers thrive on change and are very good at coming together to work on projects and then disbanding. They are not "good soldiers" and do not respond well to hierarchies and organizational teams. Whereas boomers feel the need for social and conversational groups, Xers are quite adept at working independently and then coming together, often electronically, and pooling results to produce an outcome.

For at least the next 10 years, efforts to replace retiring silents and early boomers will have to come from these comparatively few, publicly skeptical, organizational mavericks who find competitive league tables, standardized testing, and teaching a prescribed curriculum alien to their generational ethos. These strategies are seen as part of the boomers' ideology to make young people conform to their narcissistic image of the educated person. Xers view the boomers' approach to leadership and change as "wrong headed, atavistic, and chock full of arrogant self importance."[39] Many Xers have simply refused to pursue leadership positions that they believe are based on purposes with which they disagree, within a system whose values they reject. As one assistant principal in the *Change Over Time?* study stated, "I'm implementing government policy I do not agree with." With boomers staying in leadership roles longer than expected, however, and the leading edge of the next generation having now reached 32 years of age, Xers will soon be viewed as that brief interlude between the boomers and the millennials and I suspect will have little lasting impact upon education and the nature of educational leadership.

The Millennials

The transition to the millennials that will take place within the next few years raises the question: will this new generation, the sons and daughters of boomers, be any more compliant and properly respectful of existing institutions and "designer" leadership than their older siblings, the Xers? On the surface, millennials have been well prepared to perpetuate the standardization agenda. After all, this is the generation that the boomer designed educational systems have trained to conform to standardized testing, teaching, and curriculum over the past 15 years. They played the game, they jumped the hurdles, they passed the tests, and now they are ready to take on the world. Or are they? Will they meet the succession challenge and fill the leadership roles vacated by retiring boomers? They have the numbers;[40] do they have the desire? Will they be prepared? Will they make a difference? The answer I suspect is – it depends. It depends on whether this generation is "more interesting, more confident, less hidebound and uptight, better educated, more creative, in some essential fashion, unafraid"[41] or whether, as professor of English Mark Baurlein concluded, it is the "dumbest generation" that suffers from "vigorous indiscriminate ignorance." "No cohort in human history," he proclaims, "has opened such a fissure between its material conditions and its intellectual attainments." None, he asserts, "has experienced so many technological enhancements and yielded so little mental progress."[42] It is probably neither and both. The millennial generation is different from any preceding generation because it is the "net" generation; a generation of young people quite conversant with laptops, BlackBerries, and iPhones; a generation that is continually connected to the internet. Like any large generation such as the vets and boomers that preceded it, this technologically sophisticated generation will shape educational leadership and the world around it to fit its values, life goals, and ways of thinking and leading. Growing up with Facebook, YouTube, MySpace, wikis, blogging, Twittering, text messaging, and interactive games, millennials are the first global generation ever. "Net geners"[43] are "smarter, quicker, and more tolerant of diversity than their predecessors. They care strongly about social justice and the problems faced by society and are typically engaged in some kind of civic activity at school, at work, or in their communities."[44] They rallied in the hundreds of thousands to assist the victims of hurricane Katrina in New Orleans and the tragic tsunami of 2004.

Don Tapscott[45] captures this generation in eight norms that differentiate millennials from boomers and suggests that this generation is much more than a younger version of their boomer parents:

- *Freedom*. Millennials expect to determine where, when, and why they work, and to use technology to rearrange traditional notions of time, space, and purpose. After a recent workshop in Calgary, a young assistant principal asked me how you get newly minted teachers to commit to school goals. They didn't oppose, she explained, but rather ignored efforts to build cohesion. It was her perception that these young millennials "were shopping around. If they didn't like teaching after a year or two, they would choose to move into another field." They want the right to choose.
- *Customization*. Millennials like to customize their family and social lives to suit their personalities and values in the same way they customize their media. Like their boomer parents, millennials experience the confidence and optimism of a large generation growing up in generally good economic times. Boomer parents have encouraged their children to feel good about themselves, structured their homes in a more democratic fashion, and sheltered them from the excesses of society. From safety helmets for bicycle riders to graduated driver's licenses, boomer parents have tried to protect their millennial children from every conceivable hazard. This is a generation, therefore, that has been brought up to feel special and express ideas freely – that expects to be heard, and of course listened to. As the slogan I saw on a young man's T-shirt proclaimed,

"everyone is entitled to MY opinion." Given a choice, millennials would customize their jobs in ways that maintain balance in their lives. As with Xers, lifestyle balance is a major motivating force for millennials.

- *Scrutiny.* Tapscott calls this generation "the new scrutinizers."[46] As the net generation, they seem to have developed innate "crap detectors" from years of critically analyzing information from the internet. This skepticism makes them even worse soldiers than generation Xers. They are not prepared to merely accept structures, policies, and practices at face value. Like Ronald Reagan, they follow the maxim, "trust but verify."

- *Integrity.* They care about integrity for themselves and others. They expect governments, corporations, and other social organizations as well as senior leaders to be "honest, considerate, transparent, and abiding by their commitments."[47] To older generations this need for integrity can come across as brashness or even narcissism. Interestingly, they have been called the "me" generation. If this sounds familiar, it is the same epithet used to describe young boomers in their day.[48] Ironically, other authors have named them the "we" generation because of their need to collaborate with others.[49]

- *Collaboration.* Millennials are natural collaborators and team players. Generation Xers came of age with computer applications that intensified their independence and isolation, whereas more recent applications like Facebook, MySpace, and YouTube and many other networking sites promote interactivity. If the water cooler or the staff room were where previous generations shared ideas and issues with friends and colleagues, these internet sites are the water coolers of the twenty-first century. Millennials know how to use them to connect individuals around ideas and causes, as opposed to the mere dissemination of information. The 2008 presidential campaign of Barack Obama in the US, in which the Obama team encouraged millions of young people to use these interactive networks and their cell phones, BlackBerries, and laptops to organize their local communities to promote Obama's candidacy, has already profoundly changed our democratic processes. In the early days of the Democrats' primary, Hillary Clinton's team had the "big money" and the "old pros" who knew how to win primaries and other elections, and she was far ahead in the polls. They used the internet but primarily as a broadcast medium to get out her message, in the same way one might use television. This was in contrast to Obama's grassroots empowerment of supporters to use the internet as an interactive medium to build networks of workers who would get out the vote. Obama won the primary in the small state of Idaho, for example, even though he never visited it, because students in Idaho, excited by his candidacy, built collaborative internet networks of young people and others to get behind their candidate. It is generally conceded that the enthusiasm and collaborative instincts of young people to elect this young, dynamic, but relatively inexperienced black man to the presidency of the United States were major contributors to his historic election. Change agents in education will have to learn how to connect with all stakeholders and promote this kind of collaboration if genuine progress is to be made in how we educate our children. Similarly, our views of how we recruit and develop leaders will depend increasingly on how we engage future leaders in collaborative activities. The National College for School Leadership in the UK[50] and the Lutheran schools of Australia[51] among many other organizations[52] have made impressive strides in this regard. The architects of many of these programs face the task of providing leaders for educational systems that still determine policies with little opportunity for key stakeholders to influence decisions. Not surprisingly, they tend to employ the internet for broadcast purposes rather than using it to capture its interactive potential. Older generations are wary of many of the new applications and often fight changes. For example, I recently worked in a school district in which employees must have permission from superiors in the chain of command to access the internet during the school day because the "powers that be" feared that teachers and principals and others might fritter their time away accessing Facebook and MySpace.

- *Entertainment*. Millennials expect their activities including their jobs to be fun, or at least interesting and engaging. The renowned American psychiatrist William Glasser argues that as humans we have four basic needs: to care and feel cared for, to have hope for the future, to have some power over one's circumstances, and to have fun.[53] Millennials believe that their work should be intrinsically satisfying and they expect to enjoy what they are doing. They have the ability to multi-task and switch on and off tasks with a relative ease that older generations find bewildering. For example, there is a great debate in a neighboring school between the younger teachers who allow their students to wear headsets and listen to music while they do their schoolwork, and older teachers who argue that such practices get in the way of real learning.
- *Speed*. This is a generation, raised on instant feedback from video games, that finds e-mail too slow when they can get on-the-spot responses from text messaging and Twittering. In the workplace they need constant feedback. The annual review is insufficient; they expect to know how they are doing now, not next week or next year. They bridle at the snail-like decision-making processes of older generations who in turn complain that younger people make decisions too quickly and precipitously and get themselves into hot water. A significant theme of my interviews with older principals was that

many of the new generation expect after a few years of teaching that they know all they need to know to move up the ladder and can't understand why they must "pay their dues." The word "entitled" to describe this generation comes up time and again with more senior leaders. Indeed, they do feel special.[54] Howe and Strauss state that the relationship between boomers and their millennial children in the US is one in which "older generations have inculcated in 'millennials' the sense that they are, collectively, vital to the nation and to their parents' sense of purpose."[55] Hovered over by "helicopter" parents, who have monitored and managed their children's lives every step of the way,[56] pushed by anxious and threatened teachers to achieve higher and higher test scores, hectored by the press and governments to believe that their nation depends on their success, millennials "are on track to become some of the best-educated and best-behaved adults in the nation's[57] history."[58] The product of "hyper-parenting" – "the compulsive drive to perfect one's children"[59] – millennials have also lived intensified lives in and outside school and feel great anxiety to succeed as quickly as possible.

- *Innovation.* For those of us who have been around for a while, the pace of innovation throughout most of our lives has been glacial compared to the past 20 years. I can recall my father telling me how he built his own crystal set to listen to the baseball games on KDKA in Pittsburgh in the late 1920s. Some of us will remember the first TV sets in the 1950s and then some years later color sets. I remember how thrilled I was when my school district allowed me to purchase a $5,000 Mac SE for my division in the late 1980s. Millennials, however, have grown up in an age of constant innovation. Innovation is part of life; they expect it, and new products and applications are certainly not a source of awe and amazement. While I'm still reading the instructions for some new device, my grandsons have it up and working. It seems like no time since rather bulky portable phones morphed into small iPhones that can connect to the internet, text message, show movies, play music, and yes, can even be used as a telephone. Millennials expect and demand change and innovation and bridle under old hierarchal, command and control approaches to organization that inhibit collaboration, creativity, speed, and fun.

One reading of these norms is that this new generation will burst the bonds of industrial age structures and cultures and move the education of our young people into a high-tech era of collaboration, innovation, and creativity. Another reading might suggest however that this is a generation that is ill prepared for the hard work, perseverance, and sustained inquiry that educational leadership requires and is more interested in going along, getting along, and when things get tough, moving along. Judy Scotney, a boomer Australian principal with considerable international experience, commented that:

> boomers are the ones putting in the longer hours and I suspect there is simply a refusal from the younger generations to follow. They simply arrive at school at 8.00 a.m. and leave at 4.00 p.m. and what isn't done, doesn't seem to get done. They certainly have a strong desire to better achieve the desired "work–life balance." I am wondering if the boomers are still in some aspects being driven by the work ethic demonstrated to them by their parents from the 50s. They are certainly driven by a desire to achieve the very best they can. To me, and I suspect this is the case in more places than Australia from what I saw, generations X and certainly Y want their life first and work is just that. Somehow I wonder how we boomers got so consumed with the desire to live for our work. I don't think this will be as much the case in 10–15 years. I also see the Xs and especially Ys working and leading differently – with a shift to more (not always appropriate) delegation, committee work, talking, linking (yes, they are the kings of connection) and this is certainly how they operate.[60]

A retiring American principal whom I interviewed for my *Three Countries* study captured the boomer–millennial dichotomy this way:

> My generation came to early adulthood during the Vietnam era. There is an imperialism to my generation that they feel if they were right about Vietnam, that they were right about everything else too, that they never really had to ask any questions, whatever they thought was right, they were right about Vietnam. They didn't want advice and really did not want anyone to tell them what to do. They are being replaced by a current generation who wants to be trained in everything; they love training. I'm not trained to do that. Can we have a 15-minute training session? They're much nicer to work with. They're more collegial, congenial, and sharing. But there is a sense that, how do I do this? It can translate into dependence.

One of my American boomer interview respondents captured a similar idea when he paraphrased President Kennedy's famous line from his inaugural address by saying this new generation asks not "what they can do for the school system but what the school system can do for them." Still another respondent whose husband is a clergyman told me that her husband was on an interview committee in which a young man applying for a job as a church minister asked if he would have to work on Sundays.

Albert Einstein is often attributed with the aphorism that "insanity is doing the same thing over and over again and expecting different results." Regardless of how it is packaged, more and more of the same old approach to succession management, without profoundly changing our social vision and within that larger picture redefining the purposes of education and of educational leadership, is just insane. The succession challenge then is to rethink our notions of leadership and of leadership development designed "for another time" to invite, prepare, and support newer generations to assume the mantle of educational leadership.

Issues of Place and Space

There is a television advertisement in Canada in which a "thirty-something" professional woman is seen leaving her workplace, driving to her home, stripping off her dress and placing it in the washing machine, then some time later removing it and putting it on just in time for her husband's arrival home, and their hasty departure together for an evening of dining and dancing. While I can't remember what the advertisement was selling or why a professional woman had to rewash the same dress she had worn all day at work before going out again, I do know the brains behind the ad were selling a lifestyle to generation Xers and early millennials. What these two generations share is a burning desire to create balance between work, home, and a social life. What also struck me is how geographically close this woman's work was to her home and how place was an important part of her ability "to have it all." Xers and millennials not only intend to manage their time commitments to balance work and family, but also attempt to arrange their spaces to fit their chosen lifestyle. For leaders or potential leaders who are married or in committed relationships, the job prospects of their partner play a huge part in choosing locations.

By way of contrast, previous generations, especially educational leaders, impressed superiors (or fooled them) by putting in long hours, and went where they were told. For example, school district leaders expected my generation of leaders in Ontario and those boomers that followed as school-based leaders to handle any type of school situation and travel to wherever they were directed. For four of my five years as a school leader I was required to drive an hour each way to work from my home – often over snowy and barely ploughed roads. On occasion during Ontario winters I strapped cross-country skis to the roof of my car in case I got snowbound somewhere. Driving great distances to work was considered just part of the job: take it or leave it. If you happened to draw a school close to your home it was good luck rather than good management. For a number of years in my school district, as a senior leader I was involved in the placement of principals and assistant principals in schools, and rarely heard any discussion of where a prospective school leader lived and how this placement might affect his or her family. Since most of my generation of leaders were men with wives at home, or more mature women whose children were safely on their way in life, a person's lifestyle was just not an important consideration. Moreover, throughout most of my career there were lots of people who aspired and competed for leadership roles, so thinking about place was not a matter for negotiation. If you wanted the job, you went where you were told. You either drove great distances or pulled up stakes and moved your family to where the job was located. Now, with newer generations reluctant to fill up the ranks of educational leadership, addressing the issue of place becomes an important part of the succession challenge. A recent study of succession issues in Britain, with its open market approach to appointing its headteachers (principals), concluded that "the most important criterion for headteacher applicants when choosing schools to apply to was that they were near their home or a location of significance to them (such as a partner's workplace etc.)."[61]

Discussions of place and space and their relationship to how people live can thank Thomas Friedman, a well-known journalist with *The New York Times* and his bestselling book *The World Is Flat*, for placing the topic in the forefront of public consciousness. Through his extensive travels in both developed and underdeveloped nations, and his wide-ranging interviews with leaders in the public and private sectors from these countries, he contends that the world is no longer organized hierarchically, with some people and nations at the top and others in some degree dependent or subservient to them; rather, as a result of a revolution in interactive communications technologies, "the world is flat." As he states, "what the flattening of the world means is that we are now connecting all the knowledge centers on the planet together into a single global network."[62] People can bypass limitations of place and space and traditional structures and participate directly in the knowledge economy. In other words, we have conquered time and space and reduced their importance in daily living. He uses such examples as call centers in Bangalore, software development in Dalian near Beijing in China, and the trading, tourist, service, and computing centers of Dubai. He shows how cell phones and wireless internet have allowed people in less developed countries to be "wired" without going through the stage of infrastructure development such as the need for telephone wires that more developed countries went through. He provides examples of how education and medical practice and other areas of human activity use interactive communications networks to overcome limitations of place and space. Friedman shows how many service jobs in developed countries like Canada, the United States, and

England, such as preparing a will or writing up an insurance policy, are transferred offshore to cheap labour areas. For example, all a lawyer or insurance agent has to do is determine the content of the will or policy and transmit it to the overseas center, and in short order you receive the formal documents and the lawyer or insurance company makes a nice profit. In the meantime, legal secretaries and insurance company employees lose jobs. Your tax return may well have been processed in Mumbai. For those nations and individuals in the developed world that fail to adjust, he foresees only lost jobs, economic retrenchment, decline in public sector spending and services, and general economic and social distress. Friedman's answers to this "doom and gloom" are rather unimaginative, however: more education in science and math and engineering, and going green – not bad ideas but certainly under-whelming solutions for such dire predictions.

Whether we agree with this analysis or not, Friedman has raised serious questions about the importance of place and space that are also addressed by Richard Florida, an economic geographer at the University of Toronto. Through extensive, albeit controversial research, Florida argues that modern economies are driven by a creative class. This class produces a high per centage of a nation's wealth. In the United States, he contends, 50 per cent of national wealth is produced by 30 per cent of the population.[63] He argues that creative, innovative, and entrepreneurial people tend to cluster together in those places around the globe that provide access to people with similar talents, like Nashville in the US for music, Silicon Valley for innovative technology, Finland's Helsinki area which competes with Silicon Valley for leadership in the telecom industry, and so on. What these areas have in common is an openness to talented immigrants, world class educational institutions that attract and promote creativity and innovation, tolerance of people with different lifestyles and sexual orientations such as in Toronto, Boston, and London, and easy access to technology such as the Oxbridge corridor in the UK or the Vancouver–Seattle area on the west coast of North America.[64] In other words, places are more important than ever, because people are increasingly congregating in specific areas in this world based on career and lifestyle choices. Florida argues, therefore, that the world may be flat as defined by Friedman's narrow definition, but in reality it is "spiky" at the same time. Observations of our planet at night show that certain areas are lit up brightly with spikes of light in varying degrees of intensity shooting up into the darkened sky, while other areas, such as most of Africa, remain in total darkness, or with a few widely dispersed shards of light. This picture of the globe supports the notion that people congregate in certain places and not in others, and these places are the engines of economic productivity that in some cases cross national borders. For example, one such area surrounds Lake Ontario and includes Toronto in Canada and Rochester in the United States. Other spiky areas include the Boston–New York–Washington corridor and Silicon Valley in the US, London and environs in the UK, Sydney through to Melbourne in Australia, the Osaka–Nagasaki corridor in Japan, Mumbai and Bangalore in India, and the Shanghai area in China, among many others. While Friedman has captured the promise and challenges of a wired world, in his exuberance he underestimates the importance of place. The renowned economist Edward Leamer, in his devastating critique of Friedman's methods and conclusions, states that "there are many advantages that children can enter this world with including intelligence, physical power, and agility, good looks and caring parents. It also matters where you live."[65]

Where people live has a great bearing on the succession challenge in education because it determines where the students live and where the schools are built and where the leaders are required. Perhaps more challenging from an equity perspective are the needs of those places with fewer people and fewer students and fewer schools, which require quality education and first-class leaders as much as if not more than the areas in which people cluster. The succession challenge is more than just creating a plentiful supply of potential leaders; it is about the creation of a supply that can meet the expectations of diverse locations, particularly rural settings and inner cities. The combination of younger generations' reticence to assume leadership positions and their passionate desire to maintain a reasonable life–work balance compounds the problem created by the demographic issues described in Chapter 2. For example, researchers in Catholic schools in Australia revealed that life–work balance was an issue for over 50 per cent of the deputy principals who were unwilling to become principals.[66] Karen Barty and her colleagues, in their study of principal shortages in Victoria and South Australia, reported that "the smaller number of applicants for vacant positions do not necessarily indicate a decline in interest in school leadership ... but principal aspirants have become increasingly strategic in their applications."[67] This strategic approach affects rural schools most directly. A body of research in Tasmania,[68] Victoria,[69] and Queensland[70] reports that the unique demands on teaching principals in rather conservative rural communities with a idiosyncratic sense of place may discourage leaders from tackling leadership roles in such settings. Principals in these more remote areas are often assigned or hired on temporary contracts and usually stay for only a year or two, which precludes the continuity required to sustain substantive school improvement. This can often leave rural students lagging behind their urban counterparts. Financial and other similar inducements such as travel expenses designed to attract principals to these areas have had mixed success. England has similar difficulties. In his annual report on applications for leadership to British schools, John Howson uses a metric of the number of times a school has to advertise to get suitable applicants for a school head. He reports that "readvertisement rates remained at a high level in the primary sector for the fourth year in a row reaching a high of 37% in 2006/07."[71] His reports also indicate that Inner London schools, while improving in their response rate, remain a significant challenge, along with schools in the less affluent north of England and especially church schools. An Ontario report stated that:

> Of particular concern is the geographic distribution of current and future leaders. Small boards,[72] particularly in the north or more rural regions, may not have large enough pools of candidates from which to draw ... most people with principals' and/or supervisory officers' qualifications[73] live in the central and south central regions of Ontario. Board officials also indicated in interviews that the boards tend to hire from within, without looking for external candidates. Even then, however, people are reluctant to take jobs that require relocating their families.[74]

As I stated previously, supply and demand statistics are often politicized and, depending on the educational jurisdiction, of varying degrees of accuracy, but there does seem to be a general international trend that, in spite of the number of people qualified to be school leaders, shortages of quality leadership are a function of location, especially in many inner city schools and schools in more remote areas. This suggests that in addition to financial inducements such as extra pay, travel allowances, moving allowances and the like, or some form of coercion, schools and districts will have to begin to tailor their jobs, expectations, rewards, and strategies to account for changing lifestyles and the demand for a more attractive life–work balance.

Richard Florida has some advice on factors to consider in developing policies to attract quality leaders to assume positions in "location-challenged" schools and districts. When schools and school districts recruit leaders they need to look at more than financial inducements. In a comprehensive study of what creative people look for in a place to live, Florida listed the following three factors:

- *Aesthetics.* Is the location attractive? Does it have spacious parks, hiking trails, sports facilities? Were there opportunities to meet and interact with people like themselves? Was there access to culture, not just opera and symphonies, but little theater, choral groups, and the like?
- *Basic services.* Is the area affordable? Does it have decent public transportation or at least reasonable traffic conditions? Does the area have quality schools? Health care facilities? Churches?

- *Openness.* Does the community have a sense of tolerance and acceptance of diversity? Is the community safe? Does it provide economic security? Is the community leadership ethical, positive, and forward-looking?

The succession challenge requires our reassessing not only the very nature of leadership to make it more compatible with the goals, values, and life choices of new generations, but also how systems attract, recruit, develop, select, and assign new leaders to ensure that all schools regardless of location are led by creative, dynamic people, because the educational world is still not flat. In recognition of the location issue, the British National College for School Leadership provides school jurisdictions with a useful checklist to guide their recruitment practices for new leaders.[75]

In Chapter 2, I made the case that the succession challenge was more than a question of mathematics. It was also was a political issue, since it was the product of political decisions and often ideologies that moved education towards market solutions to educational issues and heavy doses of accountability that complicated the lives of existing leaders and discouraged potential leaders. This chapter has looked at the historical and geographic origins of the succession challenge. By reviewing the values, goals, and lifestyles of successive generations over the past 70 years, I have suggested that existing leadership models developed by older generations are incompatible with the values and need for a life–work balance of generation X and the millennials.

In addition, this chapter has put forward the idea that the geographic dilemma is paradoxical. On the one hand, younger people in education are increasingly reluctant to move their families to new locations in their pursuit of leadership jobs. On the other, the educational world is not flat: some locations are more or less attractive to leadership aspirants than others, which leaves governments and school jurisdictions with the dilemma of ensuring that all schools are led by quality leaders regardless of location. At the root of the succession challenge is a fundamental problem: policy makers are increasing the demands placed on educational leaders for quick and substantive improvements in students' achievement, often defined in terms of test scores, while at the same time trying to replace retiring leaders from newer generations who are committed to life–work balance and are unwilling to make the discretionary commitments as school leaders that have kept schools moving in the past. Chapter 2 and this chapter have attempted to lay out some of the broad social forces that have an effect on leadership succession. The next two chapters report on two research projects that delve more deeply into how issues of leadership and leadership succession affect schools and school systems.

Notes

1 Gladwell, M. (2008) *Outliers*. New York: Little Brown.
2 Florida, R. (2008) *Who's Your City: How the Creative Economy is Making Where You Live the Most Important Decision in Your Life.* Toronto: Random House.
3 Friedman, T. (2005) *The World Is Flat: A Brief History of the 21st Century.* New York: Farrar, Straus and Giroux.
4 The Learning Partnership (2008) *Final Report. Succession Planning: Schools and School Boards.* Toronto: Ontario Principals' Council.
5 Toffler, A. and Toffler, H. (2006) *Revolutionary Wealth*. New York: Knopf.
6 Ibbitson, J. (2009) "Boomers and whites will soon be America's new minorities", *The Globe and Moil*, 24 June: A15.
7 Strauss, W. and Howe, N. (1997) *The Fourth Turning: an American Prophecy.* New York: Broadway, p. 16.
8 Ibid., p. 16.
9 Leung, E. (2007) *Baby Boomers, Generation X, and Social Cycles.* Toronto: Longwave.
10 Chamberlain, J. (2005) "Current trends and issues in British fertility analysis". www.lse.ac.uk/collections/BSPS/ppt/Chamberlain_currenttrends_2005.ppt, 24 November 2008.
11 I promised I would name my grandsons in my book.
12 Orrell, L. (2008) *Millennials Incorporated: The Big Business of Recruiting, Managing and Retaining the World's New Generation of Young Professionals.* Deadwood, OR: Intelligent Women.
13 Lancaster, L.C. and Stillman, D. (2002) *When Generations Collide: Who They Are, Why They Clash, How To Solve the Generational Puzzle at Work.* New York: Collins.
14 Sikes, P., Measor, L. and Woods, P. (1985) *Teacher Careers: Crises and Continuities.* London: Falmer; Huberman, M. (1989) "The professional life cycle of teachers", *Teachers' College Record*, 91 (1): 31–57; Day, C. (1996) "Development and disenchantment in the professional lives of headteachers", in I.F. Goodson and A. Hargreaves (eds), *Teachers' Professional Lives.* London: Falmer.
15 Zemke, R., Raines, C. and Filipczak, B. (2000) *Generations at Work: Managing the Clash of Veterans, Boomers, Xers, and Nexters in Your Workplace.* New York: AMACOM.
16 Brokaw, T. (2004) *The Greatest Generation*. New York: Random House.
17 Lancaster and Stillman, op. cit., pp. 36–41.
18 Underwood, C. (2007) *The Generational Imperative*. North Charleston, NC: Booksurge.
19 Marks, W. (2009) "Are Principals really retiring?", Unpublished article, Sydney, Australia.
20 Underwood, op. cit., p. 114.
21 Estate agent.
22 Food-banks in Ontario collect food from wholesalers and food stores and distribute it to the less fortunate.
23 Elimination of tracking or banding.
24 See Fink, D. (2000) *Good Schools/Real Schools: Why School Reform Doesn't Last.* New York: Teachers' College Press.
25 Riley, K. (1998) *Whose School is it Anyway?* London: Taylor and Francis.
26 Fink, D. (1997) "The attrition of change", Unpublished doctoral dissertation, Open University, UK.

27 Lancaster and Stillman, op. cit.
28 See Nichols, S. and Berliner, D. (2007) *Collateral Damage: How High-Stakes Testing Corrupts American School*. Cambridge, MA: Harvard University Press; Glass, G. (2008) *Fertilizers, Pills and Magnetic Strip: the Fate of Public Education in America*. Charlotte, NC: Information Age.
29 Hargreaves, A. and Fink, D. (2007) "Energizing leadership for sustainbility", in B. Davies (ed.), *Developing Sustainable Leadership*. London: Chapman.
30 Coupland, D. (1991) *Generation X: Tales for an Accelerated Culture*. New York: St Martin's.
31 Stone-Johnson, C. (2009) "Regenerating teachers", in S. Rolls and H. Plauborg (eds), *Teachers' Career Trajectories and Work Lives*. Dordrecht: Springer.
32 Underwood, op. cit., p. 162.
33 Johnson, S.M. (2004) *Finders and Keepers: Helping New Teachers Survive and Thrive in our Schools*. San Francisco: Wiley.
34 Donaldson, M. (2007) "To lead or not to lead? A quandary for newly tenured teachers", in R.H. Ackerman and S.V. Mackenzie (eds), *Uncovering Teacher Leadership*, pp. 259–72. Thousand Oaks, CA: Corwin.
35 Wenger, E. (1998) *Communities of Practice*. Cambridge: Cambridge University Press.
36 Office for Standards in Education.
37 Paton, G. and Stewart, W. (2005) "Heads forced to quit", *Times Educational Supplement*. www.tes.co.uk/search/story/?story-id=2131152, October 2005; Moggach, T. (2006) "Too happy being number two", *Education Guardian*, 21 March: 3.
38 Underwood, op. cit.
39 Zemke et al., op. cit., p. 110.
40 Approximately 78 million in the US, according to Stephey, M.J. (2008) "Gen-X: the ignored generation?", *Time*, 16 April. www.time.com/time/arts/article/0,8599,1731528,00.html, 29 December 2008.
41 Martin, C. and Tulgan, B. (2001) *Managing Generation Y: Global Citizens Born in the Late Seventies and Early Eighties*. Amherst, MA: HRD, p. 3.
42 Baurlein, M. (2008) *The Dumbest Generation: How the Digital Stupefies Young Americans and Jeopardizes Our Future*. New York: Penguin Tarcher, p. 36.
43 Tapscott, D. (2009) *Grown Up Digital: How the Net Generation is Changing Your World*. New York: McGraw-Hill, prefers the term "net geners" to describe "millennials." For purposes of consistency I've stuck with the term "millennials," although "net geners" is perhaps more descriptive of what makes this generation different from its predecessors.
44 Ibid., p. 6.
45 Ibid.
46 Ibid., p. 80.
47 Ibid., p. 82.
48 Twenge, J. (2006) *Generation Me: Why Today's Young Americans Are More Confident, Assertive, Entitled – and More Miserable Than Ever Before*. New York: Simon & Schuster.
49 Underwood, op. cit., p. 248.
50 See www.ncsl.org.uk/leadership_network-index.
51 Jercho, A. (2007) "Leadership and succession planning: a lutheran education perspective", in N. Dempster (ed.), *The Treasure Within: Leadership and Succession Planning*. Deakin: Australian College of Educators.

52   For example, see the Ontario Principals' Council website.
53   Glasser, W.W. (1997) "A new look at school failure and school success", *Phi Delta Kappan*, 78 (8): 596–602.
54   Howe, N. and Strauss, W. (2000) *Millennials Rising: the Next Great Generation*. New York: Vintage.
55   Ibid., p. 43.
56   Marano, H. (2008) *A Nation of Wimps: The High Cost of Invasive Parenting*. New York: Braodway.
57   This quote refers to the United States but is equally applicable in other western countries.
58   Ibid., p. 44.
59   Honoré, C. (2004) *In Praise of Slow: How Worldwide Movement is Challenging the Cult of Speed*. Toronto: Vintage.
60   Judy Scotney, a personal communication, 3 February 2009.
61   Gent, D., MacBeath, J., Hobby, R., Liss, R., Benson, T., Smith, F. and Jacka, J. (2007) *Recruiting Headteachers and Senior Leaders*. Nottingham: National College for School Leadership.
62   Friedman, op. cit., p. 8.
63   Florida, R. (2002) *The Rise of the Creative Class*. New York: Basic Books.
64   Ibid.
65   Leamer, E. (2006) "A flat world, a level playing field, a small world after all, or none of the above", *Journal of Economic Literature*, 45 (1): 83–126.
66   Dorman, J.P. and D'arbon, T. (2003) "Assessing impediments to leadership succession in Australian Catholic schools", *School Leadership & Management*, 23 (1): 25.
67   Barty, K., Thompson, P., Blackmore, J. and Sachs, J. (2005) "Unpacking the issues: researching the shortage of school principals in two Australian states", *The Australian Educational Researchers*, 32 (3): 1–17.
68   Ewington, J. Mulford, W., Kendall, D., Edmunds, B., Kendall, L. and Silins, H. (in press) "Successful school principalship in small schools", *Journal of Educational Administration*, 46 (5).
69   Starr, K. and Simone, W. (2008) "The small rural school principalship: key challenges and cross-school responses', *Journal of Research in Rural Education*, 23 (5). http://jrre./psu.edu/articles/23–5.pdf, 9 January 2009.
70   Clarke, S. and Stevens, E. (2008) "Sustainable leadership in small rural schools: selected Australian vignettes", *Journal of Educational Change*. www.springerlink.com/content/0w647656071122x0, 9 January 2009.
71   Howson, J. (2008) *23rd Annual Report of Senior Staff Appointments in Schools for England and Wales*. Oxford: Education Data Survey. www.educationsurvey.org.uk_q=suystem_files-23rd+Annual+report.pdf-AdobeReader, 9 January 2009.
72   School districts in Ontario are called school boards.
73   The Ontario government for many years has required potential principals, vice or assistant principals and supervisory officers (senior executives with the ministry and school boards) to have Ontario certified qualifications, which includes university credentials above the bachelor's level.
74   The Learning Partnership (2008) op. cit., p. 90.
75   See http://forms.ncsl.org.uk/mediastore/image2/tomorrowsleaderstoday/diagnostics/tool11/formstart.asp

4

The Succession Challenge Up Close

With Andy Hargreaves, Corrie Giles and Shawn Moore

The previous two chapters covered the succession challenge with fairly broad brush-strokes. To get inside the issues, this chapter and the next report on two research projects that look at the topic from the perspective of both time and space – 30 years in the first case and three countries in the second. The investigation described in this chapter, the *Change Over Time?* study,[1] has already been widely reported. This large-scale investigation, led by Andy Hargreaves and Ivor Goodson, in which I participated along with a number of colleagues, and which was sponsored by the Spencer Foundation, examined changes in eight American and Canadian secondary schools over 30 years through the eyes of the teachers and leaders who worked there in the 1970s, 1980s, and 1990s.[2]

Leadership was one of six frames or lenses around which researchers shaped detailed case studies for each of the project schools in the *Change Over Time?* study. Among the questions researchers asked each participant were: "How did [the school] change and remain the same during the time that you were there? How did you feel about that?" This question elicited a great deal of discussion about the changing nature of leadership, particularly the principals' leadership. In addition, the open-ended nature of the interview schedule evoked considerable commentary on the tenure of various principals by teachers. While interviews with administrators were not part of the original research design, it became apparent as the research proceeded that leadership was an important aspect of the study, and insight into leadership succession an essential aspect of understanding the nature of change over time in schools and school districts. The research team subsequently conducted 20 additional interviews with present and past principals of four of the schools in the study. Interviewers asked such questions as: "How did you become the kind of principal you are (were)?" "In your own work as a principal, did it change over that period, for example, the way you spent your time?" "Can you say something about how you worked with parents over the time you were at the school?" "How did outside forces shape the school's directions?" From these data, as well as teachers' responses to the original interview schedule, we examined principals' intentions and teachers' responses as well as the way in which external social forces shaped each principal's leadership. We particularly looked at the principals' concerns when they entered their new settings, and their feelings and observations when they departed. Similarly, we reviewed teachers' reactions to the same events. From these rather extensive sources we were able to develop an understanding of principals' leadership and the effects of principals' succession beyond what had already been published.

The educational literature at the time provided only limited guidance to successful leadership succession.[3] Ann Hart is the one important exception.[4] Her two case studies, one from the perspective of faculty, and one from the perspective of a new principal hired from outside the school, illustrate how principal succession is a process of "organizational socialization" of the new leader into the school culture by the staff. From this perspective, the new leader is inducted into school culture by means of socialization tactics, stages, contexts, and outcomes. Based on one of her case study schools, Hart introduces the idea of stages in leadership transitions.[5] She describes the leadership transition at this school as proceeding through four stages: looking ahead, enchantment, disenchantment, and equilibrium.

Wenger offers a more sophisticated stage theory that provides insight into the transition process from one leader to another, both for the leaders involved in the transition and for the school affected.[6] He explains that:

> Developing a practice requires the formation of a community whose members can engage with one another and thus acknowledge each other as participants. As a consequence, practice entails the negotiation of ways of being a person in that context ... the formation of a community of practice is also the negotiation of identities.[7]

Wenger suggests that "our identities form in a ... kind of tension between our investment in various forms of belonging and our ability to negotiate the meanings that matter in those contexts."[8] Identity formation is the result of the interplay between one's *identification* with a community of practice and one's ability to *negotiate* meaning within that community. Wenger contends that as we interact over time with multiple social contexts, our identities form trajectories within and across communities of practice. The capacity of new principals to identify with their new schools, for example (and the schools' staffs to identify with them), and their ability to negotiate a shared sense of meaning of the schools' directions with their new staff, affect principals' trajectories and their identities in relationship to their new schools as communities of practice. Identity is a "constant becoming," and we "constantly renegotiate through the course of our lives."[9] Four of Wenger's trajectories are particularly appropriate for this discussion of principals' succession.

Inbound trajectories refer to individuals who join a community with the "prospect of becoming full participants in its practice."[10] Their engagement may be peripheral in the beginning but in time they expect to be an insider. The appropriateness of a new principal's inbound trajectory to a new school setting can contribute to his or her success or failure. *Peripheral* trajectories never lead to full participation, but are significant to one's identity. A person who remains permanently on the periphery, however, runs the risk of becoming marginal to the school's community of practice.

Insider trajectories grow and develop over time, as one becomes a full member of a community. The length of time to negotiate this trajectory will depend on the person and the context. New events, practices, and people are occasions for renegotiating one's identity. Conversely, *outbound* trajectories apply to those who plan or expect to move out of a community at some point. Wenger explains that what matters to a person and the community left behind is "how a form of participation enables what comes next."[11] For a school leader the question of legacy and sustainability of important changes requires the renegotiating of relationships with the former community.

While Wenger's trajectories provide insight into the leader's socialization into new settings, they constitute only one dimension of the succession issue. To see the larger picture we need to look at the issue more broadly.

Succession Cases

Two of the following three cases, Talisman Park and Stewart Heights, were chosen from among the eight longer cases in the study to provide examples of leadership transitions over a long period of time in more traditional schools. The other school, Blue Mountain, provides an interesting contrast because it was designed self-consciously as a learning organization. It tried to sustain its uniqueness by purposefully planning for leadership succession.

Talisman Park

Talisman Park is an academic collegiate-style school that opened in 1920. The staff successfully saw its mission as preparing students for university. Over 70 per cent of its students are accepted into universities and colleges. Situated in an affluent, well-established neighborhood, the school has approximately 1,200 students and a staff of 75. Staff turnover is very low. Talisman Park's traditionally middle class, white, Anglo-Saxon student population has become more racially and ethnically diverse over the past 10 years. From 1919 to 1987, Talisman Park had six principals in 68 years, compared to the 13-year period between 1987 and 2000 when four principals followed one another in rapid succession. Bruce Riley lasted only three years before his promotion to superintendent in 1990 and was seen by staff members as so upwardly mobile that he had little lasting influence on the school. Bill Andrews (1990 to 1995), whom we will meet again when we look at Stewart Heights, followed Riley, and in turn Charmaine Watson (1995 to 1998) and then Ivor Megson (1998 to 2003) succeeded Andrews. One department head who had worked under five of Talisman Park's principals expressed the growing cynicism of many of his colleagues when he stated:

> What I noticed as time went on and principals changed, was that the principal was less interested in the school and more interested in his own personal growth. There's nothing wrong with trying to be upwardly mobile and looking at the next step to being a superintendent, but don't sacrifice what you're doing at the school for that. You could tell as some of these other principals came in, they spent more time outside the school than they did inside the school and right away that was a danger flag for me.

Staff viewed Bill Andrews as a change agent. An experienced principal, Andrews pushed Talisman Park's school community to confront issues of change in broad conceptual and systemic terms as well as pragmatically. He advocated an inclusive approach to planning and problem-solving and involved students in the process. He had his strong advocates, as the following statement from a counselor attests. He also rubbed some people up the wrong way, especially women.

I loved Andrews! Loved him! He was my favorite. Every single day he'd say, "How are we doing? Are there concerns that we need to know about? How are the kids liking this?" He would be out in the parking lot at lunchtime wandering around the school talking to kids and trying to get to know everybody. Now he didn't do all the handwritten notes ... That was above and beyond the call of duty. But he did get around and try and meet as many people as possible. And I thought he brought a lot of changes in that were good.

Issues unrelated to his school leadership resulted in the district's moving him rather abruptly to the district office to assume a regional role in 1995. The precipitous nature of the move left little time for planning the transition, and the new principal Charmaine Watson had little opportunity to interact with Andrews or the staff before she assumed the role. There was no exit strategy: one day Andrews was principal, and the next he wasn't.

For Talisman Park, this rapid movement of principals (and assistant principals) made it difficult for school administrators to become an integral part of the school's culture, and to maintain the momentum of their leadership efforts. Most, it would appear, have remained on the periphery and as a result their change efforts tended to be replaced by new initiatives under the next principal. Many staff members have become reluctant to invest their energies in new school structures and practices that they anticipate will change again in two or three years. After five different principals in his tenure at the school, a department head concluded that:

[School leaders] have responsibility that I think is getting more and more onerous ... They are forced into an administrative role and are becoming, unfortunately, more detached from what we do in the classroom ... They're getting dumped on too. Principals generally come in and they have grand visions and plans and somewhere along the line ... they seem to always have an ulterior motive ... Maybe they want to go to another school or be a superintendent.

Watson, who replaced Andrews, had taught at Talisman Park before she became its principal and understood the school's history and ethos. Many of the school's mainly white and middle class staff members had been at the school a long time. Almost 30 per cent had been on the faculty in the school for over 16 years, 45 per cent for over 11 years, and 80 per cent for over 6 years. A coffee circle of experienced, long-serving teachers met every morning before school to socialize and to share opinions on government initiatives, school board policies, and administrators' decisions. This circle group, composed for the most part of teachers who taught the core subjects in the curriculum areas like mathematics, science, and English, helped to set the tone for the school. This group, according to one of the school's assistant principals, was an influential subculture within the school that jeopardized the "administration's efforts to build morale." According to a new teacher:

> I do go [to the staff room] every now and then. But I find that it is just mostly gossip. People just go there to complain about the way things are run within education. I think it is important to socialize with the staff. But on a regular basis I just don't want to hear all the crap.

This staff group, and the other micro-politically powerful department heads' group, had traditionally determined what changes would occur in the school and what would languish. These groups supported innovations in their own academic subjects, but were skeptical and often cynical about larger-scale reform agendas that altered the essential "grammar" of the school.

Once she became the principal, Charmaine immediately set out to alter the balkanized culture of the school that had produced departmental fiefdoms. She democratized the school's decision-making by taking major decisions to the staff as a whole, rather than depending on the heads of department as a decision-making cabinet. The circle group's and department heads' influence in the school gradually shifted to the staff as a whole. Watson provided leadership opportunities beyond the formal leadership structures, and developed a whole-school strategic school plan that focused on improving assessment strategies for student work, and engaging students in instructional technology. She participated actively with staff in professional development activities, and took every opportunity to challenge teachers to diversify their teaching to meet the changing nature and needs of the school's students. With key staff members, Charmaine initiated a strategic plan that involved all the major stakeholders in the Talisman Park community and developed a statement of purposes for the school. After four years in the school, researchers reported that most staff members were quite supportive of her directions or at least willing to go along.[12] While some of her strategies in her early years can be described as instrumental, she gradually empowered people and opened leadership opportunities widely as her tenure progressed.

In spite of her best efforts, however, there remained a small but influential element of staff, composed largely of long-serving staff, who continued to resist her efforts to develop the school as a learning community. A male teacher who had related well to Andrews complained: "At times I find that she is direct. At other times I find that I am second guessing to find out what it is that she really means." A female colleague commented, "she is always so busy I feel I'm infringing on her time." When Charmaine was absent from meetings, their cynicism would occasionally surface. Efforts to develop school-wide goals such as integrating computers into the curriculum often became bogged down in issues such as students' tardiness in arriving at classes. In her own way she presented a powerful personal presence in the school, but as the small group of naysayers suggests, she still had much to accomplish to achieve her goal of building a learning community that focused on school-wide issues. Even though she had the credibility of teaching at Talisman during its "glory" years, and was seen by most staff as a caring and capable leader, she had not yet become an insider. A few influential staff members never considered her to be part of the school's community of practice. Unfortunately she would never get the chance to work from the inside out – to "sail" the school, "steering from the stern" rather than "driving from the front" as she had during most of her tenure.[13]

In June 1998 the West School District, which includes Talisman Park, experienced a number of unexpected retirements among its school leaders. As a result, in July, after school had adjourned for the summer break, the school district abruptly transferred Charmaine to a school that was experiencing serious leadership problems. The district had obviously given little thought to Charmaine's exit or for that matter the preparation for leadership of her successor at Talisman Park. The officials who moved her seemed more concerned to place a principal with considerable experience into a challenging situation than to consolidate her four years of attempted reforms at Talisman Park. She was in her own words "devastated" by the ill-timed move. Charmaine had little opportunity to draw her tenure to a conclusion or even to say goodbye, although she attempted to attend to her own exit strategy by arranging with the school district for the placement of Ivor Megson as the school's new principal.

Megson's preparation included a short stay as vice (assistant) principal at Talisman Park, and involvement in a system-sponsored school improvement program that included Talisman Park. While Megson was cognizant of the cultural side of change, his approach to leadership predominantly reflected his background as an engineer – rational, managerial, and strategic. His arrival coincided with significant government initiated changes hitting the school with their full force.

In response to the numerous mandates from the government and the staff's feelings of being under siege, Megson abandoned the many years of effort to change the school's culture under Andrews's and Watson's leadership and turned to formal leadership structures to ensure compliance with top-down initiatives. The circle group regained its influence as stressed teachers met to complain about the latest government requirements, and department heads once again made most of the important decisions. Like many principals, Ivor felt that his main responsibility was to protect or buffer his staff from the deluge of reforms that descended on the school. He allowed the staff to focus on the "bubble" students who were slightly below the median on the provincial literacy test in order to boost achievement and gain a higher ranking for the school. In the process, teachers tended to provide less assistance to those students most in need of intensive support in language development, but who would not contribute to a positive school language profile. Ironically, Charmaine Watson in her new school developed a program of literacy across the curriculum that did not achieve the kind of immediate gains of the Talisman Park approach but, within three years, contributed to this disadvantaged school achieving the second highest score in the district and outpacing the much more socially advantaged Talisman Park by a considerable distance.

Principals from the school's earlier days stayed long enough in the school to move from the periphery to become insiders. Earlier leaders, while in the "great man"[14] tradition, were able to influence the school's community of practice and sustain not just structural changes but attitudinal and social changes. From 1987 to 2003 the rapid rotation of principals has created the revolving door syndrome,[15] which has resulted in staff members going along with reform initiatives but withholding total commitment. This case suggests that principals who intend to sustain change over time need sufficient time to negotiate their identity within the school's community of practice to move from the periphery to become insiders. At the same time, a prolonged stay as an insider could result in complacency and a rigorous defense of the status quo. Virtually all the principals in this case, regardless of the length of their tenures, were able to involve significant numbers of staff members in the pursuit of important educational changes. Charmaine Watson, for instance, engaged the discretionary commitment of all but a minority of staff and was approaching insider status at the time of her departure. What she and her predecessors and their staffs enjoyed was considerable voice in the directions the school would follow. Ivor Megson, however, inherited a situation in which neither he nor his staff colleagues had any significant influence in the school's directions. The district and the provincial government predetermined the school's goals in the name of educational reform. Ivor's job became one of ensuring compliance. The learning community that Charmaine Watson was close to achieving disintegrated in the face of these external forces, and Ivor Megson felt he had no alternative but to use instrumental strategies to ensure he kept his job.

Stewart Heights

Located in the same school district as Talisman Park, our second case Stewart Heights presents a similar picture. Stewart Heights is an old and established collegiate located in what was once a tightly knit, white, largely Anglo-Saxon rural community. While the small-town feel remains on Main Street, the housing boom of the 1990s resulted in a sprawling, culturally and ethnically diverse community. The school has experienced the same demographic shifts; it has become a microcosm of the multicultural nature of southern Ontario. A sea of portable classrooms dwarfs the original building. When the school board assigned Bill Andrews to the school in 1998 he assumed responsibility for a staff that was largely white and middle aged and in some ways oblivious to the changing nature of the school. Thirty eight per cent of the staff had taught at the school for more than 20 years, and 65 per cent had taught at the school more than 11 years.

Andrews replaced the long-serving Fred Jackman who had led the school for the previous 10 years. A staff member described Jackman as "a delightful guy and absolutely fabulous man". In general, the teachers that knew him respected him and his administrative team, which was often described as "very stable". Jackman referred to himself as a "principal-teacher" and believed that a major part of his job was to help make it easier for teachers to do theirs. This he believed was both his strength and his weakness. As he stated:

> One of the difficulties I found for my personal approach to leadership was that I didn't have a particular direction or goal for my school. I simply wanted to facilitate the relationship between teachers and students, and I thought my job was to take as much of the administrivia and annoyance and pressure from outside sources off the teachers so that they could work effectively with kids.

After 10 years of stability and a focus on teachers' needs and concerns, Andrews replaced the popular Jackman. Stewart Heights was Bill Andrews's third principalship. He had spent five years at Talisman Park and two years in a system-wide role in the district office. A policeman's son, Bill was tall, confident, and scholarly. His considerable inbound knowledge allowed him to move confidently, quickly, and energetically, to shake the school out of its insularity and redirect staff members' efforts towards the interests of students and the community. Two very capable and experienced assistant principals, one male and a visible minority and the other female, ably supported him. By articulating firm expectations for staff performance and students' behavior, and by demonstrating through example that change was possible, he succeeded in moving the school to a point where it was beginning to function as a professional learning community by the end of his second year as principal. He led by example. When guidance counselors[16] demanded more help because they said changing students' timetables was impossible, he brushed them aside and did it himself, to demonstrate that indeed it could be done within existing resources. Perhaps frustrated by his inability to alter the bureaucratic nature of Talisman Park, in his new school he aggressively addressed the dominance of the department heads' group and the perceived lack of influence of the assistant heads and staff as a whole. He immediately took steps to address such building issues as the tawdry appearance of the school, and he also initiated a process to mobilize the staff behind a coherent set of school goals. To heighten staff awareness, he presented the staff with survey data showing that 95 per cent of staff were satisfied with the school but only 35 per cent of students and 25 per cent of parents; this created a common problem which staff had to solve together. When confronted with these data, many staff members reacted with disbelief and attacked the credibility of the research. While Andrews was generally responsive to staff opinions, there was no doubt who made the final decisions and who was in charge.

Andrews had his critics at Stewart Heights, just as he did at Talisman Park. Interestingly, many of the critics were women, as they were at Talisman Park. "I think he has ideas of where he wants to go and I think he's going to, but his overall style is almost an imposing kind of thing that will be – 'this is how it will be.'" "[He has been] insisting that there's certain things he has to do because this is his mandate from the board." "He's a change agent and an instigator, but it sometimes is decreed to be done." Andrews never tried to move from a peripheral trajectory. It was his goal to transform the prevailing community of practice as quickly as possible. He used instrumental strategies to achieve his goals because more empowering strategies require time and staff receptiveness and capacity.

After only two years at Stewart Heights, Bill received an appointment to a position at the district office. In addition, the school board appointed one of his assistant principals as the principal of another school in the district, and also moved the second assistant principal to a nearby school. There was no time to consolidate their legacy through building leadership networks, and limited opportunity to connect with the incoming leadership team. The needs of the system clearly came before the needs of the school. It was into this situation that the board parachuted Jerry West, a new principal appointee, and two newly appointed vice principals. The departure of Andrews's assistant principals, and their replacement by inexperienced appointees, exacerbated West's feelings of being overwhelmed and isolated. As West observed: "The previous principal had had 10 years' experience. Now he was here only for two years. But he came in with a certain skill set, having had 10 years' experience. I came in with no experience ... so I had to develop some other skills ... as well as running the school." At the time of his appointment to Stewart Heights, West had just settled into his second assistant principal position in a large and complex urban school after five years as an assistant at a small rural school.

Despite his strong work ethic and experience as an assistant principal, he found the first 18 months of his new role daunting. His inbound trajectory had not prepared him for the challenge of replacing such an experienced and high-profile, indeed charismatic, leader like Andrews, or for dealing with the sheer volume of mandated external reforms. West was the third principal appointed to Stewart Heights in four and a half years. This pattern compares to the period from 1970 to 1998, when the school had four principals in 28 years. West found himself dealing with a staff that felt that "we are not going to have a principal come in and tell us what to do." Like many novice principals, West had received little formal induction to the role or to his new school. Historically, the school board had provided strong staff development opportunities for prospective and existing principals in the system; however, funding cutbacks at the time meant that there were no programs available for new principals like Jerry West.

West felt frustrated by the circumstances of his appointment. Only a few years before, West would have been able to count on an assistant superintendent or an experienced colleague to orient and mentor him. By the time he arrived at Stewart Heights, the board had cut the number of superintendents to reduce the district's budget, so that two assistant superintendents served 26 secondary schools compared to six only two years before. In addition, the few senior colleagues who had not taken advantage of early retirement were themselves on overload. Although he knew that it was important for Stewart Heights to keep progressing, and he had demonstrated in his past schools that he was an enthusiastic change agent, West felt he needed a year "just getting to understand the school." Because the school had had such a rapid turnover of principals, West also sensed that some of the staff were ready to "outwait" him and so block or ignore any changes that he proposed. As he explained, "it's only been one plus years but teachers are coming to me already and asking how long am I going to be here."

Unfortunately, the pressure of events denied West the opportunity to negotiate an entry process that would enable him to build meaningful relationships with staff members. His promotion had occurred at the same time as the pressure to implement the standards agenda of the provincial government was at its peak. Unlike Andrews, West had limited opportunity to develop a sense of directionality with his staff; his efforts were pushed aside by prepackaged mandates from outside the school and its community. As he stated, "sometimes the rules change, day by day by day, in terms of what we can and can't do." He added that, "as we were making our own changes, moving forward in the direction that we believed we need to go, other changes and outside pressures have been imposed on us as well. So things that you want to do have to take a back seat sometimes and that can be quite frustrating."

Observations at the school climate meetings chaired by West indicated that with the previous principal's departure, student-centered policies now gave way to a more conventional behavior code. Rules replaced common sense, punishment replaced encouragement, and negativity replaced affirmations. Teachers' issues had superseded students' issues, and in this regard the school tried to resurrect the comfortable, avoidance culture of the Fred Jackman era.

The early achievements of school improvement at Stewart Heights under Andrews faded quickly. Hierarchical structures such as the department heads' group that had dominated before Andrews's arrival reasserted their authority, and West went along because he needed support to ensure compliance with ministry curriculum and assessment requirements. In effect, the school-wide learning community that Andrews had initiated now fragmented into a number of micro-political units. Certainly the clumsiness of the board's approach to replacing Andrews and his assistants contributed to West's difficulties, but the complexity of government reforms and West's own lack of preparation set him up for failure.

While very different in many ways, Andrews and West both remained on a peripheral trajectory. Often charismatic leaders like Andrews remain peripheral to their new school community, achieve considerable short-term change in an organization, and then move on. While such leaders may add to their personal reputations as "movers and shakers," their legacies, like Andrews's, are usually short lived; their real legacies are often the disappointment and cynicism of those staff members who worked with the leader to effect change, and now feel abandoned and used. As a result of the circumstances of his succession, Jerry West remained peripheral to the school's existing community of practice, and never became an insider. West continued to operate on the periphery and found himself permanently marginalized by the staff and ineffectual as a leader. Ultimately his health suffered and he was hospitalized and never returned as principal to Stewart Heights. Interestingly, Andrews the transformational leader, and the beleaguered West, both employed instrumental strategies to achieve their purposes – Andrews by choice, and West by circumstance. West, who by nature and belief favored more empowering strategies, had to deal with teachers who, like those at Talisman Park, were withdrawing their discretionary commitments. He had to revert to traditional bureaucratic structures and instrumental strategies to ensure compliance with district and ministry fiats.

Blue Mountain High School

By way of contrast to both Talisman Park and Stewart Heights, Blue Mountain High School provides an example of carefully planned principals' succession in which attention to the sustainability of a school's purposes, culture, and structures were built into its very design. In 1994 the South School Board opened Blue Mountain High School as a "lighthouse" school to challenge the "grammar" of secondary schooling in Ontario. Situated in a middle to upper middle class neighborhood, the school began with 600 students, and now has a student population of over 1,000 students. Established with an experienced and imaginative principal, Ben McMaster, with a carefully selected staff, many of whom had former connections with McMaster, and with the advantage of a full year's advanced planning, the school in its first five years established great technological, structural, and curriculum innovations.

Structurally, the school had no subject-defined departments, its staff workrooms were mixed, and school documentation declares that "no subject or extra-curricular area dominates another with respect to importance." The initial leadership team comprised eight "process leaders" in areas like technology, or assessment and evaluation, rather than the customary group of subject department heads. In addition to their own subject area, all teachers belonged to at least one process team that met regularly. Leadership in the school involved all teachers either formally or informally: indeed, assuming leadership was a shared expectation.

Architecturally, the school has a relaxed meeting space in the entrance area, its main hallway resembles a shopping mall, and the gymnasium and fitness center are widely used by staff and community as well as students. Blue Mountain is fully integrated for technology, with every student having access to the internet and all staff members having laptop computers and being expected to model the use of technology to students. The assessment and reporting system is computerized and achievement data are regularly collated, analyzed, and shared with parents.

The school was self-consciously a learning organization. For example, leaders modeled "systems thinking" in staff meetings (all announcements are distributed electronically to make space for this), and teachers model such thinking in classrooms when school issues are discussed. Many of the highly dedicated and enthusiastic staff were omnivores of personal and professional learning outside school as well as within it.

Ben McMaster planned for his own successor from the outset. McMaster, a former professional athlete and special education teacher, anticipated his own departure by working hard to create a school structure that would perpetuate his devotion to the idea of a "learning community" when he eventually left the school. McMaster's influence was pervasive at Blue Mountain; his imprint was everywhere in the school's philosophy, organization, design, and culture. He was especially alert to the threats to his work posed by the possibility of an ensuing principal importing a significantly different philosophy. He explained that "I negotiated very strongly [with the district] to have my assistant principal appointed principal." After four years, the system did in fact move him to a larger "high-profile" school in the system, and promoted his assistant principal Linda White to principal.

Blue Mountain's second principal had impeccable insider credentials as its founding assistant principal. She continued to stress the relationships theme. In her first year, as she worked to renegotiate her relationships with staff as the principal, she and her leadership team were described by many of the staff as "wonderful," "supportive," "spectacular," and "amazing" – people who were "still teachers at heart". She was highly valued as being "very caring" and as someone who recognized that "family comes first." White worked hard to be open and accessible. She dedicated herself to maintaining the originating philosophy of the school. As she explained:

> Before [McMaster] was moved to another school we talked – we talked about how we could preserve the direction that this school was moving in. We were afraid that if a new administrator came in as a principal, that if he or she had a different philosophy, a different set of beliefs, then it would be quite easy to simply move things in that particular direction and we didn't want that to happen.

As principal, she stated that "I'm on the same road, and any detours I take will only be for a few moments in the overall scheme of things before I come back onto the main road again."

Events got in the way of her intentions. The full impact of the government's massive reform agenda descended on the school at the same time as she became the school's principal. As time went by, the staff began to notice that the twin pressures of time and complexity had created a perceptible change in her leadership style. As one staff member explained:

> It's because so much has to be done in so little time. We [used to] meet to decide as a group how best to go about a process. Well there's been no meeting. We've just been told these classes are closed ... And never in my whole career has that ever happened ... There isn't that opportunity to share information ... And now it's just sort of "top down" because there's only time for top down.

She had become more of a manager of the external agenda than a leader of the school's values and ideas. Some staff members perceived the way White tried to "talk up" change as being somewhat forced and not fully sincere – the effect of having to manufacture optimism in a policy environment that repeatedly seemed to defeat it. They recognized her dilemma but also saw its effects:

> I think we've gone from an organization that was kind of a shared responsibility, at least in appearance, to a very linear one now based on, because of time. And [Linda] is fairly directive, and likes to be in control of lots of things, but she's also a humanist with you on that. But I think we've lost some of that shared responsibility because of outside direction.

Like Megson and West in the other two cases, the overwhelming pressure from external influences gradually forced her, perhaps unwittingly, to abandon the empowering leadership strategies of the learning community and adopt more instrumental approaches. Budget cuts initiated by the school district undermined Blue Mountain's mid-level leadership structure by reducing the number of members of the school's leadership team, and increased teachers' teaching loads which in turn interfered with disciplinary and cross-disciplinary activities. A number of the original team leaders subsequently retired and were not replaced.

In many ways, Blue Mountain had been a model of distributed leadership,[17] but Secondary School Reform in Ontario and the accompanying budget decisions forced the new principal of Blue Mountain to adopt more hierarchical decision-making structures and to employ more instrumental strategies to ensure compliance with government requirements. The external reform agenda constrained White's ability to lead in ways that were consistent with her intentions and values and with the founding philosophy of the school, and undermined her credibility with a staff that still aspired to the idea of Blue Mountain as a learning community. After three years as principal she was moved to another school and, like other model schools, Blue Mountain has regressed to the mean.[18]

Ben McMaster, in his five years at Blue Mountain, enjoyed a unique opportunity to empower people. As the principal of a new school, he hired his staff with his vision of a learning community in mind, and he encouraged his colleagues to take personal ownership of the directions of the school. To this end he provided the time and the spaces, as well as the organizational structures such as process teams, to encourage a culture of collaboration and distributed leadership. During his tenure he had sufficient time and autonomy to inspire his colleagues to develop a genuine learning community. He carefully attended to his outbound trajectory by ensuring an appropriate successor, and perhaps equally important ensuring that leadership was widely distributed in the school.

His successor, Linda White, also tried to use inclusive and empowering strategies but in the name of predetermined organizational changes, and in the process appeared to some staff members to be inauthentic and to others Machiavellian. Her inexperience as a principal, as we have seen in the cases of Megson and West, made her particularly vulnerable and unable to resist the external forces. An inexperienced vice (assistant) principal in another of our study schools articulated this feeling when she confessed: "we are trying to say 'no' you don't have to do that. That's a hard thing to do. And it's hard because my principal is a second-year principal and I am second-year assistant. You are not going to balk your superiors." Inexperienced principals appear to comply more readily with external mandates, and revert to managerialism, out of their own insecurity and their inability to negotiate or renegotiate an identity with their schools' community of practice.

While both Talisman Park and Stewart Heights had immature learning communities and long histories of bureaucratic leadership, they might well be expected to revert under pressure to traditional structures and cultures. Blue Mountain provides a cautionary example of the vulnerability of a well-developed learning community, and of the fragility of empowering leadership strategies in a climate of planned chaos and leadership turnover.

Planned and Unplanned Succession

One of the initiating questions of our study asks: "Does the planned or serendipitous nature of the transition affect a principal's ability to maintain or alter school directions?" This suggests two dimensions for analysis: first, to what extent is a transition planned or unplanned; and second, to what degree does the transition contribute to continuity with past directions or promote discontinuity? The planned–unplanned dimension assesses the degree to which the agents[19] who initiate and/or are responsible for the transition act on a well-developed succession plan.[20] Such plans include:

- sufficient time to enable the participants in the transition to execute exit and entry processes
- open and timely communications among the initiating agents, the participants in the transition, and the school personnel involved in the transition
- consideration by the initiating agents of the compatibility of the educational philosophy and abilities of the new appointee and the developmental needs of the school.

The continuity–discontinuity continuum assesses the degree to which a new appointee to a position sustains[21] or substantively alters (either advertently or inadvertently) the philosophy, policies, and practices of his or her immediate predecessor. The interrelationship of these dimensions produces four possible scenarios, as shown in Figure 4.1.

	Continuity	Discontinuity
Planned (purposeful)	Planned continuity	Planned discontinuity
Unplanned (accidental/ unintentional)	Unplanned continuity	Unplanned discontinuity

Figure 4.1 *Planning and Continuity*
Hargreaves, A. and Fink, D. *Sustainable Leadership* © 2005. Reprinted by permission of the publisher John Wiley & Sons, Inc.

Planned continuity occurs when the hiring or assigning of a new principal (or school head in a British situation) to a school reflects a well-thought-out succession plan and is intended to build on the general directions and goals of his or her predecessor. Sustained school improvement over long periods and across multiple leaders depends on carefully planned continuity. The replacement of Ben McMaster by Linda White at Blue Mountain provides the best example of planned continuity. Ben McMaster and the school board carefully orchestrated this transition to preserve the uniqueness of Blue Mountain. Unfortunately, over time, coercive outside pressures created discontinuity that had never been planned, and White found herself behaving in ways that were quite inconsistent with the culture of the school and even with her own leadership philosophy.

Planned discontinuity occurs when the initiating agents such as a superintendent or school governors assign or appoint a principal or school head to a school based on a well-conceived plan which expects, intends, and is successful in ensuring that the principal will move the school in directions that are substantively different from the principal's predecessor. A new principal hired or assigned to "turn around" a failing school, to give a jolt to a "cruising" school,[22] or to implement a "top-down" reform agenda would fit this category. For example, Bill Andrews was an experienced principal with a reputation for making significant changes in schools when his school board assigned him to Stewart Heights. Not only was his placement planned, but the discontinuity his placement produced was also part of his mandate. Unfortunately, his premature departure led to unplanned discontinuity.

Unplanned discontinuity takes place when senior leaders or school governors assign or hire principals or heads to a setting with very little forethought and planning. Unplanned discontinuity often results when ineffective principals abdicate leadership in ways that disrupt previous goals and directions. Inexperience or other kinds of incapacity may mean that some principals are unable to advance or even maintain the improvements achieved by their predecessors. Unexpected and unusually demanding reform pressures may also push incoming principals aside from maintaining their school's internal improvement dynamic. In these senses, unplanned discontinuity is often paradoxical and perverse. It may be discontinuous with immediately prior improvement efforts, while re-establishing long-term continuity with the less innovative and effective practices that preceded them.

The replacement of the dynamic Bill Andrews at Stewart Heights by the inexperienced Jerry West provides an example of unplanned (or at least poorly planned) succession. Saddled with two totally inexperienced assistant principals and facing a massive government reform agenda, West crumbled under the pressure. The resulting leadership vacuum produced an anarchic situation in the school as various micro-political units such as the former department heads and the younger acolytes of Andrews sought to assert their power.

Unplanned continuity occurs when the initiating agents thrust a principal into a school without much forethought and the principal perpetuates existing patterns of school goals and operations. Unplanned continuity can arise when principals are appointed or assigned without any clear understanding of the needs of the school, when schools are used as mere placeholders for leaders who may have lost their effectiveness or are cruising into retirement, or when deeply entrenched cultures of long-standing staff have the knowledge, experience, and tenacity to outwit and outlast even the most innovative incoming principals.

Unplanned continuity occurred at Talisman Park when Ivor Megson replaced Charmaine Watson in July after the school year had ended. Watson had hoped that the appointment of a former assistant principal would maintain the directions that she had tried to establish in spite of considerable resistance from entrenched elements like the department heads and the circle group. Pressure to comply with government mandates, and his more technocratic style of leadership, led Megson to fall back on traditional structures such as the rather entrenched department heads' group to get staff cooperation to implement unpopular government changes. As a result, the school reverted to the culture of elitism and conservatism that Charmaine Watson had worked so hard to change.

As the case studies show, all these characteristics – continuous and discontinuous, planned and unplanned – are possible in the succession process. Continuity is not always desirable. Sometimes discontinuity is more appropriate. What matters most is that these directions are planned with the best interests of students and all those who support them in mind.

The *Change Over Time?* study provided a unique opportunity to explore changes in leadership in general, and principals' succession in particular, over a 30-year period. Principals' transitions have often given rise to problems, challenges, and upset for teachers and principals alike. However, this study indicates that the accelerating turnover of principals, resulting from the aging of the baby boom generation and the pressures of the standardization agenda, has created additional difficulties that threaten the sustainability of school improvement efforts and undermine the capacity of incoming and outgoing principals to lead their schools. On the basis of these cases, four major factors have made principal succession increasingly problematic.

First, over the years of the study 1995 to 2003, the turnover of principals accelerated at an ever increasing rate. Talisman Park had six principals in its first 68 years; it then had four in just 12 years. From 1970, Stewart Heights had four principals in 28 years, then three in quick succession in the next five years. These and other cases reaffirm that in order to bring about sustainable improvement, principals need sufficient time (more than five years) to negotiate or renegotiate an identity and an acceptance within their school's community of practice. Yet in almost all cases, district succession and rotation practices limited leaders' abilities to create and leave a lasting legacy. This study seriously questions the effectiveness for the school of regular, rapid, and bureaucratically predictable principal rotation, especially in turbulent times. "Revolving door" principalship only breeds staff cynicism, which subverts long-term, sustainable improvement.

Second, leaders like Watson, Andrews, and McMaster, who made strides in influencing their schools, were able to access or develop the inbound knowledge that prepared them for their jobs. However, as more and more leaders like Watson take early retirement, and others like Andrews and McMaster are promoted to higher levels of the system, less experienced successors have had to manage the standardization agenda. In a compliance culture, demands from on high for quick results and evidence of quick changes in student achievement on standardized tests have denied these successors the time to engage in an entry process that would help them to engender the trust of their staffs, and gain insight into the cultures and micro-politics of their schools. Inexperienced and unprepared principals like West and Megson are condemned to ensuring that teachers comply with outside mandates as best as they can, rather than working with their colleagues to achieve shared, internally developed improvement goals for their schools. In the context of current reform movements, these latter-day principals typically have neither the inbound knowledge and training, especially if they come from outside education or have been rushed through accelerated leadership programs, nor the confidence that comes with experience, to colonize external mandates for their internal improvement purposes.[23] New principals are increasingly left to fend for themselves without the time or the conditions to move from a peripheral trajectory to an insider one. Instead of leading from the center, they are left to manage from the edge. Creating and protecting substantial support systems for new principals that can pass on, share, and develop the essential inbound knowledge of incoming leadership, in light of the "succession challenge," would seem to be of paramount importance.

Third, the transition from McMaster to White at Blue Mountain provides evidence that thoughtful succession plans can really help to sustain school improvement. They provide considerable lead time, they develop shared understanding and commitment among faculty through meaningful communication, and they harmonize the new principal's inbound knowledge with the outbound knowledge of the departing principal and his or her concern to maintain and build on what has already been achieved in the school. Yet, the vast majority of our data in the three cases in the *Change Over Time?* study as a whole point to most succession events being unplanned or at least poorly planned. In the main, unplanned or hastily arranged successions seem to serve only as an enemy of improvement.

Finally, the *Change Over Time?* study not only revealed a lot about leadership succession but also highlighted changes in leaders themselves. In almost all our schools, not just the three cases described in this chapter, teachers reported great changes in leaders and leadership between the period ending in the mid to late 1970s, and that commencing in the mid 1990s. In this characterization of leadership now and then, leaders in the 1960s and 1970s were remembered as larger-than-life characters who were attached to their schools, knew most people within them, and stayed around long enough to make a lasting impression. By comparison, leaders by the year 2003 were typically perceived as being more like anonymous managers than distinctive leaders. They were less visible around the school, seemed more attentive to the system's agenda and their own careers rather than the needs of the students and teachers, and were more of a passing presence in the school than a lasting influence on its development.

The changing nature of leadership cannot be separated from the frequent changes among leaders themselves. Principals like Ben McMaster of Blue Mountain build powerful learning communities that sustain change over time by employing empowering strategies that engage teachers in working together to achieve meaningful goals for students' learning. Instead, increasing erosion of leaders' and teachers' autonomy has forced more and more principals to use instrumental and managerial tactics to achieve the short-term shifts that comply with standardized reform. The study suggests that leaders who empower others need considerable autonomy and time to work with their school communities to establish and achieve meaningful school improvement goals. When governments mandate reforms that preempt most school-based direction setting, they reduce school leaders like Jerry West to mere functionaries. Under these circumstances, while standardized reforms often create short-term movement, they fail to produce sustainable improvement.

The evidence of the *Change Over Time?* study exemplified by the three preceding case studies suggested that the standards/standardization agenda that has dominated public policy for the past 15 years or more has contributed to an emerging model of leadership that is reactive, compliant, and managerial. This model discourages and deters younger aspirant leaders, who might be capable of inspiring learning communities that promote deeper and higher learning for all students, from becoming principals or heads or assuming other formal leadership roles. In the interplay between design and emergence, design has overwhelmed emergence. Conscious of the themes and findings of the *Change Over Time?* study, the next chapter describes an investigation carried out in 2008 and 2009 among principals and heads in the United States, Canada, and the United Kingdom that carries the succession story forward by examining in some depth the issues discussed in this chapter and their influence on the "succession challenge."

Notes

1   Hargreaves, A. and Goodson, I. (2003) *Change Over Time? A Study of Culture, Structure, Time and Change in Secondary Schooling*. Project 199800214. Chicago, IL: Spencer Foundation of the United States.

2   Hargreaves, A. and Goodson, I. (2006) "Educational change over time? The sustainability and non-sustainability of three decades of secondary school change and continuity", *Educational Administration Quarterly*, 42 (1): 3–41.

3   Morris, V., Crowson, R., Porter-Gehrie, C. and Hurwitz, E. (1984) *Principals in Action: the Reality of Managing Schools*. Toronto: Merrill.

4   Hart, A.W. (1993) *Principal Succession: Establishing Leadership in Schools*. Albany, NY: SUNY Press.

5   Ibid.

6   Wenger, E. (1998) *Communities of Practice*. Cambridge: Cambridge University Press.

7   Ibid., p. 149.

8   Ibid., p. 188.

9   Ibid., p. 154.

10   Ibid., p. 154.

11   Ibid., p. 155.

12   Hargreaves, A., Shaw, P., Fink, D., Retallick, J., Giles, C., Moore, S., Schmidt, M. and James-Wilson, S. (2000) *Change Frames: Supporting Secondary Teachers in Interpreting and Integrating Secondary School Reform*. Toronto: Ontario Institute for Studies in Education/University of Toronto.

13 Hopkins, D. (1992) "Changing school culture through development planning" in S. Riddell and S. Brown (eds), *School Effectiveness Research: Its Messages for School Improvement*. Edinburgh: HMSO.

14 Hook, S. (1955) *The Hero in History: A Study in Limitation and Possibility*. Boston: Beacon.

15 Macmillan, R. (2000) "Leadership succession, cultures of teaching and educational change", in A. Hargreaves and N. Bascia (eds), *The Sharp Edge of Educational Change*. London: Falmer; MacMillan, R. (1996) "The relationship between school culture and principals' practices at the time of succession". Unpublished thesis. OISE/UT, Toronto.

16 Pastoral care.

17 Spillane, J.P., Halverson, R. and Drummond, J.B. (2001) "Investigating school leadership practice: a distributed perspective", *Educational Researcher*, 30 (3): 23–8.

18 Fink, D. (2000) *Good Schools/Real Schools: Why School Reform Doesn't Last*. New York: Teachers' College Press.

19 In many American and Canadian school jurisdictions, officials of the district, with the approval of elected school board members, are responsible for the placement of principals. Increasingly, school governors or school councils composed of locally elected or appointed community representatives are responsible for the choosing and placing of school leaders. In some educational jurisdictions such as New South Wales in Australia, Ministry of Education officials are responsible for principals' placements.

20 Rothwell, W.J. (2001) *Effective Succession Planning: Ensuring Leadership Continuity and Building Talent from Within*, 2nd edn. New York: AMACOM; Souque, J.P. (1998) *Succession Planning and Leadership Development*. Ottawa: Conference Board of Canada.

21 For a detailed discussion of sustainablility in educational settings, see Hargreaves, A. and Fink, D. (2006) op.cit.

22 Stoll, L. and Fink, D. (1996) op.cit.

23 Goodson, I. (2003) *Professional Knowledge, Professional Lives: Studies in Education and Change*. Buckingham: Open University Press; Woods, P., Troman, G. and Boyles, M. (1997) *Restructuring Schools, Restructuring Teachers*. Buckingham: Open University Press.

5

The Succession Challenge Up Really Close

Leadership was only one of six dimensions of *the Change Over Time?* study described in the last chapter, and leadership succession was an important but only one aspect of the overall study. Moreover, the study concentrated on succession planning and never delved deeply into succession management. The *Leadership Succession in Three Countries* study outlined in this chapter builds on the *Change Over Time?* study and looks into both succession management and succession planning in more depth. By looking at three cases – the South School Board in Ontario, Canada, the Eastern School District in the United States, and the Midlands Local Authority in the United Kingdom – this study provides a comparative look at the "succession challenge" as it affects three quite different school systems in the three national contexts. With the help and support of local school officials anxious to address their succession issues, principals and assistant principals in the Canadian school jurisdiction, and heads and deputies in the UK, completed an extensive 80-item questionnaire which asked respondents to determine on a five-point Likert scale how important they considered each item, and how closely they felt the item applied to their school board, district, or local authority.[1] In the latter category I included an "uncertain" option to determine policies and practices which senior levels of government had not communicated well, or about which school leaders, for one reason or another, felt uninformed. These processes enabled me to compare the respondents' views of the ideal with the reality of their particular setting. A typical item would look like Figure 5.1.

Importance	(A) Identification and recruitment	Describes district local authority
1 2 3 4 5	1 A major task of the principal is to identify and recruit potential leaders.	1 2 3 4 5

Figure 5.1 *Example questionnaire item*

Unfortunately for my overall design, the response rate from the Eastern District with only 10 schools was not sufficient to draw any valid conclusions based on the questionnaire. As a result, comments related to this American district are based solely on interviews and discussions with six principals and one senior official during a four-day visit to the district office in early 2009. Both the structure of the questionnaire, and the subsequent analysis of its results and of the interviews in each school jurisdiction, were built around the following five themes derived from the *Change Over Time?* study:

- succession management
- succession planning
- frequency of moves
- politics of succession
- succession and the self.

Research Design

A key part of the research was a one-hour interview I conducted with a cross–section of school leaders in each of the three areas. In each jurisdiction, a senior official selected a representative group of principals or school heads in the UK based on my categories of age (generation), gender, experience as a principal, ethnicity, and school type (elementary/secondary), who agreed to participate in the interview. I recorded the responses of six principals in the Eastern School District, 21 in the South School Board, and 18 in the Midlands Local Authority to a structured interview.[2] Although my samples for both the questionnaire and the interviews were not random in a statistical sense, they were what Stephen Ball would call "naturalistic coverage."[3]

To set up the questionnaire and the interview and the subsequent analysis of succession management I drew upon Figure 5.2 as my organizer of a comprehensive succession management program. Beginning with the identification and recruitment of prospective

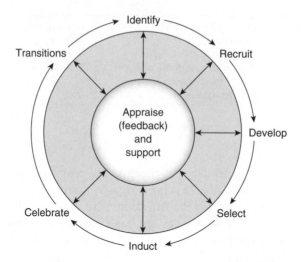

Figure 5.2   *Successtion management*

candidates, the program moves successively through their development, their selection for positions of responsibility, their induction, and ultimately the celebration of their accomplishments before their transition to retirement or another career phase. Every stage requires support and performance appraisal.

Since space precludes a full reporting of this research I will attempt to highlight some of the key findings in the following paragraphs.[4]

Succession Management

Recruitment and Induction

One of the more pleasing aspects of the many interviews that I conducted was meeting school principals and heads of both genders, baby boomers and Xers, of various ethnic and religious backgrounds, who in spite of all the obstacles were still keen, motivated, and determined to do their best to promote the learning of each child in their care. When asked why they wanted to assume the leadership of a school, regardless of whether it was in the American, Canadian, or British context, they all said: "to make a difference for children on a larger scale than a solitary classroom." While many respondents expressed disappointment with the way the "compliance culture" has undermined their autonomy and ability to improve learning, most still had the spark of enthusiasm and excitement for the job. As a newly appointed school head in a small school in the midlands in England declared, "I adore my job, it is exactly what I wanted." A recently retired school leader in Ontario said, "I wanted to be a principal after I did my work in special education because what I learned was I love to have the big picture in education. As much as I loved being in the classroom, and teaching children, the more I got involved in the larger aspects of education, the more excited I was about it. I loved being in a school, knowing what was happening and, more importantly, why it was happening. I wanted to be part of that." A long-serving American principal recalled.

> I think there was a more a sensibility of wanting a bigger piece of the pie. There was a sense that I was involving myself in a number of things ... I also liked certain aspects of the role and seemed to be able to do it – speaking publicly, I cared about traditions. I had a reputation as a good teacher and the idea that I might be able to extend that to others.

Reflecting on their own motivation for assuming leadership roles, principals and heads in all three countries believed that as incumbent leaders, they had a major role to play in the identification and recruitment of new people. A number of school leaders in all three settings expressed concern that perhaps they had oversold the trials of leadership and failed to communicate the joys of the job. When asked if the demands of the job were inhibiting the recruitment of new people, 66 per cent in Canada agreed, with 18 per cent uncertain, and 83 per cent in the UK agreed with only 9 per cent uncertain. A senior Ontario principal suggested that, "it's important for the current leaders to talk about the great stuff about the job, instead of always talking about – 'it's so busy, there is this to do and that to do.'" When asked about where the idea of moving up the ladder started for them, most pointed to a motivational leader who stoked their ambitions as young teachers; a few referred to dysfunctional leaders who made them think "I can do better than that"; and others had undertaken challenging leadership roles inside and outside their schools and enjoyed the satisfaction of accomplishing important goals. As a result, virtually every head or principal interviewed, and over 90 per cent of respondents to the questionnaire, saw that "a major task of the head (principal) is to identify and recruit potential leaders." As one principal said, "I think good principals bring along good talent."

Similarly, over 90 per cent in both Canada and England saw it as important that senior system leaders actively promote leadership, and most gave their authority or school district high marks for doing so. However, 25 per cent of the Ontario respondents to the questionnaire disagreed that "senior system leaders actively encourage prospective leaders to apply for promotion." While principals and school heads in all three settings felt their systems were interested and somewhat active in promoting leadership, they felt that their own efforts to promote leadership were too often thwarted by hiring decisions that selected external candidates over internal people. As an American principal explained, "we've had enough of the white knights. Somebody who comes from afar, who's perfect and shiny and shows up, and by October we find out it's a real human being with warts and problems and deficiencies, just like the person who's been in the school already and tested." A Canadian principal used similar logic:

> I was very frustrated being told several times that I was a competent administrator and I was good at recognizing strengths in other people and yet carefully putting teachers' names forward that I felt would be wonderful leaders, and then, finding out that they didn't even get an interview. If you're asking us to support people that we believe should be good leaders, and you're telling me that I am a good leader, why are you not at least giving an internal person an interview when they've done all the work that needs to be done, and I've signed off on my support?
>
> I think bringing people in from the outside is a good thing because you always need to have a fresh set of eyes to look at things. But I think if we have internal administrators who we have carefully looked at as potential leaders, who we have watched grow and develop their leadership skills, and are at the point of saying this person is ready for an interview, I think we should listen to our internal people and at least give them the interview opportunity.

There appears to be only a limited effort in the three jurisdictions to recruit new leaders that reflect the increasing diversity of their student populations although, as a senior official in the Eastern District observed, the topic is on their radar:

> We're very committed to increasing the number of diverse staff members that we have within the system to more closely match our student population because we're not there by any means. So I'm working, forging relationships with some different universities in the area that have more diverse student populations, and I'm working with a team representative of teachers and administrators in our system to put together an actual recruitment and retention plan for the system. So we're just taking the first baby step.

When asked if their school board had a policy or plan to encourage greater leadership diversity, 46 per cent of the Canadian respondents didn't know and 27 per cent agreed that such a policy didn't exist. Principals who had participated in interview committees were quite convinced that no particular effort was being made to recruit minority candidates. Similarly, in the British authority 63 per cent were unaware of efforts to engage minority candidates.

In all three jurisdictions identification and recruitment followed traditional patterns, with very little if any effort expended to develop innovative practices to encourage younger people to come forward. This lack of foresight can perhaps be explained by the relative ease with which all three areas have filled vacant leadership jobs over time. Senior officials in all three settings however, recognized that a "replacement planning" strategy based on enticing leaders from other school jurisdictions was ultimately unsustainable and were at various stages of developing leadership preparation programs to augment what their respective governments required in terms of leadership training.

Leadership Development and Support

The role of governments in the certification and training of new leaders varies widely from jurisdiction to jurisdiction. In Ontario, the government conducts required leadership courses, usually paid for by prospective leaders, who apply to participate, and access is quite open to qualified people. In England, the National College for School Leadership in conjunction with other government agencies operates the basic leadership requirement through the NPQH[5] program which in times past allowed fairly easy admission to interested candidates, but more recently has required a much more rigorous entry process. Candidates will often have part or all of their fees and expenses paid for by their school's budgets, however. Prospective leaders from the Eastern School District can get state certification by enrolling in courses offered by private contractors, usually universities and colleges, and for the most part at candidates' own expense.

The three jurisdictions' contributions to leadership preparation, induction, and long-term development also vary widely. As a very small school district, the Eastern District has virtually no succession management process and depends on weekly principals' meetings and central office advisory support to assist principals. Ongoing professional development of principals was pretty much left up to the individual. The district does have a "foundation" supported by the community that makes funds available for approved professional activities. The Ontario school board's succession management plans are a "work in progress." It has resurrected its historical leadership development programs in the past few years, and offered induction programs for new appointees which new principals have found very helpful. Most experienced principals however, had little idea of ongoing professional development opportunities available and took it upon themselves to continue their own professional development through professional reading, university courses, or programs offered by the Ontario Principals' Council.

By far the most extensive and comprehensive succession management package is that offered by the Midlands Authority in England. The fact that over 65 per cent of the leadership of schools in the authority comes from within, in a central government mandated open leadership market, speaks well of the preparation programs of the authority. Even those participants who eventually leave the authority, do so well trained for the challenges of educational leadership, and help to sustain the quality of leadership in smaller or less advantaged authorities. Built around a consistent model of school leadership for England, prospective and existing school leaders can enroll in such courses as "Developing High Performance Teams", "Authentic Leadership", "Developing Mental Toughness," "Managing Performance Management", "Curriculum Leadership", "Induction Programmes", and "Leading the Small School". Each participant must pay to enroll, but as mentioned previously, the government allots money to schools for professional training. When you factor in special training programs required to support the innumerable government initiatives, however, the array of required and voluntary courses and programs available to school leaders is mind-boggling to the outsider, and as I found out in the interviews, to many of the insiders as well.

The demands on all three sets of school leaders to be involved outside the school for one reason or another was a source of real consternation for all the participants in the interviews. They saw themselves as leaders of learning, but priorities imposed upon them kept getting in the way of what they saw as 'job one'. Many suggested that staff resented their many absences from the school. Over 90 per cent of both British and Canadian school leaders agreed that spending over 90 per cent of their time as leaders of learning was important, but only 35 per cent in both countries believed they measured up to this intent, and 40 per cent, especially at the secondary level, felt constrained in their attempts to do so. The same theme permeated my American interviews as well.

Principals and heads in all three countries believed that developing professional learning communities was important, that they understood the concept, and that their schools were in fact learning communities. In addition, virtually all agreed that they distributed leadership widely in their schools. My interviews with principals and heads, however, suggested that there are a wide variety of meanings and practices involved when people talk about "professional learning communities" and "distributed leadership".

One significant difference between the British and the Ontario approaches, as reported by practitioners, appears to be the British emphasis on management as opposed to "leadership for learning". In response to the item "the focus of leadership development programs is on good management rather than leading learning for students", 50 per cent of the British respondents agreed and 20 per cent disagreed, compared to only 22 per cent who agreed in Ontario and 45 per cent who disagreed. By way of contrast, however, British heads felt that governments at various levels were more interested in leadership and more prepared to pay for it than their Ontario counterparts. This difference in approach shows up when respondents were asked if the government's support for their initiatives was satisfactory: only 14 per cent in the UK disagreed as opposed to 40 per cent in Ontario. The more positive response of British educators may reflect their government's generous support of the National College for School Leadership and its multiplicity of activities, as well as the 2007 government initiative to identify and assign a "school improvement partner" (SIP) to every school.

Two school heads in my British sample had qualified as SIPs to work with heads in other schools. One of my respondents, a SIP, visits five other schools six times in the school year, three in an advisory category and three as a SIP. Some authorities split the roles between two people, particularly at the secondary level. She explained that during the advisory days, the supported school head determines the agenda. In contrast, the SIP days are "about school improvement and driving school improvement, and we have to challenge the headteacher, we have specific paperwork we have to fill out." "So you've got to be very careful about whether you're going as a SIP or an advisor." "As a SIP I'm just there to look at data, challenge the data. Raise questions of what we're doing with the data."

While this project is "early days", there is some general skepticism on the part of a number of heads, including the SIPs, about the efficacy of the process, and a feeling that an idea with lots of promise is being compromised by the propensity of senior levels of government to micro-manage the procedure. The program does give experienced and successful heads the opportunity to exercise much wider leadership, but as at least one SIP suggested, at a cost to her time commitment to her own school.

Selection

Each school district in my study uses a different approach to the actual selection of a new principal or head. The Eastern District in the US uses an open application method, and a very elaborate screening and selection process that involves finalists presenting to the parents and teachers of the school with the opening, and final selection by the district's superintendent and approval by the school board. I discuss this process more in Chapter 7. The South School Board in Ontario invites applications from both inside and outside the school board. A committee of senior leaders and principals sorts the applications and chooses those it wishes to interview. From these interviews, the committee creates a shortlist for formal approval by the school board and ultimate placement by the board's senior officials as jobs become available.

Since each school's governors are responsible for personnel in the UK, processes tend to differ from school to school. In general school governors, with help from the authority's advisory services, will select a group of applicants to be interviewed. The selected applicants are usually required to make presentations over the course of one or two days to one or more teams of governors before the school's governors arrive at a final decision. Over 70 per cent of respondents in both England and Ontario considered their respective selection processes "fair to all applicants", that the pre-interviewing screening was thorough, and that "selection rises and falls on the quality of the final interview." Selection criteria appear to be better known in the British context (68 per cent), perhaps because it is school specific, than in the Ontario board (40 per cent) where principals are hired to the school board and then placed. Unsuccessful candidates in the Midlands Authority schools get more useful feedback (85 per cent) than in the South School Board in Ontario (44 per cent), which probably reflects the fact that the number of applicants to one school will probably be far fewer than applicants to a school district. These data in general are probably perceived in a more favorable light by the respondents to the questionnaire and interview, given that all had successfully traversed the selection hurdle.

Induction

Once new principals and heads are hired, both the British authority and the Ontario school board respectively provide special support programs which involve group networking, mentoring, advisory support from senior principals, and formal study. These programs, however, evoked quite different responses. Over 90 per cent of British heads agreed that their authority provided good support to new heads, and supported them with mentors, and that fellow heads created a collegial environment for all heads. In Ontario the results were much more mixed. Only 32 per cent agreed that the system assisted entry to a new school and 42 per cent disagreed; 65 per cent believed new principals had mentors and 22 per cent disagreed, although over 80 per cent felt there was a culture of collegial support in the district. One of the two non-Caucasians in my Ontario sample, a young woman of Asian heritage, supported this view. She said that when she came to the South Board from a neighboring board, she was "accepted totally and right away." The mixed nature of these responses may reflect the newness of support programs in the South Board or the difficulties of communicating in a fairly large school system.

The small size of the American district precludes a formal program similar to the other jurisdictions that I studied, although each new principal is required to attend a program on how to observe teaching "so that we're all speaking the same language." As a result the induction process in the Eastern District tends to be *ad hoc* and serendipitous. As one experienced principal explained:

> I don't think we do a very good job of mentoring our new principals. We have a principals' group which meets every other week on its own. And at that time we try to support new principals and usually a new principal hits it off with one of us and, you know, we try to informally mentor that person.

Leadership Appraisal

As befits a small district with only 10 principals, the superintendent of the Eastern District in the United States evaluates all the principals on a two-year cycle. The process is quite informal, but very open and perceived as quite useful by participants. A principal whose responsibility goes across a number of schools explained that:

> The superintendent has goal setting meetings with me and then on a regular basis he comes to a site where I have the classrooms and I go with him to visit those classrooms and then we have an opportunity to sit and talk about what he's seeing and what my thinking is around certain aspects of my practice. I provide him with a detailed accounting of what I'm doing every year and all of the demands on which I am reviewed and he writes my evaluation based on this information.

A soon-to-retire American principal describes his participation as a two-way street between himself and the superintendent and how he can help the superintendent:

> The paper evaluation is probably the last thing I look at. And my first couple years I looked at it very closely. There's a comma here, wait a minute, what does that mean? But now it's much less the paper and it's the relationship [with the superintendent]. I think that for principals in a small district that's a key relationship. The relationship that you have

with the superintendent – the idea that he can float ideas that can remain confidential; the idea that he can talk his way through without having it be disclosed if there's a new plan for something that he was just trying out loud; the idea that there are certain parents in the school system that he's having problems with.

Superintendents who are responsible for a "family" of related primary (elementary) and secondary schools evaluate a principal's performance in Ontario (the role is "family of schools superintendent"). They in turn report to the chief executive officer, the director of education, who is responsible to the elected school board. A recently retired primary principal described the operation of her family of schools:

> We have a superintendent that we meet with regularly and collectively, all the administrators from the family. There are two families in each of the areas, six families in the district. We meet secondary and elementary. My family met once a month, all of us, and the agendas were driven by the needs of the principals and vice principals. They are the planning teams and work on what it is we want to know for our own learning. I think that your support system to a certain extent depends on your superintendent, how interested they are in being out and about in the schools.

A female elementary principal explains how her superintendent attends to appraisal:

> We certainly have a conversation – questions are given to me in advance. There's a long visit. The superintendent comes for at least two to three hours. We do sit down, talk about the school effectiveness plan, how I'm dealing with challenging teachers, that kind of thing. We do a walk about the school and then that would be followed up with a letter at some point.

The primary message in the questionnaire data for the South Board is that principals' appraisal lacks consistency in application and efficacy. For example, when asked if the appraisal system is dedicated to professional growth, 43 per cent agreed, 31 per cent disagreed, and 25 per cent were uncertain. Similarly in response to the question whether the appraisal system was based on agreed goals, 34 per cent agreed, 34 per cent disagreed, and 31 per cent were uncertain. Moreover, 35 per cent were uncertain whether the appraisal system was the same for everyone, and only 40 per cent agreed that the system was fair. Items related to the professional purposes of appraisal, the importance of student results on standardized tests on principals' appraisal, and the criteria for appraisal all received very mixed results, with "uncertain" the most frequent response. The value and usefulness of the family superintendent's support and approach to principals' appraisal appears to depend totally on the interests, ability, and energy of the individual superintendent. With considerable recent turnover of superintendents, it seems obvious that this aspect of performance management in the South Board requires review.

In England the governors of each school carry responsibility for reviewing the performance of the school head. To do this, the school appoints two or more from the full governing body to act as the performance review committee. This committee is charged with:

- reviewing the head's performance
- setting new objectives
- agreeing and implementing arrangements for monitoring performance against objectives
- depending on local school policy, be involved in setting or making recommendations on the head's pay.

The government's directive on performance management[6] urges school heads to be actively engaged in the process if they are to have ownership of the results. The ostensible intent of the process is to be supportive and promote an open, challenging and professional dialogue that encourages the headteacher to:

- reflect on their performance and achievements over the past year
- assess their needs for personal development
- suggest key priorities for moving forward.

The school's school improvement partner (SIP) has a part to play in the performance management of the heads. The SIP "advises" the governor reviewers on the performance of the headteacher, and assists the governors in preparing a review and planning statement. This statement summarizes progress towards agreed objectives over the previous 12 months, provides overall performance and pay recommendations by the governor reviewers to the governors' pay committee, and helps to formulate agreed objectives for the next 12 months. This involves:

- evaluating the evidence
- drafting advice for the governors
- meeting the headteacher to discuss their performance
- meeting the performance review committee to help them to review performance and to set out new objectives
- attending the performance review meeting

- advising the governors on monitoring procedures
- drafting the performance review statement (if required).[7]

Materials are confidential between the reviewer and the person whose performance is under review. The local authority has no role in the process other than to train SIPs and coordinate their activities.[8]

By way of contrast to the Ontario school board, heads in the Midlands Authority responded quite positively to items on the questionnaire related to the British approach to performance management. Over 75 per cent of respondents in the Midlands Authority agreed that the performance management system "is dedicated to professional improvement, is based upon agreed goals, accounts for a head's experiences, is fair, is based on well known and agreed upon criteria and is based on multiple measures." They are uncertain about its consistency across schools, and how much the results on standardized student tests matter in their evaluation.

There is, however, an undercurrent of fear and apprehension that comes through in many of the interviews about the overriding role of OFSTED and the "sacking" of heads. In addition to advice from SIPs, OFSTED reports are also part of the evaluative package. While only governors can hire and fire, OFSTED reports appear to carry a great deal of weight with school governors. The perception among principals seems to be that a poor OFSTED rating can lead to fairly arbitrary dismissal. As one head who is involved on a national scale declared:

> If I was working in a tough school or a tougher school where things were more difficult, there's no doubt with the new OFSTED framework coming out that there's more pressure on heads taking over schools like that. And certainly how I perceive the profession to have changed is that heads' jobs are much less secure. Somebody quoted a figure, which I didn't believe, something like 150 headteachers got the push last year. Because I'm on this [national principals'] council I tend to listen, tend to hear more. There's a field officer who was working with people like that. It's frightening the number of obviously good headteachers on their second or third headship, actually go to a school that's in difficulty, they've not been given time and they're out. At my age I can't afford to lose my job and get sacked. In another 10 years' time I'll probably be a bit less bothered about it. I just think at the moment that's the big thing is that teaching used to be a job for life and certainly headteaching probably did.

The accountability practices of OFSTED inspectors are too often seen as unfair, inconsistent, and impractical in terms of timelines, particularly for schools and heads of schools in disadvantaged areas. This rather pervasive perception has the potential to compromise the good intentions and exemplary practices of performance management in the Midlands Authority that to date have strong support from the majority of school heads.[9]

Celebration

I've called the next to last phase of the succession management process "celebration" as a way to highlight the need to acknowledge the contributions of school leaders before they move on to other settings or into retirement, not only as a way to honor the past, but as a way to interest younger people in following in their leadership footsteps. Successful sports franchises do this well. One of the most prestigious ice hockey teams in North America is the Montreal Canadiens. Written in bold letters in its locker room, for all new coaches and players to see, is the Canadiens' motto: "To you from failing hands we throw the torch. Be yours to hold it high." Like the New York Yankees of baseball, and Manchester United of soccer, the Canadiens connect their past and their present with their plans for the future by honoring star players and outstanding coaches, preserving retiring players' numbers, holding "old timers" games, celebrating important milestones in club history, and hosting other events that uphold their long and successful tradition. In general in education, we do this poorly if at all. For example, when asked if the local authority honored retiring heads in the Ontario board, 26 per cent of current respondents replied in the negative and 56 per cent were uncertain. Conversely in the British authority, 60 per cent responded in the affirmative and only 24 per cent were uncertain. Almost 60 per cent of British heads agreed that the local authority helped soon-to-retire heads prepare for retirement, as opposed to only 15 per cent in the Ontario board where the Ontario Principals' Council fills the vacuum left by school boards by conducting retirement seminars. The difference in response probably reflects the fact that British heads are hired to a school, and the Ontario principals to the school board, which by its very structure tends to be large and impersonal. One important discrepancy that probably shows the more pressurized British situation for heads, however, emerged in answers to the item: "heads (principals) want to retire as soon as they can." Only 15 per cent of British heads disagreed, whereas over 40 per cent responded in the negative in Ontario.

Succession Planning

The final piece of succession management is the transition part in which leaders retire or move on to other pursuits, or continue to cycle into other positions within education. These transitions from a system's perspective constitute succession planning, which I have defined elsewhere as ensuring that the right person is in the right place at the right time for the right reasons. In the South Board in Ontario, succession planning decisions are corporate because the senior leaders of the system decide which principal goes where, when, and for what reasons. The cases in the last chapter reflect the Ontario approach. I explain this strategy in more detail in Chapter 7. Since the Eastern District in the US invites applications for a principal at a specific school, aspirants self-select because they decide whether the advertised school fits their particular interests, career trajectory, and lifestyle. The district through its selection committee chooses the self-selected candidates that fit the school, and the superintendent makes the final decision. Similarly, through open applications potential school heads in England decide if they feel they are the right person at the right time to meet the advertised requirements of a school.

In spite of different approaches to leadership placement, the Ontario and British systems seem to take an informal and almost serendipitous approach to succession planning. For example, when asked if their school system "carefully planned" the process, both the Ontario (40 per cent agreed, 38 per cent uncertain, 22 per cent disagreed) and British (38 per cent agreed, 44 per cent uncertain, 18 per cent disagreed) responses were similar. As we saw in the last chapter, entry processes in all three jurisdictions depended almost entirely on the goodwill of the departing principal or school head and the enterprise of the incoming school leader or head. A British head explained the transition in his case:

> I had a brief meeting with the previous headteacher and during that meeting he gave me three big bunches of keys, told me the combinations to all the door locks, and gave me a list of parents who would cause me grief, and that was it. It's staggering to think about. But that was it – that was his handover process.

A Canadian principal told a happier story:

> Before I took over, Debbie spent almost five days with me. By the time she left she wanted to be able to say that I knew everything I needed to know to take her place, but I could still call. When I was first informed that I was coming here I called Debbie to introduce myself. One day I told her I just want to come, she didn't even need to be here, I just wanted to walk through the building, so I came and I walked through the building and got a feeling for it and talked to the few people that were here in July. The second time I came she took me around and she introduced me to more people.

On the questionnaire, only 33 per cent of Ontario principals agreed that "each principal has an entry process focused on understanding the new context", and 44 per cent responded in the affirmative in the Midlands Authority. When asked if the local authority or school board insisted on a dialogue between the incoming and outgoing leaders, most respondents were uncertain and over 30 per cent in Ontario definitely disagreed. Judging by my interview subjects, most transitions are largely unplanned and few can recall any mandates from governors or from senior officials in their district, board, or authority. It would appear from both the interviews and the questionnaire that none of the three systems insist on either an entry or an exit process. Dialogue between incoming and departing leaders is largely informal, with little structure, and varying widely in commitment and efficacy. Over 80 per cent of respondents either disagreed or were uncertain as to whether their district or authority even required dialogue between outgoing and incoming school leaders. Over 60 per cent of both Canadian and British respondents to the questionnaire either disagreed or were uncertain as to whether they entered their new school with a specific mandate from the school board in the Canadian situation, and governors or the authority in the British setting. Certainly this sense of direction appears to be changing in the UK with the very prescriptive performance management system, and in Ontario with its increasing emphasis on accountability. Whether there was a plan behind transitions depended on each situation. The data suggest that most transitions lack a clear sense of direction.

The American district with its very limited turnover of principals presents a somewhat different picture, which makes it hard to generalize. Respondents in the Eastern District suggested that their exhaustive hiring process enabled the final candidate for a school's principal job to get a good idea of the issues facing her or him when they assumed responsibility for the school. In addition, the small size of the school district and the very limited turnover allowed system personnel and particularly the district's superintendent to remain closely engaged with the school in support of its new principal.

A second transition question emerging from the *Change Over Time?* study related to the continuity–discontinuity issue. The difference in pressure from government between the South Board and the Midlands Authority shows up when respondents to the questionnaire were asked whether principals or heads new to a school should quickly put their own stamp on the school. Here 55 per cent of Canadian principals disagreed with the item, whereas only 16 per cent of British heads disagreed. Since the American principals had all been in their schools for a minimum of nine years, questions related to entry were ancient history and not terribly relevant to the world of "No Child Left Behind". Most principals and heads were left pretty much on their own to determine whether they would maintain continuity with past practices or move quickly to change the direction of the school. Most tended to wait at least a year until they had a real understanding of the school before making any significant changes. One Ontario principal explained how she gradually reshaped the culture:

> The one thing is that I think when I came Helen used to be in everything and she orchestrated everything. Things would come up and I would say, what is happening with this or that, oh, Helen always did that. Oh, I see. Well what did she do? Since then I've been putting things into committees because I don't believe one person should be the one who knows and does everything and so forth. So we almost have a committee for everything now. That's how you build leadership amongst your staff. They're learning how to run things and all the intricacies of getting people on board and willing to set up for them or take down for them or whatever. It's a little different now.

Frequency of moves

The length of a principal's or head's tenure in an individual school differs significantly among the three systems. In both the US and the UK, once school leaders are selected they tend to remain until they decide to leave, or in a few cases, the superintendent or governors ask them to leave. With one exception, all my American interview respondents had been in their school for at least nine years and one principal had been 26 years in one school. The principal of the secondary school had served for 24 years as principal. A number of my British interviewees had remained in one school for over 10 years. None of the Ontario principals had more than seven years in one school. This discrepancy across the three jurisdictions raises questions that I will return to in Chapter 7. For example, when does stability become immobility? Is there an optimum length of time school leaders should remain in a school? Should school leaders move after a certain number of years in one setting? The answers to these questions from my respondents tended to correspond to the system with which they were most familiar. The South School Board principals and vice principals overwhelmingly support some form of leaders' movement among schools. A recently retired female principal offered this opinion:

> I was the vice principal under two very different principals so I learned lots of things. I think those were important experiences and I would hope that

any VP would have at least two different kinds of schools before they were, become a principal. I had too many vice principals at Park School – one year and out, one year and out. That's useless to the principal and to the vice principal. I don't think that's a good learning experience. Two years is great. And I say that because I think three opportunities at two years each would be perfect for a vice principal if you could do it. The five years as principal in my first school was perfect. I got a chance to look at things, get a sense of where the school was, before I made any decisions about what I want to do to move it forward. Then I had a chance to make some moves but actually see them through and pull something together. And then at my second school I was there for seven years. I felt blessed to be there for seven years. At the end of six years I thought, you know, I need another year here. I need to continue on, to finish up and see some things through. During the seventh year I knew I had to leave. I could sense that it was time to go. I knew there were certain things I did well, I knew there were certain things I didn't do well. Somebody else needed to go in there and look at those parts of the school, I felt, to keep it moving in a positive direction. So I think five years minimum for a principal. I wouldn't move a principal before five years but the seven was great.

Over 60 per cent of her Ontario principal colleagues felt it was important to move principals to "keep them from becoming stagnant." Only 30 per cent of the British sample agreed with this proposition.

Principals in the Eastern District, all of whom are long serving in their present schools, generally oppose rotating school leaders. They all believed good principals don't get stale and could reinvent themselves because the challenges of leadership keep changing. When one considers the size of the system, such an approach might be impractical anyway. The senior official responsible for recruitment said, "I'm not in favor of just continually moving people just to move them but I can see where moving around can have its benefits." A long-serving boomer principal believed staying in one school was necessary because building a community takes a long time. As she stated:

After nine years I am just now feeling like that's my school. It takes a long time. I was in the shadow of the principal before me who was there for 33 years, the last 11 as the principal. It took a long time to stop hearing people say, well Joyce would do it this way. I graduated my first class last year from K to 8 this year. Now it feels like whatever happened with those kids, I can't blame Joyce, I can't blame anybody else. They came through on my watch. It's my school. It takes a while to feel that way. You have to stay at least through a whole children's cycle, and change is hard and takes a long time.

Interestingly, in the British case there is more openness to the idea than one might expect. When asked if "Rotating from school to school on a timed cycle is a crucial part of a leader's development",

41 per cent agreed, 26 per cent disagreed, and 38 per cent were uncertain. While British heads were quite mixed in their views on some kind of leadership rotation to refresh or reenergize leaders, most saw the market approach to British education and the variable salary structure to be huge impediments. A male head in his ninth year at his present primary school, when asked about leadership rotation, responded:

> I mean personally I would have no problem at all. You do become flat because in your initial years you're trying to get the school in the model you want that school to be in and once you achieve that it's a case of continuing on. And the children change, and the parents change, and the staff sometimes change. But for me, a move wouldn't be for promotion. It would just be to take on something different and I'd want a very different sort of school to experience that. I think a lot of heads feel that the thought of staying in the same school for 20 odd years is beginning to die out.

Another head that was completing her 12th year in a medium-sized primary school replied to the idea of periodic move this way:

> I think if that were the system I'd quite happily go with that. I think the problem is in Britain we choose to move. If I knew I was going to be moved after a certain number of years then I would look forward to that with the anticipation of what that would bring. I guess the governors here have been quite clever in that I'd have to move to a very much bigger school to actually get paid as much. Now, I'm not money driven but I don't think anybody would actually move for a pay cut.

While most principals and heads had very clear ideas about rotation at their level, they held a wide variety of views on the rotation and even status of vice (assistant) principals or deputies. In response to the question, are vice principals or deputies, principals or heads in training or are they in career positions, 94 per cent of the Ontario principals considered them "principals-in-training" as compared to 75 per cent of British heads who held this view. Over 90 per cent of the respondents in the South Board in Ontario agreed that vice (assistant) principals should move every two to three years to get a variety of experiences, whereas only 9 per cent in the Midlands Authority agreed with this idea. When asked if after a period of time vice principals or deputies who failed to apply or were unsuccessful in applications for principal or head should step aside to give others the opportunity to train for principalship or headship, both Ontario principals and British heads were evenly split between those who supported this admittedly controversial idea and those who opposed.

Succession and the Self

A leadership transition is one of the most traumatic events in a school's history. In *Sustainable Leadership,* Andy Hargreaves and I reported on the emotional toll that transitions take on the leaders involved. In the cases outlined in Chapter 4 one principal felt "devastated" by her move to another school, and another confessed to being "overwhelmed". Since British and American school leaders choose to apply for their positions, there was little emotional language concerning transitions in their interviews other than being "pleased" or "thrilled" to get chosen. The Ontario system, where the school district decides who goes where and why, evokes more emotional language among principals and their assistants. Some interview respondents expressed "disappointment" at leaving a school, "bewilderment" at why they were being sent to such and such a school, or just "relief" that their new school was in a pleasing location. In general the emotive language I heard differed significantly from the words we heard during the *Change Over Time?* study that was conducted at a time of great turbulence in Ontario education. For the purposes of this study I particularly tried to discover how school systems attended to the emotional stress experienced by school staffs before and during a transition. I was interested in knowing whether any special steps were taken to keep staff members informed and connected to the transition process. In the Eastern District, the requirement that final candidates for a principal's position address the staff of the prospective school as an integral part of the hiring process gave staff a meaningful role in the selection process and went a long way towards addressing staff anxiety. Like the American school district, schools in the UK also hire to the individual school. Although a teacher and a non-teacher staff member are part of a school's governing council, there is little evidence from the interviews or from authority sources to suggest that school governors involve the teachers and other school staff members in any meaningful way in the selection process for heads and deputies, or that any particular effort is made to prepare a school's staff for the transition. There might be some school governing councils that attend to staff concerns, but they would appear to be exceptions. Only 10 per cent of the school heads that responded to the questionnaire agreed that processes existed to prepare staff for the arrival of a new head; 60 per cent disagreed and 30 per cent were uncertain. The Ontario school board's system provides little time to prepare staff for a transition. An Ontario principal who has led three different schools described what happens when transition of a principal or vice (assistant) principal becomes imminent:

I think that staffs recognize there's going to be transition of administrators. They don't have any say in it. They worry, it's funny watching the staff and I've done it for so many years now, every time that it's getting close to announcing administrative changes you can see them getting tense, what's going to happen, who's going to be here, who's not going to be here? And if you're moving, we're sad to see you go, who's coming in, what are they like, what do we need to know, and they very much worry. Then of course they start listening to stories from other people because it's all they have to go on. So preparing the staff, no, I get the information and the first thing I would do is go straight to the staff in that next break to let the staff know what the information is before they hear it from somebody else. That's it for the prep.

The data from the questionnaire confirm this observation. In the South Board, over 60 per cent indicated that the school board had no process to prepare staffs for a new leader, and 28 per cent were uncertain. It is therefore safe to conclude that how a school staff responds emotionally to leadership moves is not considered significant enough to alter the processes in Ontario and the UK. At least in the Eastern District staff preparation is a consideration. One principal saw the process to engage staff as mere window dressing and inconsequential; others viewed it as an important way to engage a school's staff in the transition process.

Politics of Succession

Leadership succession is inherently political. Many groups and individuals have an interest in who becomes a principal or head or an assistant; some of those groups and individuals have more power than others, and often their interests and relative degrees of power conflict. As one would suspect, the source of power in matters related to succession differs widely in each of the three school jurisdictions. In the US and Canadian examples, senior leaders decide on selection processes and make the final decisions on who is chosen. In both cases elected school board members usually "rubber-stamped" the corporate decisions. In the UK school governors, some elected, some appointed, were intimately involved in the selection, appraisal, and rewarding of their school leaders.

In general there was, among the respondents to both the questionnaire and the interviews in all three countries, a consensus that principals and heads had lost considerable political clout over the past 15 years. Yes they are consulted, but one American principal described it as "process liberalism" in which everyone is consulted but then the policy originators ignore the advice and do what they were going to do in the first place. A Canadian principal recalled that:

> At the beginning as an administrator I felt that we were listened to for our opinion and how decisions were affecting schools and children in our schools, which is what I loved about the job. As time went on I felt that more and more lip service was paid to listening to us … and I started to feel, "oh yes, we heard what administrators had to say but we're going ahead and do it our way anyway."

Politics in a very small jurisdiction such as the Eastern District is very up-front and personal. As one soon-to-retire principal explained:

> And when Phil [the superintendent] came he said, is there any advice you can give me? I said, when you have to do something because of the politics of it, tell us. Just tell us, you're going to have to hold your nose on this one, guys. Because we do politics in the building all the time. It's not like we're talking to a bunch of virgins. I mean, we do politics all the time. And if you have to do it don't waste your time trying to just dress this thing up and undermining your own authority just to say, you know, this is politics, I understand. I understand you'd like me to cut the gifted and talented director when we're getting into real budget cuts, I can't do it politically. Thank you. End of discussion.

The most important succession question for most principals is the choice of their assistant (vice) principal or deputy head in England. The role of the principal differs markedly. In the American case, the principal is a very active player and makes the final decision. A long-serving principal described the process this way:

> The human resources person [for the system] comes in and gives the charge to the interview committee and then they are gone. Then at the end I pick finalists, two or three, and I meet with them and with the superintendent and he advises me; tells me what he sees, and then it's my decision. I've had five vice principals in 10 years; they've all gone to be principals. I feel somewhat good about it except I have to keep starting all over every two years. That doesn't feel so good. I have a new vice principal this year. There were two finalists and the superintendent liked the other person better than the one that I picked. When I told him, before I contacted the person I chose, I called and I said, I'm going to pick this person and this is why. He said, fine, it's your decision; you have to live with it. Just wanted to give you my perspective. I believe I've made the right choice. Although the other person might've been fine, it's not that the person I chose hasn't worked out.

In England school governors may or may not involve the head in the process of choosing a deputy head. An experienced and knowledgeable British colleague from an authority near the Midlands Authority explained the involvements of various participants in the selection process in England this way:

> Authority advisors advise [school governors] on both headteacher and deputy headteacher recruitment, however [their role] does vary in terms of deputy heads as to how involved they are – it can range from no involvement to full involvement at the request of the school governors. The involvement of governors [one is the norm] is usual for any appointment to the teaching staff although it tends to be more so for the higher-level posts. A deputy headteacher recruitment process can be very similar to a headteacher, one with involvement of governors from shortlisting to interview [for a headteacher appointment the full governing body has to ratify the appointment]. Deputy headteacher appointments vary from school to school and are perhaps more rigorous and more like a headteacher appointment in the secondary sector. Appointment of heads of department in secondary schools usually involves at least one governor, but essentially it is a headteacher's decision.[10]

A primary head from the Midlands Authority described how the appointment of a new deputy involved him in a meaningful way:

> I put that, the central criteria together for the governors. When people applied, the governors and the school advisor and I shortlisted from the candidates who applied. Then on the day, I helped to choose the questions and in a way without directly guiding the governors, essentially let them know this is who I would work with and this is who I couldn't work with. I think that makes a big difference in the school. They asked my opinion because we had three very good candidates and we could've appointed any one and it came down to who I could work with, who I thought my staff could work with, that personal chemistry where I think well, they're not going to fit in, or their way of working is so different than ours, it might be a hindrance. But I was highly involved in the whole process and did have quite a lot of say, not the final say but I got the person I wanted.

These two scenarios reveal the sources of political power and the relative degrees of influence of the various participants. The Ontario picture is quite different. The senior leaders in the system assign vice principals to a school. I have participated in these decisions and most decisions are made with the best of intentions such as balancing or supporting the leadership style of the principal, creating gender balance in the leadership of a school, acknowledging the diversity of a school, or providing the new vice principal with a training opportunity. In some cases an assignment was purely to make the jigsaw of placements work. Principals' engagement in the process is for the most part minimal. They can express their desires to their family of school's superintendent, but whether he or she can deliver depends on that superintendent's influence among colleagues. Placement of principals and vice principals centrally in a large system requires a great many political tradeoffs, which may or may not benefit the school or the individuals involved. As one Ontario principal explained:

> I was never asked about a vice principal staying or not staying, coming or not coming. I sometimes was asked about, how did I feel about particular vice principals as far as their abilities or where they were in the continuum as far as moving towards a principalship. Sometimes I was asked for that input, not always. It was always a shock to me that I was losing another vice principal. I never knew who was coming in until after the fact, until the person was named.

In my experience, gaining access to leadership opportunities was often a political process in that you had to know the right people. We have all heard of the "old boys' network" or now the "old girls' network." I asked my respondents if "who you know" is as important as "what you know", and generally speaking all systems seemed to think that jobs were genuinely open. However, the response to the questionnaire item "do you have to know the right person" elicited 25 per cent agreement, 59 per cent uncertain, and 16 per cent disagreement in the South Board, and 20 per cent agreement, 28 per cent uncertain, and 52 per cent disagreement in the Midlands Authority. This suggests that "who" you know may still be as important as "what" you know.

From a political perspective, school leaders in all three systems have only a modest influence over leadership selections above the department head level. In all three, principals chose their department heads and also selected staff. In the American system, the human resources department acted in an advisory capacity to the school principal who after consultation with the superintendent made a decision. In the British situation a school governor usually sat on interview committees, but governors generally allowed heads to select their leadership team with the exception of the deputy. The authority usually acted in an advisory role if requested. In the Ontario setting, principals selected their own school leaders within system guidelines, with the exception of vice principals. The general sense I got in the interview process was that principals felt they were losing political influence over policies and practices that had a direct bearing on their abilities to meet their commitments, and that more and more of the decision-making that had enabled them to do their jobs well had been usurped by other levels, particularly district, state, provincial, and in the British case, national governments. This loss of autonomy that we saw emerging in the *Change Over Time?* study made them feel more vulnerable, more risk aversive, and move inhibited in doing their job. Perhaps at the heart of the succession challenge is the observation by younger potential leaders that their leaders have lost their political influence and their autonomy, and these young people have opted to exercise their innate leadership abilities in other ways.

Over the course of this book I have attempted in Chapter 1 to answer the question of why leadership succession is so important, and in subsequent chapters to probe the reasons that there is a problem in the first place. Chapters 2 and 3 have looked at the issue in a somewhat generic way, while Chapter 4 and this chapter have tried to get inside the issues by exploring two research projects that look at leadership succession "up close". The next two chapters, Chapters 6 and 7, focus on what we can learn about leadership succession from the business world, from various succession programs, and from the three school districts I have looked at in depth in this chapter.

Notes

1   Copies are available from the author at deanfink@cogeco.ca.
2   A retired head kindly conducted six of the Midland's Local Authority interviews for me.
3   Ball, S.G.(1984) "Beachside reconsidered: reflections on a methodological apprenticeship", in R.G. Burgess (ed.), *The Research Process in Educational Settings: Ten Case Studies*. London: Falmer, p. 54.
4   For a more complete write-up of the research and the instruments, please contact the author at deanfink@cogeco.ca.
5   National Professional Qualification for Headship.
6   Department of Education and Skills (2006) *School Teacher Performance Management (England) Regulations No. 2661*. www.tda.gov.uk/upload/resources/pdf/t/the_education_(school_teacher_performance_management)_(england)_regulations_2006.pdf, 20 July 2009.
7   Department of Children, Schools and Families (2009) *A New Relationship with Schools*. www.ncsl.org.uk/media-13c-f7-sips-brief-edition-3, 20 July 2009.
8   Department of Children, Schools and Families (2008) *Guidance on Head Teachers' Performance*. www.thegrid.org.uk/leadership/sips/secondary/documents/sip_handbook_appendix6.doc
9   Marley, D. (2009) "Bullying academy head given £45k to go", *Times Educational Supplement*. www.tes.co.uk/article.aspx?storycode=6017941, 20 July 2009.
10 My thanks to Wendy Jackson for helping me to sort out the intricacies of the British system. Any mistakes my British readers may find are the product of my inability to get my head around the vagaries.

6

Pipelines, Pools, and Reservoirs

In the past few years, shortages of willing leaders have forced governments around the world such as the United Kingdom, many American states, most Australian states, and most Canadian provinces to spend substantial amounts of money to fill up the leadership pipeline with qualified candidates for leadership positions. As I outlined in Chapter 2, this "replacement planning" strategy has foundered on the shoals of ever increasing demands placed on educational leaders and, as described in Chapter 3, the reluctance of generation X and the millennials to compromise their personal lives for the pressures and workload of leadership positions. As a result, we are seeing a subtle but important shift in thinking over the past few years among some educational decision makers in more progressive jurisdictions such as Iowa in the United States and New South Wales in Australia. Where once money spent on leadership recruitment and development was considered a cost, it is now viewed as an investment in the future. As a result, some school authorities and districts have shifted focus from replacement planning in which specific people are identified to fill certain jobs, usually through open competition, to a "succession management" approach which involves "the accelerated development of a select group of high-potential individuals for both current and future roles that may not be identifiable at present."[1] Rather than "hire and hope", these school authorities have adopted a "grow your own" philosophy.

While "grow your own" doesn't preclude hiring high-quality candidates from outside the school or system, it has the potential to reduce mistakes because pool members are known, "warts and all". It allows effective use of resources of time, money, and human energy, and since good development positions like assistant principal are limited in number, pools provide an alternative development opportunity for valued staff members. "Grow your own" ensures a ready supply of prepared leaders even in a crisis, reduces the expense of recruiting widely, precludes the high costs of turnover and demotivation when outside hires are brought into established settings, and reduces the amount of time for new leaders to "get up to speed" because they already understand the structures and culture of the organization. In the business world, Jim Collins contends that "grow your own" is the most effective strategy. He states that the findings

> across multiple studies (*Good to Great, Built to Last, How the Mighty Fall* and our on-going research into what it takes to prevail in turbulent environments)[2] show a distinct negative correlation between building great companies and going outside for a CEO.[3]

Developing this pool, however, depends in large measure on the reservoir of leadership capacity in an organization and, perhaps most importantly, the willingness of potential leaders to come forward. This chapter moves beyond the discussion of leadership pipelines in Chapter 2 by first examining leadership pools and then looking at how organizations build reservoirs of leadership capacity through distributed forms of leadership.

Filling the Pool

By observing successful business approaches to pool development, Mark Busine and Bruce Watt suggest that pool members should be allowed to enter from any level and at any age. A good pool development process allows participants to:

- get assignments that offer the best learning and highest visibility opportunities
- spend less time in routine assignments
- receive stretch assignments
- get more training
- attend development activities designed just for them
- have an assigned mentor
- prepare for a job – but they are not guaranteed a job.[4]

They suggest that the following steps are required to ensure the systemic development of pool members:

- a definition of success at key leadership levels
- an objective process to identify people with high potential as future leaders

- a comprehensive diagnosis of the development needs of participants based on their experience, knowledge, capabilities, and personal style
- specific job actions that involve on-the-job assignments, coaching, and targeted training.[5]

Some school districts, such as the Eastern School District in the US described in the previous chapter, continue to rely on replacement planning because they still get lots of applicants. As long as this plentiful supply exists, they can continue to "hire and hope", although mistakes can be costly in terms of student success, teacher morale, community support, and severance expenses. Some areas where shortages of principals and other educational leaders have become a major concern, such as in certain authorities in the UK, have moved aggressively into a succession management model. The National College for School Leadership (NCSL), with its multiplicity of programs designed to meet the needs of leaders at various career stages, has generally taken a pipeline approach to produce a number of qualified potential leaders from which school governors can choose. In more recent times, in light of the concerns that qualified people are not applying for the reasons described in Chapter 2, and particularly in high-need areas, NCSL in concert with the British Department for Children, Schools and Families (DCSF)[6] and other agencies has moved to a more targeted pool approach like more progressive businesses, in which the development of promising pool members is purposely accelerated. For example, the *Future Leaders Programme*

> seeks to expand the pool from which headteachers can be found for urban complex schools by recruiting from non-traditional sources and providing a model for changing attitudes to recruitment of senior staff. The intention is that people on the scheme should seek headships after about four years. The scheme consists of a rigorous selection process, some foundation training, and a one-year residency as a member of a senior leadership team in a London secondary school, after which participants apply for positions as deputies or assistant heads. There is ongoing support through coaching and training sessions.[7]

Similarly, in Scotland a pilot program entitled *Flexible Routes to Headship* creates a pool of potential leaders through a one-on-one coaching model.[8] However, as Peter Gronn and John MacBeth have pointed out, this program doesn't necessarily augment the pool but rather provides an alternative track for people already in the pool. A third of the pilot group studied got headships during the 18-month program and so that meant their participation was redundant or served little point. In the US the New Leaders for New Schools program invites potential leaders drawn from both the education and non-education sectors to apply to become part of an accelerated program with a view of providing leadership for difficult to serve schools.[9] Even privately funded foundations such as the Broad Foundation in the United States, which supports training programs of potential superintendents drawn from a variety of fields including 12 military generals, have got into the act.[10] Programs such as these however beg the question: do accelerated leaders, especially those from non-educational backgrounds, have the knowledge, experience, motivation, and aptitude to be leaders of learning, or are they just emergency appointments that governments have rushed into schools and other educational agencies to ensure that schools adhere to a political agenda that has more to do with good politics than with students' learning? There are so many programs around the world,[11] with and without non-educator leadership aspirants, that aim to develop a pool of potential leaders that it would be impossible to list and analyze them all and do them justice, although the work of Jacky Lumby and her colleagues[12] and Neil Dempster[13] provide good starting places.

Henry Mintzberg, noted management expert, has identified five general approaches to leadership development that apply in business, which from my observations of programs in various parts of the world are also relevant in education:[14]

- *Sink or swim.* This is the least expensive approach in the short run, and by far the most prevalent approach to leadership development in education. It promotes leaders from within or hires from outside and then places them in leadership roles, and lets them sink or swim. Districts that have historically thought in terms of replacement planning usually consider leadership development in education a cost for schools and school districts, and find it less expensive in the short term to advertise a position and then hire and hope that a person works out rather than to invest in pricey leadership development processes. The long-term costs of this approach, while hard to quantify, can be significant if the appointment turns out to be hopeless.
- *Moving, mentoring, and monitoring.* There is a general consensus in the business literature that rotating potential leaders through a number of leadership experiences provides a variety of challenges that encompass the spectrum of the company's activities and provides the neophyte leader with the greatest opportunity for learning. McCall found that prospective business leaders agreed with this approach because it gave them the opportunity first to witness experienced leaders deal with complex issues, and then to address such matters themselves with the support of their mentors.[15] He provides two rules

of leadership development: first, leadership development is a personal responsibility; and second, challenge can be provided to encourage this self-development, notably by rotating people through a series of challenging jobs that stretch their abilities. Such roles range from managing a start-up to "providing strong direction in the face of ambiguity, to managing the turnaround of an existing business to learn about overcoming resistance and incompetence."[16] There is, however, some evidence that suggests that the disruption caused to schools by the regular rotation of principals and assistant principals far outweighs any gains that might accrue to the individuals involved.[17] As we found in the *Change Over Time?* study, transitions in times of turbulence can be particularly problematic. At the same time, as described in Chapter 5, principals in the Ontario district in the *Three Countries* study, which moves principals on a five- to eight-year cycle and assistant principals on a three- to four-year cycle, felt that their moves as assistant principals sometimes two and three times were invaluable in their development as leaders. They saw a variety of leadership styles, coped with different contexts and challenges, and learned what to do in certain circumstances and sometimes what not to do. At least 10 of the 21 people I interviewed continue to stay in contact with former principals and make use of them as mentors and coaches.

- *Spray and pray*. This approach refers to the practice of credentialing leaders through leadership development courses offered by school districts, universities, and private consulting groups. From a system's point of view, these often uncoordinated courses vary widely in efficacy, tend to stress teaching over learning, and offer generic answers to contextually based issues. As Mintzberg has observed, "deep managing and deep learning depend on personal engagement, not just on a detached expertise that 'knows better.' So managers learn most profoundly when they have significant responsibility for all aspects of the learning process, including its design."[18] He concludes after years of teaching management courses for potential leaders that "setting out to create leaders in a classroom, whether in a short program or full degrees, too often creates hubris. People leave believing they have been anointed."[19]
- *Learning in action*. Positioned somewhere between the context-based "moving, mentoring, and monitoring" and the decontextualized course work of "spray and pray", "learning in action" involves potential leaders in field projects and activities followed by serious reflection that creates a learning laboratory for leaders. Schools and school districts have often organized potential leaders into problem-solving committees to address a system's problems. Mintzberg concluded in his critique of action learning that "learning is not doing: it is reflection on doing. And reflecting is not an escape but an

essential part of the management process – and probably its weakest part in today's hyper world."[20]

- *Corporate academies.* There is an increasing trend in the business world for large corporations to establish academies that provide coordinated, contextualized leadership development that focuses on developing leadership potential to ensure a continuing supply of quality leaders. Such companies as Boeing, General Electric Motorola, and even McDonald's have adopted this practice. Perhaps the closest educational equivalent is the National College for School Leadership (NCSL) in the United Kingdom, although various states and school districts support leadership assessment centers and development programs. For example, the South School Board in Ontario offers two leadership programs for potential leaders and a program for newly appointed leaders. These programs are conducted by school board or authority personnel and experienced educators within the system. Mentoring connections are promoted in all their programs. The Eastern School District in the US is part of a consortium of school districts linked with a large and prestigious local university and relies on the university to provide preparation for aspirant leaders. The Midlands Local Authority, as I outlined in the last chapter, provides a full range of offerings to meet the diverse needs of school leaders.

Some models are more useful at different stages of a leader's career and some are quite unsuitable. For example, "spray and pray" might be of limited efficacy for a leader on an inbound trajectory, but reinvigorating for an experienced leader. All these approaches are based on the questionable assumption, however, that people are interested in becoming or continuing to be leaders and the even shakier notion that they want to be leaders of learning.

Mentoring, Coaching, and Counseling

Regardless of the general approach, mentoring and coaching in recent years have become important parts of virtually every important leadership development model.

A mentor is defined as someone with "experience, expertise, wisdom and/or power who teaches, counsels and helps less experienced and less knowledgeable persons to develop personally and professionally."[21] In the educational literature, the terms "mentoring", "coaching", and "counseling" are often used interchangeably. Bruce Barnett and Gary O'Mahony, in their very useful survey of mentoring purposes and practices, describe coaching as a short-term interaction in which a more skilled or experienced coach helps a person through an immediate difficulty such as how to use a particular computer program, interpret district policies, or deal with a difficult parent.[22] Counseling also involves a short time frame; however, "the focus is on attitudinal, motivational or behavioral issues that interfere with someone's job performance."[23] Mentoring is more inclusive and includes both coaching and counseling when appropriate. It is usually carried out over a longer time frame and it is intended to encourage formal and informal career development, reciprocal learning between mentors and mentees, reflection for personal and professional growth, and trust between mentors and mentees.[24] Barnett and O'Mahony suggest that mentoring should only be a part of a leadership program and not the program itself.

Program designers, however, need to be aware of some of the limitations of mentoring as a development and support process. It has been argued that some mentors perpetuate the status quo,[25] often lack the commitment to be of any real help, attempt to clone themselves, and attend to personal agendas that have little to do with the needs of the neophyte leader. The most frequently reported limitation to effective mentorship or coaching programs is a lack of time for partners to engage in professional dialogue. All three school divisions involved in my research have some form of mentorship, which for the most part participants, mentors, and their protégés find to be quite useful. The common complaint, however, was a lack of time to deepen and extend relationships. As a result, mentoring in these districts tends to be informal and *ad hoc* and usually dependent on the new leader's support network. A 35-year-old female acting head in England explained that:

> I haven't had anything in the line of mentorship or anything like that, which I think is something that perhaps needs to be looked into because there are courses for people near to headship, they're assigned a mentor and I didn't have any of that. So I took on the acting role, now, just over 12 months with none of that support really, just my school advisor. I am involved in two local cluster groups, which aren't facilitated as such by the authority. One's an excellence cluster and one's the large schools' cluster. That one is a sort of self-sustaining group of some headteachers who got together and did that one. They have been my biggest source of support.

An experienced American principal explained that in her district, "When I was first appointed, the superintendent used to assign a mentor principal to us, but it was never really formal and I was never quite sure when I was supposed to see Heather, what the expectations were for me from her." Similarly, a mid-career principal in Ontario, now in her second school as principal, ascribes her success to the ongoing support of her principal when she was a first-time vice (assistant) principal eight years previously. Even though her principal is now retired, she finds that he is a useful sounding-board for ideas, a source of encouragement, and a sympathetic ear when she needs to vent her frustrations. An experienced Ontario principal in a nearby school finds himself the mentor to three of his former assistant principals who are now new principals. He says a day rarely goes by without a call to discuss an issue, get information, or ask advice. While deemed effective by participants, this informal approach leaves out people who are new to the system, and people who never had the good fortune to work with a principal who took the mentoring role seriously. To rectify some of these inequities the Ontario Ministry of Education has invested $4 million in an impressive and ambitious province-wide mentoring program as part of a larger leadership development strategy.[26] Based on my 21 interviews with principals in an Ontario school board, the government's plan appears to be very slow in getting off the ground and its effect upon schools and principals to date is negligible. The strategy really begs the question: does more money address the systemic problem of recruiting and developing new leaders and supporting existing leaders? Successful mentoring programs seem to be emergent, and to evolve as a function of collegial relationships, rather than to be designed at a distance or even imposed, regardless of the financial support.

A leading source of information on approaches to mentoring and coaching is the UK's National College for School Leadership. Since its inception in the late 1990s, mentoring, coaching, and networking have been integral parts of its varied and impressive programs. Its mentoring and coaching are based on six propositions about the role of school leaders, which provide a rather succinct summary of why school districts and schools who want to address the succession challenge should look at mentoring as a key component:

- Leaders have a moral responsibility to promote everyone's learning, both adults and pupils.
- Leaders have a moral imperative to develop the next generation of school leaders.
- High-quality coaching in schools supports professional development, leadership sustainability and school improvement.
- Leaders therefore have a responsibility for providing the processes, structures, and resources to support coaching.

- Central to these propositions is the role of learning conversations, which make tacit knowledge explicit and engage staff in open and honest feedback.
- Leaders should model the dialogue and personal approaches that create a culture of high-quality coaching interactions across the school.[27]

While there are plenty of mentoring schemes available to provide guidance and advice, and innumerable very useful leadership programs that provide examples of very good practices that schools and districts can adapt, the question remains of how we encourage potential leaders to "jump into the pool". One important answer is to build reservoirs of people who are engaged in productive leadership activities.

Developing a Reservoir

I belong to a very fine golf club, which for the past 100 years has drawn water to keep the course green and lush from a creek that winds its way through my hometown. Even in the summer when southern Ontario usually experiences a drought, the course maintenance personnel continue to use the water from the creek. But times have changed. My sleepy village has become part of a major metropolis with an expanding commercial and residential base. As a result, the local conservation authority has limited the amount of water the golf course officials can extract from its historic source, which in turn has forced the club to build a large and expensive reservoir to conserve the spring rain and the winter snow for use during the dry months of the summer. Like my golf course, I suggest that schools and districts need to build a reservoir of prepared and available leaders by taking advantage of the leadership capacity inherent in any organization and directing it in ways that give teachers and other educational workers opportunities to exercise their latent leadership potential in rewarding and productive ways. In practice this means distributing leadership across an organization rather than depending solely on historic vertical structures. As Peter Gronn explains, "distributed leadership invites consideration of an organisation's overall capacity for leadership, rather than helping to perpetuate the idea of the power of one."[28] Various authors, particularly in the UK, hold out great hope that distributed forms of leadership will spread within schools and across schools within local authorities and create new patterns of networked leadership that not only address recruitment difficulties but inspire systemic improvement in educational standards. David Hopkins and his colleagues predict that meeting the contemporary challenges of schooling will require school leaders to "consider new models of leadership and governance to appropriately distribute an increasing range of responsibilities to a wider and differentiated pool of leadership expertise."[29] In a similar vein, Alma Harris writes that the present leadership situation in the UK invites

> new forms of leadership and decision making processes that are *widely distributed* within, between and across schools plus partner organisations. It will require leadership that is distributed across into the "community" in its widest and most diverse sense. It will require:
>
> - Leadership that crosses structural, cultural and personal barriers,
> - Leadership that builds capacity within schools, communities and systems,
> - Leadership that generates relational and social capital,
> - Leadership that sustains performance,
> - Leadership that supports re-design and self-renewal.[30]

The enthusiasm for distributed forms of leadership is well placed as long as certain conditions prevail. Harris argues that changes in British education are "predicated on greater freedom and autonomy for schools and the system as a whole."[31] She has succinctly captured the essence of what is required on a policy level to ensure that schools and districts realize the potential of distributed leadership models.

David Hartley's less sanguine opinion of distributed forms of leadership suggests that:

> The emergence of distributed leadership is very much a sign of the times: it resonates with contemporary culture, with all its loose affiliations and ephemeralities, and it is yet another sign of *how* the public sector *purports* to legitimate policies by appeals to the new organizational forms within the private sector ... But what it is to be distributed remains very much within the strategic parameters and targets set by government. It is the teachers, not the strategy, which are available for distribution. Hierarchical forms of accountability remain.[32]

In a recent publication, the National College for School Leadership provides practical examples of schools and networks of schools that have purposefully attempted to build leadership capacity by distributing leadership.[33] From these examples, the authors concluded that each school and local authority had three strategic targets for its leadership development. At an individual level, spreading leadership around can actively enhance individuals' career potential. Such approaches to leadership can also add value to schools' improvement agendas and build capacity to meet those demands, and can nurture a pool of talented leaders for the future able to apply for leadership roles within their own or other schools.

By examining a number of case studies of shared approaches to leadership, the College publication indicated that individuals reported "they had increased confidence and self-belief and are now keener to aspire to a leadership role in future and, in a number of cases, their careers have progressed." Within the schools, "staff motivation levels rose and the capacity of the school increased. Leaders were focused on school improvement, which had a direct influence on the quality of provision and pupil outcomes including achievement." And finally, "these approaches contributed to the pool of leadership talent available within a local area and further afield." Nevertheless:

> Aside from lack of time and finances, interviewees highlighted two specific barriers to progress in their schools:
>
> - the view that talented leaders should be retained within the school rather than feed the system persists,
> - there is some resistance to the idea of younger, less experienced staff assuming a leadership role.[34]

At the moment I remain an agnostic on whether distributed forms of leadership are the hope of the future or the same old top-down change model presented in a shiny new package. Are distributed forms of leadership just a less coercive way of spreading unrealistic demands across organizations to already stressed people, or of pushing them onto overloaded teachers and other educational professionals? Peter Gronn asserts that "distributed leadership is merely a linguistically made-over way of talking about delegated responsibility – nothing more, nothing less," just "as 'management' was given a linguistic makeover and became 'leadership'."[35] In a similar vein, Andy Hargreaves and I also asked if distributed leadership is really anything new or different or just a more subtle way to spread the leadership load to other people:

> The hardest questions about distributed leadership are moral and democratic ones. What kind of distributed leadership do we want, and what educational and social purposes will it serve? Are such forms of leadership merely more subtle and clever ways to deliver standardized packages of government reforms and performance targets in easily measurable areas like literacy that have more to do with expedient politics than with sustainable educational change? ... can distributed leadership be a key principle in a coherent and inclusive democratic consensus that joins the entire community in the pursuit of a compelling social vision?[36]

There are two ways to look at distributed leadership. The first is *normative*: the more distributed leadership we have, the better. The second view is *descriptive*, pointing to all the leadership that is already there based on the premise that leadership is always distributed in some way or other. Jim Spillane argues that leadership is an activity, a social practice that stretches across many people and includes the situation in which leadership activity takes place: "School leadership is best understood as a distributed practice, stretched over the schools' social and situational contexts."[37] Spillane uses the metaphor of two people performing a dance – the Texas two-step. The actions of the individuals in the dance are important, but it is the interaction *between* individuals that is the practice or activity of the dance. Music becomes an important part of the *situation*, and therefore the dancers' interaction with the music becomes part of the activity. If the music changes, so does the dance. The point is to show how the distribution occurs. Spillane's activity-based approach is a good way to audit existing leadership practices.[38] It draws attention to leadership contributions that might otherwise go unrecognized.[39] It can highlight emerging leadership talent. And it validates the leadership achievements of the group, beyond the gallant individuals who usually get the credit.

When the normative and descriptive positions are combined, what we learn is that all leadership is always distributed – even in an autocracy (which creates resistance). It is distributed either deliberately or by accident, and in a good way or a bad way. Sustainable leadership is distributed leadership. But not all distributed leadership is sustainable leadership. Nor do all forms of distributed leadership contribute to the idea of a reservoir of leadership. It depends on how the leadership is distributed and for what purposes. Different forms of distribution reflect the interplay of design and emergence, as described in Chapter 1. The more design, the more control by the formal structures, and the fewer opportunities for leadership to emerge spontaneously. As more leadership activity emerges, the formal structures have less ability to direct and control.

A Distributed Continuum

The evidence of the *Change Over Time?* study described in Chapter 4 suggested a continuum of distributed leadership that reflects the relationship between design and emergence and can be represented on a thermometer (Figure 6.1).[40] As the mercury ascends the thermometer, distributed leadership occurs primarily through structural means of roles, committees, and formal procedures at the bottom; then factors in

Too hot!

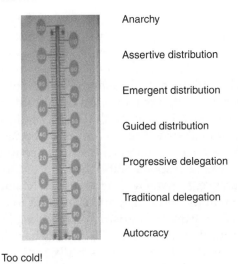

Anarchy

Assertive distribution

Emergent distribution

Guided distribution

Progressive delegation

Traditional delegation

Autocracy

Too cold!

Figure 6.1 *Raising the temperature of distributed leadership*
Hargreaves, A. and Fink, D. *Sustainable Leadership* © 2005. Reprinted by
permission of the publisher John Wiley & Sons, Inc.

cultural forms of distribution through communication, relationships, and group life in the middle; and adds in further political ingredients of assertiveness towards the top. The following sections outline the stages in this continuum.

Autocracy

At the bottom end of this spectrum there are schools, fortunately very few, in which the principal, sometimes assisted by a small group of formal leaders such as department heads, makes all the important decisions. Such leaders not only fail to engage the leadership abilities of others within the official structures of the organization, but also invite a backlash from emergent groups that need outlets for their leadership abilities. In the *Change Over Time?* study we found that if leadership is not deliberately distributed in ways that engage teachers with the goals of the school, it will end up being distributed by default. Leadership will emerge to subvert and sabotage the principal's plans at every step. There may be times when autocratic approaches are a reluctant necessity to be used as a last resort – when teachers abdicate responsibility for poor performance, for instance.[41] But in general, autocratic leadership does not just fail to sustain important changes but leaves them stillborn, and in the process pollutes the leadership reservoir.

Traditional Delegation

The next ascendant level, delegated responsibility, tends to be the way most large bureaucratic institutions work. The leader, for example a secondary school principal, works closely with his or her department heads, delegates leadership to them within their subject areas, and works with them to develop broad school policies, manage day-to-day operations, and react to outside reform initiatives. Under duress, principals in all three of the cases outlined in Chapter 4 reverted to traditional structures to ensure compliance with outside mandates. If the leader has sufficient confidence in their abilities to manage their areas of responsibility, they are left to attend to them without interference. Bureaucracies move slowly since their purpose is to maintain stability and order, and they tend to colonize external change efforts. Department headships have the potential to be the incubating ground for leadership at higher levels, but my observations from the *Three Countries* study indicate that they have become career jobs with little turnover and in some cases represent a barrier to aspirant leaders. Leadership opportunities within traditional delegation tend to be serendipitous and depend on the style of the individual department head. Rather than actively suppressing emergent leadership like autocrats, bureaucratic leaders frustrate it. Distributed leadership means more than delegated leadership. At its worst, delegated leadership amounts to assigning tasks to subordinates that are menial, uninteresting, or unpleasant. Student discipline, routine committee work, unimaginative and unpopular teacher evaluation procedures: these are the stuff of traditional delegation. They get the existing work of the school done, but do not really change or challenge it. At its best, some department heads might enjoy opportunities for prestige and power and possible advancement and promotion. But for staff members who feel ignored, their dissatisfaction and alienation are expressed by withdrawing into their classrooms, disengaging from school activities, and exercising their leadership abilities through quiet subversion of school-wide change.

Progressive Delegation

Progressive delegation occurs when schools break out of the vertical delegation mode and adopt more horizontal engagement of staff members from across a school or district by creating committees that address school-wide issues such as assessment of student performance or the integration of information technology into the curriculum. This can result in a larger percentage of school staff becoming involved and gaining insight into issues beyond their teaching areas, and also exercising some leadership within the limits of the school's formal structures.

The more progressive patterns of delegation in schools redirect their schools' structures towards supporting improvement. But they succeed only as long as the formal leaders are around to guide them and the teachers involved remain committed and supportive. While a few teachers might get to exercise some leadership, the constraints inhibit all but the super enthusiasts from pursuing more leadership opportunities. The legacy of investing oneself in such school-wide efforts, only to have them fall apart upon the departure of the key leaders or replaced by another top-down initiative, can result in frustration, long-term cynicism, and leadership exercised in negative ways.

Guided Distribution

The building of a culture and accompanying distribution of leadership in guided distribution is always firmly directed by the close watch and controlling hand of the principal or head. Guided distribution can create strong professional learning communities but it is unlikely to sustain them over time. Guided distribution is so dependent on the senior leader that the sustainability of significant change is confined to the period of their tenure. Within this structure a few potential leaders have an opportunity to shine and assume leadership roles. As they do, they have the guidance of the formal leaders to help them along their way. This oversight provides a form of mentorship that often builds personal bonds that may not sustain the school as a learning community but can support the neophyte leader's ambitions even after the guiding leader departs.

Emergent Distribution

Emergent distribution occurs when formal and emergent leadership tracks blend seamlessly to contribute to a school as a professional learning community. Leadership certainly flows through the designed formal roles and structures, though many of these are explicitly innovative and improvement oriented. But if a professional learning community works well, leadership is stretched across the school in ways that are creative, spontaneous, and emergent – leading to temporary structures and committees, unexpected and inspirational initiatives that engage staff members in meaningful leadership activities, and the building of reservoirs of leadership potential.[42]

Assertive Distribution

Assertive distribution means that teachers in a school feel free to challenge the principal or head, and are actively empowered to do so, provided their assertive leadership strengthens and does not undermine the overall vision for sustainable learning and improvement. Assertive leadership moves distributed leadership to a higher, more risky and overtly political plane. It calls for courage and self-confidence among senior leaders who are able to endure, encourage, and empower assertive distribution that furthers the school's or system's goals (even though it may challenge the means). And it requires an activist orientation among teachers as change agents who are committed to social and educational missions that unite them in confronting bureaucratic and political obstacles to socially just and educationally justifiable improvement and reform.

Governments and bureaucracies do not always occupy the high ground on change and reform. And assertive distributed leadership repeatedly emboldens successful leaders of schools in difficult circumstances to challenge government or district bureaucracies which impede their path to achieving authentic improvement, and make it unnecessarily hard for them to engage with the cultures of and intellectual differences among their diverse students.[43]

Anarchy

The line between autocracy and anarchy is a thin one. Autocracies foment resentment and rebellion. Lacking government, anarchies give rise to lawlessness and disorder. Anarchies result from distribution by neglect. The designed structures have broken down and no longer counterbalance emergent and potentially divisive and corrosive emergent leadership. The circle group at Talisman Park in Chapter 4 is but one example. Senior leaders who cannot maintain clarity or unity of purpose, who are weak or afraid, or who only want to be liked – all of them create a leadership vacuum that others are more than eager to fill. This kind of emergent leadership is often divisive and self-serving – even callous and cruel. There is no moral glue to hold the emergent leadership together.

Like weak or inexperienced teachers who inherit a class from a controlling colleague, transitions from micro-managers to ones who are inexperienced or ineffectual provide optimum conditions for the emergence of anarchy. The shift from autocracy to anarchy can be frighteningly fast. At Stewart Heights, described in Chapter 4, Jerry West became the school's principal. He replaced Bill Andrews, a dynamic and charismatic change agent. Andrews, in his two years as principal, distributed leadership widely, but always retained control and oversight. The transition from the firm hand of Andrew's guided distribution to first-time principal Jerry West's desire to just watch the existing culture and wait led to destructive political infighting, reassertion of departmental self-interest, punitive purges on student behavior by the school climate team, and (as in an autocracy) the contamination of the leadership reservoir.

The degree of distribution in a school will move up or down the distribution "thermometer" in response to outside pressures and the unique features of the school's context. Drawing on the school scenarios from the previous chapter, we can see that Talisman Park, which was an example of guided distribution, responded to innovation overload by moving to greater design and delegated distribution through the formal department heads structure to ensure compliance, and in the process limited emergent leadership opportunities. The principal of Blue Mountain School, Linda White, an exemplar of emergent distribution, reacted to external pressures by adopting more managerial strategies and guided approaches to distribution. Stewart Heights, which under Bill Andrews modeled guided distribution, found the combination of outside pressures and inexperienced leadership after Andrews's departure so unsettling that the school became anarchic as various micro-political factions emerged to fill the formal leadership vacuum; distributed leadership was purely accidental, with too much emergence and not enough design and stability. I would suggest there is an inverse relationship between outside pressures for rapid and often overwhelming change and the facility with which a school distributes leadership: the more pressure, the more the formal structures focus on risk reduction and conformity and controlling leadership emergence. Conversely, the reduction of external pressures allows leadership to emerge because formal leaders feel sufficiently comfortable to take some risks that mistakes could be made. As Alma Harris has suggested, distributed leadership needs "freedom and autonomy."[44] Jim Collins explains that in the business world "when bureaucratic rules erode an ethic of freedom and responsibility within a framework of core values and demanding standards, you've become infected with the disease of mediocrity."[45]

In this chapter, I have suggested that most jurisdictions have or are in the process of moving beyond merely filling the pipeline of qualified potential leaders as a way to address the succession challenge to developing pools of potential leaders who would be ready to assume leadership roles when incumbent leaders retire or move on. There are, I sense, some subtle shifts taking place at policy levels, from looking at leadership recruitment and development as a cost to viewing them as investments, from relying solely on replacement planning to introducing a "grow your own" strategy, from hiring based on existing proficiencies to recruiting people with potential to become a school or district leader. The question remains, however: are these strategies producing leaders of learning?

As I have written elsewhere,[46] developing leaders of learning takes time, resources, and energy, because prospective leaders require

- the opportunity to undertake significant and challenging activities early in their careers that "stretched" them intellectually and professionally
- leadership development opportunities that enabled them to meet these challenges
- supportive mentors who assisted them as they met their challenges
- the opportunity to observe and learn from powerful models of successful educational leadership (and from some negative examples)
- feedback on their performance that was honest and constructive (although not always positive).

Accelerated leadership programs may attend to the short-term challenge of filling some jobs with warm bodies, but creating environments in which leadership is distributed in ways that produce reservoirs of potential leaders of learning will depend on a change in the policy environment internationally. Let us now move on to look at specific examples of how a few educational jurisdictions are addressing the succession challenge within their policy contexts.

Notes

1 Busine, M. and Watt, B. (2005) "Succession management: trends and current practices", *Asia Pacific Journal of Human Resources*, 43 (2): 225–37.
2 Collins, J. (2001) *Good to Great: Why Some Companies Make the Leap and Others Don't*. New York: Harper Business; Collins, J. and Porras, G. (2002) *Built to Last: Successful Habits of Visionary Companies*. New York: Harper Business; Collins, J. (2009) *How the Mighty Fall: And Why Some Companies Never Give in*. New York: HarperCollins.
3 Collins, *How the Mighty Fall*, op. cit., pp. 94–5.
4 Busine and Watt, op. cit., p. 230.
5 Ibid., p. 230.
6 Previously called the Department for Educations and Skills. As policy changes, the name keeps changing.
7 Early, P., Weindling, D., Bubb, S., Evans, J. and Glenn, M. (2008) "Evaluation of the Future Leaders Pilot Programme". http://www.ncsl.org.uk/evaluation-of-future-leaders-3.pdf, 6 March 2009.

8   Gronn, P. and MacBeth, J. (2008) "Towards a mixed economy of head teacher development". http://www.docstoc.com/docs/3623265/Towards-a-Mixed-Economy-of-Head-Teacher-Development-Evaluation-Report, 6 March 2009; see also https://www.ltscotland.org.uk/cpdscotland/what/prd/frh.asp.

9   See http://www.nlns.org/Become.jsp.

10 Broad Foundation (2009) "12 military generals, school district executives, entrepreneurs chosen for national superintendents training program", press release, 14 January http://broadeducation.org/asset/0-090114tba2009class. pdf, 9 March 2009.

11 Some examples I'm personally familiar with are local authorities in England such as Bury, Kent, and Buckinghamshire, states such as Iowa, Nebraska, and Virginia in the US, states such as New South Wales and South Australia in Australia, and extensive state–university collaboration in New Zealand. Descriptions are easily accessed on the internet.

12 Lumby, J., Crow, G. and Pashiardis, P. (eds) (2008) *International Handbook on the Preparations and Development of School Leaders*. New York: Routledge.

13 Dempster, N. (2007) *The Treasure Within: Leadership and Succession Planning.* Deakin: Australian College of Educators.

14 Minzberg, H. (2004) *Managers Not MBAs: A Hard Look at the Soft Practice of Managing and Management Development.* San Francisco, CA: Berrett-Koehler.

15 McCall, M. (1988) "Developing executive through work experience", *Human Resources Planning*, 11 (1): 1–11.

16 Ibid., p. 9.

17 Macmillan, R. (2000) "Leadership succession, cultures of teaching and educational change", in A. Hargreaves and N. Bascia (eds), *The Sharp Edge of Educational Change*. London: Falmer.

18 Mintzberg, op.cit., p. 211.

19 Ibid., p. 215.

20 Ibid., p. 208.

21 Danielson, C. and McGreal, T.L. (2000) *Teacher Evaluation to Enhance Professional Practice*. Princeton, NJ: Educational Testing Service, p. 251.

22 Barnett, B. and O'Mahony, G. (2008) "Mentoring and coaching programs for the professional development of school leaders", in Lumby et al., op.cit.

23 Ibid., p. 238.

24 Crow, G. and Matthews, L. (2003) *Finding One's Way*. Newbury Park, CA: Corwin.

25 Danielson and McGreal, op. cit.

26 Ministry of Education (2008) "Ontario Leadership Strategy". http://www.edu. gov.on.ca/eng/policyfunding/leadership/leadersSupport.html, 26 March 2009.

27 National College for School Leadership (2005) "Leading coaching in schools". http://www.ncsl.org.uk/research/research_activities/coaching/research-researchactivities-coaching-more.cfm#propositions, 3 February 2009.

28 Gronn, P. (2002) "Distributed leadership", in K. Leithwood, P. Hallinger, K. Seashore-Louis, G. Furman-Brown, P. Gronn, W. Mulford and K. Riley (eds), *Second International Handbook of Educational Leadership and Administration*. Dordrecht: Kluwer, p. 17.

29 Hopkins, D., Higham, R. and Antaridou, E. (2009) *School Leadership in England: Contemporary Challenges, Innovative Responses and Future Trends*. Nottingham: NCSL, p. 9.

30   Harris, A. (2009) "Future leadership: challenges and implications", presented at *Invitation Seminar 21st Century Schools,* Department for Children, Schools and Families (DCSF), London, 27 March.

31   Ibid.

32   Hartley, D. (2007) "The emergence of distributed leadership in education: why now?", *British Journal of Educational Studies,* 55 (2): 211.

33   National College for School Leadership (2009) "Identify and grow your own leaders: a practical guide and case studies". http://www.ncsl.org.uk/identify-and-grow-your-own-leaders.pdf, 15 July 2009.

34   Ibid., p. 26.

35   Personal correspondence, 29 May 2009.

36   Hargreaves, A. and Fink, D. (2008) "Distributed leadership: democracy or delivery", *Journal of Educational Administration,* 46 (2): 229–40.

37   Spillane, J. (2006) *Distributed Leadership.* San Francisco, CA: Jossey-Bass.

38   Ibid.

39   This argument is also made in Ryan, J. (2006) *Inclusive Leadership.* San Francisco: Jossey-Bass.

40   See Hargreaves and Fink, op. cit., for a detailed description of this idea.

41   Stoll, L. and Myers, K. (1998) *No Quick Fixes: Perspectives on Schools in Difficulty.* London: Falmer.

42   Heifetz, R.A. and Linsky, M. (2002) *Leadership on the Line: Staying Alive Through the Dangers of Learning.* Boston: Harvard Business School.

43   Lewis, J. and Caldwell, B. (2005) "Evidence based leadership", *The Educational Forum,* 69 (2): 182–91.

44   Harris, op. cit.

45   Collins, *How the Mighty Fall,* op. cit, p. 56.

46   Fink, D. op. cit. pp. 142–6.

7

The Good, the Bad, and the Ugly

When I asked my daughter what it was like meeting her old boyfriends at the recent reunion of her secondary school she said, "I met the good, the bad, and the ugly." With a little imagination, it could be said that my daughter's description is an apt way to categorize leadership succession practices from around the world. In this chapter, I will concentrate on what I think are good practices, describe a few bad practices to avoid, and ignore "the ugly". To this point in the book, I have attempted to make the case that the succession challenge is more than just recruiting warm bodies to resolve a mathematical mismatch between leadership aspirants and available jobs. The real challenge of leadership succession is to find and assign the right warm body to the right place, at the right time, for the right reasons. While timing and location may not always be controllable, hiring for the right reasons is always possible. Educational leaders, regardless of their roles, must see themselves as leaders of learning – their own, their teachers' and other staff, and of course their students'. They must be "passionately, creatively, obsessively and steadfastly committed to enhancing 'deep' learning for all students – learning for understanding, learning for life, learning for a knowledge society."[1] From this perspective, there is a succession challenge of major proportions looming in most western countries to replace the vanishing leaders with new leaders who have the commitment, values, qualities, and intellect to advance student learning to new heights of genuine achievement and accomplishment. The succession challenge, as I have suggested, is the product of four interrelated themes: shifting demographics, the attractiveness (or lack of it) of leadership jobs, conflicting generational aspirations, and geographic inequalities. Many of the younger people who are quite capable of replacing retiring principals and other educational leaders see their jobs as unattractive. From a generational perspective, these jobs are incompatible with their lifestyles and career goals. Moreover, some areas of the world are more succession challenged than others. As I indicated in Chapter 3, the world is not flat but spiky, and some areas have an abundance of potentially great leaders and others suffer from a dearth of quality, much to the detriment of their students. In this chapter, I use examples of good and not so good practices from first the private sector and then various educational jurisdictions around the world, particularly my three cases from Chapter 5, to provide some guidance and suggestions for those who have to wrestle with the succession challenge, without getting lost in long lists of "best practices".

I've long been suspicious of the search for the "holy grail" of best practice.[2] There may be best practices in manufacturing processes, drawing up a will, or producing an insurance policy, but non-linear, unpredictable, emergent activities like teaching and leading do not lend themselves to long lists of best practices. Similarly, leadership succession is so context dependent that lists of best practices would be relatively useless. We can, however, learn and adapt from the many good practices and in some cases not so good practices that various school jurisdictions around the world have employed, and also from the private sector which has invested much more time, energy, and study into succession management and planning over the past 20 years than has the public sector.

The Private Sector

The traditional private sector method of succession management, according to William Rothwell, "helps ensure the stability of tenure of personnel."[3] In practice this meant that businesses tried to match individuals to statically defined positions. "This approach, however, is outdated and conflicts with the rapidly changing needs of today's organizations."[4] Contemporary approaches to succession management in business take a much broader view on the succession processes, and now focus on leaders' ability to learn, adjust, and create rather than on their capabilities for existing proficiencies of a specific job.[5] The present fetish in education and other public sector areas, supposedly based on good business practices, to nail down every job to a "laundry list" of easily observed principals' competencies fails to account for shifting job requirements, changing contexts, and the evolving needs, interests, and life circumstances of children. Hiring based on this approach may be suitable for replacement planning but is of limited use for succession management:

> The National Academy of Public Administration defines succession management as a deliberate and systemic effort to project leadership requirements, identify a pool of high potential candidates, develop leadership competencies in those candidates through intentional learning experiences, and then select leaders from among the pool of potential leaders.[6]

Rothwell explains that it is an important tool of organizational learning because it should ensure that:

> the lessons of organizational experience – what is sometimes called institutional memory – will be preserved and combined with reflection on that experience to achieve continuous improvement in work results. Stated another way, [it] is a way to ensure the continued cultivation of leadership and intellectual talent and manage the critical knowledge assets of organization.[7]

Just as demographic problems contribute to leadership succession issues in education, so early retirements, downsizing, and reengineering have created critical shortages of middle and top leaders in the business community,[8] to say nothing of the massive reorganizations resulting from the economic downturn of 2009. To attend to this ongoing problem, business observers contend that organizations must embark on systemic succession management programs to replace the departing and soon-to-depart leaders.[9] While different authors emphasize various aspects of the succession process, I have listed here some "good" procedures practiced by the better companies.[10] It should be added that just because a company is private doesn't mean that its succession management and planning are effective or strategic. The best companies, however, search for potential leaders, and expend considerable time, energy, and money to prepare them for future leadership. My list is as follows:

- The succession process should be directly connected to the strategic purposes and values of the organization.
- The chief executive of the organization should champion the organization's succession management.
- Line managers must take ownership of succession management so that staff support the process.
- Potential and existing leaders should be judged on their ability to learn and to develop the learning of others in the organization.[11]
- Managers should be held accountable for human resources reviews and for implementing their outcomes.

- Succession management is fully coordinated with the corporate human resources system and strategy.
- The succession process is simple and focused on people not technology.
- Succession management is tailored to the organization's unique needs, culture, and history.
- Succession management drives leadership development programs.

While these guidelines are useful and generic, their application in various educational jurisdictions will depend on the distinctive context of each setting. My three school districts in three countries illustrate the variability and uniqueness of each situation and the limitations of best practice.

The Eastern School District

The three school systems described in Chapter 5 share a need for quality leadership but face quite different issues and as a result emphasize different aspects of the succession process. But each in its own way provides some examples of good practices that deserve a closer look. As I have stated before, the Eastern School District in the US has no problem recruiting high-quality leaders and invests very little time or money in the development of its own people as leaders. The system compensates by devoting a great deal of time, expense, and human energy to its selection process. When a principal's job becomes available, a committee, chaired by a senior district official and made up of a cross-section of the system, including teachers, principals, and school board members, thoroughly checks applicants résumés, interviews the suitable qualified applicants, and then reduces this group to a workable number of candidates, who are subsequently required to address and respond to questions from community members and the teaching staff of the school with the vacancy. After putting the candidate through these steps, the committee then reduces the shortlist to two or three who are deemed suitable and their names are forwarded to the superintendent[12] who makes the final selection. While comprehensive, this approach does tend to discriminate against internal candidates. As one experienced principal explained:

> The superintendent uses his superintendent's network to bring in strong candidates. He is exceptionally good on reference checks – maybe too thorough – if you talk to enough people you will find something wrong. The district has tended to hire vice (assistant) principals from within but go outside to fill principals' jobs. Such a small system creates problems to hire from within – you might hear that when he taught grade four he shouted at kids and that would eliminate an internal candidate.

As a result, a staff member from within the system who aspires to be a leader must first seek leadership training at one of a number of private or university training centers, and then look outside the Eastern District for promotion. My interviews with principals in the Eastern District suggest that this approach causes considerable resentment within the system and undermines the collegiality of the district. System leaders have recently recognized this dilemma and are in the early stages of developing a leadership pool of internal candidates that would be capable of competing with outside applicants. While few school districts, especially larger districts that have to hire a number of new leaders annually, could emulate the Eastern District's thoroughness in its selection processes, the district's procedures highlight the importance of an in-depth approach to leadership appraisal at the time of selection. As most districts well know, once hired, ineffective school and district leaders are difficult and expensive to dislodge.

Interestingly, one of Eastern's succession practices that virtually every principal I interviewed applauded was one that the system abandoned a few years ago. A previous superintendent arranged for principals new to a school to spend a day meeting with a cross-section of usually five or six staff members of his or her new school. Teachers were paid and the superintendent arranged for meals and refreshments in a restaurant. The superintendent trusted that the resulting discussion would enable the new principal to get a good idea of the climate and culture of the prospective school. The principals remarked on how useful it was in getting to know the school and how it really helped ease their entry into this new setting. Most used this group as a "principal's advisory council" during their first year in their new school. Sadly, budgets and time have relegated this approach to the wastebin of good but expensive ideas. The Eastern District's selection and discarded entry processes provide examples of good practices that have worked well in a particular setting, but hardly best practices for all situations.

The South School Board

In a similar vein, for much of the South School Board's history it has succeeded for the most part in placing quality leaders in its schools, but times have changed and what worked in the past is not working as well now. The South School Board until the mid 1990s always hired from within. It had a long history of succession management that goes back to its initiating director[13] in 1969, who believed that a significant investment in leadership was the way to develop a strong school district. For over 20 years the board[14] financed a leadership program for aspirant leaders and operated on a "grow your own" philosophy. This policy shifted dramatically in the 1990s, when budget cuts forced the board to move to a replacement strategy and to hire more and more leaders from outside the board. As a prestigious jurisdiction in a desirable area, it has had little trouble recruiting or as some might suggest "stealing" quality applicants from other school boards, especially larger, more culturally and racially diverse neighboring boards. But even these applications are falling off so that, within the last few years, senior leaders have revived some of the more successful practices from the past as well as initiated newer programs to engage potential leaders from within. For example, it invited all of its secondary principals to bring two or three of their school's outstanding department heads to an evening session in which senior board officials encouraged them to look at more senior leadership positions. Fifteen years ago such a meeting would have been redundant because there were lots of aspirants for leadership jobs in secondary schools. A recent round of hiring,[15] however, suggests that either these efforts are not yet yielding suitable internal candidates or the board has a deliberate but unstated policy of going outside its boundaries to fill its vice principal openings, because all five shortlisted elementary vice principals and all four of the secondary vice principal appointees came from the South Board's neighbors.

With applications from both inside and outside the school board in hand, a committee made up of senior officials of the board and representatives of the principals' associations choose what applicants to interview from their résumés, and based on the interviews develops a shortlist that must be approved by the school board. As jobs become available, school officials assign the new appointees to schools based on their appropriateness for a particular setting.

As I pointed out in Chapter 5, principals and vice (assistant) principals are hired to the school board and not to a specific school as is the case in the Eastern District and the Midlands Authority. As a result, system officials move principals and vice principals from school to school based on the needs of the system, the school, and the individual school leader. Virtually all of the principals of the South Board that I interviewed strongly supported some form of leaders' rotation. Ken Sutton was the principal of Lord Byron High School[16] in the late 1990s. Lord Byron was his third principalship. Before that he had been a department head and an assistant principal in two secondary schools. He felt his varied experiences in a number of schools enriched his leadership preparation. As he stated:

> From what I've read, the height of your effectiveness [as a principal] seems to be somewhere between the five and seven years period. Then after that it doesn't have the same dramatic rise and it tends to level out if you look at a graph in terms of your effectiveness. Going into a new setting is always rejuvenating and for me it was exciting because every school has its own sense of community, its own history, its own way of doing things, and its own ethos. It's very easy to follow into a nice rhythm and routine and just stay where you are. Whereas this forces you to meet new challenges and I learned from every single setting.

An experienced secondary principal now leading his third school in his career observed that "Each move rejuvenates you. I don't think it is healthy for a principal to be in a school for 12 or 15 years. I believe the optimum cycle is to begin preparing an exit after five or six years and move after at least eight to reflect the life cycle of a school." The system seems to work well for most schools and for most leaders.

Each school reports to a superintendent who is responsible for all aspects of a family of interrelated elementary and secondary schools. The oversight and coordination aspects of this role are comparable in some ways to the British idea of executive headships. As part of his or her responsibility, the family superintendent develops a career profile with each principal and vice principal in the family. This career profile includes qualifications, experiences, lifestyle considerations such as home location and aspirations. Armed with the career profiles and each school's development plan, the six 'family of school's' superintendents try to balance system needs, school needs, and individual needs. My interviews with principals, however, suggest that this very rational approach breaks down when six differently experienced and skilled superintendents meet to make personnel decisions. Some superintendents are far more sensitive to individual school and career needs than others, and some are far better at negotiating on behalf of their principals and vice principals than others. As one recently retired principal explained, "Some people thought, oh, good, they listened because look I got what I wanted. And some people thought, oh, they never look at [my career profile] because it was so out of left field. From my perspective it was dependent on the superintendent."

Conscious of the criticism of the predictable rotation of school leaders,[17] the South Board now tries to leave principals in schools from five to 10 years and vice principals for at least three years. Its officials also strive to respond to lifestyle requests of school leaders. But as one superintendent explained, this doesn't always work out and sometimes you have to say to a principal or vice principal you are "taking one for the system." Sudden retirements, moves, promotions, and illnesses can also upset the delicate balance. For example, virtually every principal agreed that as vice (assistant) principals their periodic moves helped them to develop professionally, although most believed that a minimum of three years in a school was vital to achieve anything worthwhile. As one experienced principal who mentors a number of neophyte principals explained, two years as an assistant principal was too quick a turn-around because "they get lots of opportunities to start projects but they never get to experience the successes or failures and the next steps in the cycle." Also with the best of intentions, senior leaders make mistakes. For example, a senior principal explained how the system promoted his last assistant principal after only two years in the role to a principalship in an inappropriate setting for which he felt she was unprepared:

> Without consultation with either her or me, she was placed in Mapleton,[18] a French immersion school that was involved in a provincial study – a perfect storm. She was set up for failure. If I had been asked I would have said it is not a place for her, even with the skills set she has. She has had a rough go there ever since then. It was unfortunate, there have been points in time where it could have broken her and that is certainly what you don't want to do.

Another school I visited has had three different principals in three years and four different assistant principals in five years. While all of the departures are logically explained in terms of retirements, promotions, and long-term health concerns, and for the most part are beyond the control of senior officials, the school staff is "worried about what's next." The present principal is retiring this year and the vice principal had previously retired and returned as an emergency replacement, and will leave as soon as he can. Needless to say, any attempts to initiate new directions in this school are met by understandable upset, cynicism, and apathy.

The South Board provides an example of a jurisdiction that is trying to develop its own while infusing it "with new blood" from outside. On the surface this would seem to be a good practice and to ensure a steady flow of quality leaders. Initial evidence, however, suggests that a balance has yet to be achieved and it would seem that quality internal candidates have not yet come forward. There is also some evidence that the performance of some external candidates was better in their interviews than it has been in their schools. Since the South Board would find background checking much more onerous than a smaller school district like Eastern, a process that depends almost solely on an interview or two is built on pretty shaky ground.

The Midlands Local Authority

It is difficult for a local authority in the British setting to promote mobility or to even develop a well-thought-out and effective succession program because most of the succession variables are in the hands of local school governors or the central government. All decisions on recruitment and selection are made by 15 to 20 governors, who are chosen in different combinations depending on the type of school. All schools will have some governors elected by parents of that school, some chosen by religious officials if the school is a church school, some chosen by a sponsor if the school is an academy, and a few chosen by the local authority. The basis of selection of a new school head or deputy will vary widely depending on the makeup of the school governors. For example, some religious schools have particular challenges recruiting heads because of stringent faith requirements. Since school size often determines salaries of heads and deputies, remuneration can vary widely and act as either an inducement to apply or in many cases a deterrent. The Midlands Authority has over 600 schools and they vary in size from primary schools of under 50 to schools of over 500 students, and secondary schools of under 200 students to schools over 1,000. While smaller schools require unique individuals who can blend a fairly heavy teaching load with burdensome headship requirements and pressures, the salary structure actually works against the hiring of capable people who can do both jobs well. For example, some senior teachers would either lose money or gain very little except more pressure by leaving the classroom for an administrative position, and a head in a large school would find it difficult to move and receive a similar salary.

At the same time, the central government determines the certification requirements for headship and the expectations of leaders through a detailed "framework"[19] and then judges the competence of school leaders through its OFSTED inspectors who report to a school's governors with recommendations for improvement.[20] In spite of its lacking the autonomy enjoyed by districts in the US and school boards in Ontario, the Midlands Authority received very high marks from its heads in both the questionnaire and the interviews for its course offerings for potential and incumbent leaders, the support of the authority advisor assigned to the school, and the efficiency with which the authority came to the rescue in emergencies. Even heads that came from other authorities commented on the rich support they received from the authority and how it had helped them adjust to the new culture more easily. More than one head remarked that there is "always a capable person at the other end of the phone" whether you need help on educational issues, business matters, or human resources questions. The authority's advisory services thrive in spite of a "pay as you go" system. All resources to operate schools are allocated on a per-pupil formula directly to the schools for the governors to oversee and the school head to administer. This includes not only money for educational materials and building maintenance but also salaries for teachers and teacher's assistants and for heads, deputies, and other leadership positions. Schools must therefore purchase support from the authority, and this support from schools determines the efficacy of the authority's role in supporting schools. A somewhat unconventional program offered by the authority that has proven very popular among heads is one called "executive coaching", in which senior leaders such as school heads receive one-on-one personal coaching from a private company with a background in sports psychology who are contracted to assist leaders in the authority to enhance their personal performance, develop their strengths, and build personal resilience.

The governance model of the Midlands Authority and the other areas of my study suggest a continuum of succession practices, ranging from an almost entirely corporate approach such as in the Eastern District, where the superintendent as chief executive makes the final selection of a new leader after an exhaustive selection process orchestrated by senior professional staff; through the Canadian example, in which a selection committee of senior officials and principals creates shortlists of leadership appointments and transfers; to the Midlands Authority, in which a group of individual community-based school governors, some democratically elected, do the selecting. My Canadian and American districts are examples of corporate models of leadership succession because both rely on an expert panel to recruit, select, and ultimately train new leaders. Elected school board members tend to "rubber-stamp" the professionals' selections and placements in both cases. The Midlands Authority, like every other local authority in England, depends on non-professional school governors to actually recruit and select new school leaders. While the local authority in which the school is located makes the services of professional staff members available to governors in an advisory and facilitative role, the degree of their involvement varies from school to school. Selection and dismissal of school leaders is a direct responsibility of these school governors.

Spain and Brazil: Elected Principals

If the Eastern District and South Board are at the corporate end of a succession continuum, and the Midlands Authority chooses leaders through some elected community-based school governors, then at the even more democratic end of the spectrum are some areas of Spain and Portugal. These provide examples of representative and direct democracy in action that involve teachers in the selection of their principals. Both countries and a few of their former colonies, such as Brazil, provide some of the most interesting but cautionary examples of the democratic approach to leadership succession. After long years of political dictatorship ended, both countries adopted overtly democratic institutions at the school level as a way to emphasize democratic values and to give the principal legitimacy with various stakeholders. Rather than a traditional corporate model of top-down selection and placement, each Spanish primary (elementary) and secondary school elects a school council made up of community members, teachers, and students, with teachers as the majority. Each council chooses a teacher from the respective teaching staffs to be the school's principal, usually for a three-year term. This system "established a temporary, non-professional, and collegial and participatory model of principalship, departing sharply from the prevailing model in OECD[21] countries, which is permanent and professional."[22]

While no leader can stand alone at one extreme, leaving leadership to the "democratic" whims of a teaching staff also has its limitations. For example, Antonio Bolívar and Juan Manuel Moreno in their study of Spanish schools assert that 50 per cent of principalships remain unfilled because prospective candidates feel that as elected leaders they would lack the independent agency necessary to provide effective leadership, especially in a climate of fast-paced external reform.[23] The state has filled the other 50 per cent with a temporary principal until one could be elected. The major problem for elected principals who must return to their teaching roles is to promote change that is required by the state while not alienating colleagues with whom in time they must associate as peers. The result places principals in a bind that most appear to resolve by becoming "captives" of their colleagues and acceding to their desire for stability and little upset. In times of relative stability this approach works reasonably well, but it is quite ineffective in contexts requiring rapid change and leadership of learning. As Bolívar and Moreno state, "If the ultimate problem is reconciling democratic participation with professionalism, the question is how to move towards a professional model of principalship without bypassing the participation model."[24] They argue that appointed professional leaders might be a better idea, especially in times of change, balanced by a different concept of democracy that shifts from representative democracy to a form of deliberative or participatory democracy through parental involvement in important decisions, and some form of distributive leadership which allows for teacher engagement but at the same time provides the principal with institutional legitimacy.

John Myers's study of schools in Brazil, and particularly one school in Porto Alegre, paints a more positive picture of principal elections as an approach to leadership succession.[25] After years of often brutal dictatorships, Brazil like Spain has tried to inculcate democratic values and practices at many levels including schools by allowing the teaching staff, students, and parents of each school to elect its principal for a three-year term. Teachers' choices clearly have the advantage because their votes count for half the total and parents and students votes combined make up the other half. Myers concluded:

> Empowerment for the teachers of Porto Alegre was experienced as increased control over their professional lives in terms of being able to teach in ways that they desired. These teachers believed that the election of principals created a more democratic school culture, which allowed them to introduce novel teaching and curricular approaches to the classroom.[26]

While he suggests that the democratic experience motivates more innovative and change-oriented teachers, he is unsure of how it impacts on those who are quite content to do as they always have done. Elections have also been criticized because they advantage teachers' perspectives and self-interests over those of students and parents. The real purpose behind elections of principals, Myers argues, is that the process is "an experience of learning democracy for the school community"[27] because it teaches some of the values and procedures of democracy based on the premise that the best way to learn democracy is to practice it. While election of principals appears to be a stage of development for emerging democracies such as in Africa,[28] and the nation of Georgia,[29] western nations can learn from their inclusiveness in involving students, teachers, and community members in meaningful ways in the selection of principals for their schools.

Finland: An Integrated Approach

Finland provides an example of a nation that faces many of the demographic and generational problems of leadership succession that bedevil other nations and states, but it has addressed them within the context of a societal and educational transformation and not as a stand-alone problem.[30] Over the past 20 years Finland has successfully integrated educational and economic policies with an unswerving commitment to social justice without becoming caught up in mechanistic strategies for educational change, and has transformed itself from an economic and educational backwater to one of the world's most competitive economies[31] with a highly successful but quite decentralized educational system. In the OECD's 2003 PISA results,[32] Finland's 15-year-olds ranked top in reading, mathematics, and science, while in equity terms the country displayed the lowest variance between schools – just one-tenth of the OECD average.[33] Ironically, this world leader in measured student performance does so without an emphasis on individual testing or measurement-driven high-stakes accountability. Learning rather than measured performance defines the focus and the form of systemic distributed leadership.

Leadership development in education in Finland begins with a highly qualified and respected teaching profession. Learning and teaching are valued throughout schools and society; learning starts early but is unhurried and untested; and learning is broad and life-long rather than concentrated on test preparation. Teacher quality and performance are addressed at the point of entry through a careful preparation and vetting process. All teachers require master's degrees. Principals in Finland are required by law to have been teachers themselves, and most continue to be engaged in classroom teaching for at least two to three hours and many up to 20 lessons per week. They can do this, as one leader explained, "Because, unlike the Anglo-Saxon countries, we do not have to spend our time responding to long lists of government initiatives that come from the top."[34] Indeed, principals and national government officials actively moderate the number, pace, and range of reforms so that schools do not spend excessive time reacting to initiatives from the outside.

Improvement of schools that employ these highly capable and trusted professionals is achieved by processes of self-evaluation within learning organizations that are allocated national and local government resources so they can solve problems for themselves. "System leadership, in this sense, is leadership for learning, leadership by learning, and leadership as learning – not leadership for performance and testing."[35]

At the heart of the human relationships that comprise Finland's educational system and society is a strong and positive culture of trust, cooperation, and responsibility. Finnish leaders are commonly recruited from the ranks of the schools where they have taught for many years of their careers. This norm may not be easily transposable to more mobile societies, but the lesson to be learned is to develop leadership capacity among those that poorer communities have come to trust, wherever possible. They share resources and support each other across schools, through a sense of common responsibility for all the young people in their town or city. Principals and teachers are trusted, to a degree, because of their high qualifications, expertise, and widespread commitment and responsibility. If principals become sick or ineffective, the community of teachers takes over because it sees that the school belongs to all of them. Yet trust is not blind or indifferent. Rather, active trust is built through deliberately created structures and initiatives. This is evident in:

- *Networks.* National projects always have "very strong and big networks" for cooperating with national authorities, in forums where people "learn and work from each other." Municipalities stress the importance of all teachers participating in local and school-based processes as well as in curriculum development, not to implement government strategies and initiatives but to spread ideas transformatively and interactively through non-linear processes of learning and experimentation.
- *Shared targets.* These are produced at the local level through action plans rather than imposed by political or administrative means.
- *Self-evaluation.* This is the key to continuous improvement, as compared to imposed inspection or test-based accountability that ranks schools competitively on the basis of their test scores.
- *Local principal cooperation.* Even at the secondary level, principals across schools share financial and other resources when needed, and feel genuinely responsible together for all the children and young people in their town and city – for their community's future – rather than competing only for the advantage of children in their particular schools.

While it would be difficult to import this model of educational change and leadership development to other contexts, other settings can learn from its example and address its issues of leadership success, succession, and capacity by:

- developing a broad and inspiring social as well as educational mission beyond the technicalities of achievement gaps or beyond lofty yet vaguely stated advocacy for goals like "world class education"

- recognizing that the most important point of exercising quality control in relation to leadership performance is at professional entry where the motivating incentives of status, reward, and professional as well as social mission should be most emphatic
- increasing leadership capacity by reducing and rationalizing unnecessary demand in terms of the pace, scope, and intrusiveness of external initiatives and interventions
- developing political and professional leadership that can build greater trust and cooperation as a basis for improvement
- building greater lateral leadership not merely through loose and geographically dispersed professional networks but through area-based cooperation that is committed to the welfare and improvement of children and citizens within a community
- narrowing inequalities of opportunity and achievement by integrating strong principles of social justice into systemic leadership as it becomes founded on clear practices of the strong helping the weak within and beyond schools' immediate communities
- extending leadership teams and distributed leadership within schools to increase leadership capacity across them
- paying diligent and detailed attention to learning (curriculum and pedagogy) as a basis for high performance, rather than giving primacy to measured performance in the hopes that it will serve as the main lever for improving teaching and learning
- challenging the necessity for achieving improvement by employing expensive and extensive systems of high-stakes testing.[36]

This chapter has described some illustrative approaches to leadership succession from a few school jurisdictions with quite different governance models. These range from the corporate models of the South School Board in Canada and the Eastern School District in the United States, through the quasi-democratic model of the schools of the Midlands Authority in England, to the democratic approaches of Spain and Portugal and some of their former colonies, and to the comprehensive model of Finland, which has integrated its education into its systemic approach to social wellbeing and economic development. Each model presents ideas that with modifications others might want to emulate – the good – and some ideas that have serious limitations – the bad. As promised, I have refrained from describing the ugly. Now to move to the next and final chapter, in which I try to pull together some of the insights from the previous seven chapters into a series of policy alternatives that I believe those concerned with understanding and resolving the succession challenge in their context will need to address.

Notes

1   Fink, D. (2005) *Leadership for Mortals*. London: Chapman/Corwin, xvii.
2   Fink, D. (2004) "Best practice: a technocrat's dream." International Confederation of Principals, http://www.icponline.org/content/view/81/50/, 1 May 2008.
3   Rothwell, W.J. (2001) *Effective Succession Planning: Ensuring Leadership Continuity and Building Talent from Within*, 2nd edn. New York: AMACOM, p. 5.
4   Eastman, L.J. (1995) *Succession Planning: an Annotated Bibliography and Summary of Commonly Reported Organizational Practices*. Greensboro, NC: Center for Creative Leadership, p. 54.
5   Government of Western Australia (2001) "Managing succession in the Western Australia public sector". www.mpc.wa.gov.au, 14 September 2008.
6   National Academy of Public Administration (1997) *Managing Succession and Developing Leadership: Growing the Next Generation of Public Service Leaders*. Washington, DC: NAPA, p. 7.
7   Rothwell, op. cit., p. 7.
8   Byham, W.C. (2001) "Grooming next-millennium leaders", *Society for Human Resources*. www.shrm.org/articles.
9   Schall, E. (1997) "Public sector succession: a strategic approach to sustaining innovation", *Public Administration Review*, 57 (1), 4–10; Liebman, M. Bruer, R.A. (1994) "Where there's a will there is a way", *Journal of Business Strategy*, 15 (2): 26–34; National Academy of Public Administration, op. cit.
10 Souque, J.P. (1998) *Succession Planning and Leadership Development*. Ottawa: Conference Board of Canada; Rothwell, op. cit.
11 Institute for Educational Leadership Task Force on the Principalship (2001) *Leadership for Student Learning: Redefining the Teacher as Leader*. Washington, DC: IEL, p. 1.
12 The chief executive officer who reports to the school board of five members.
13 Chief executive officer of a school board in Ontario.
14 A school board in Ontario serves the same policy function as a district school board in the US. In Ontario, trustees are elected locally and serve a three-year term. Depending on the size of the jurisdiction, a board such as the South board can have 10 or more trustees. Since remuneration is relatively small (c. $5,000 per year), trustees are not always representative of the diversity of communities. Unlike the local authority in the UK, which is part of the local government and has responsibility for a broad range of children's service, the South Board is quite independent of local governments but quite beholden to the provincial government and focuses solely on educational issues.
15 The announcements came out in May 2009.
16 For a study of Lord Byron over times see Fink, D. (2000) *Good Schools/Real Schools: Why School Reform Doesn't Last*. New York: Teachers' College Press.
17 See chapter 3 of Hargreaves and Fink (2005) op. cit.
18 I have used pseudonyms throughout. Mapleton is an upscale community with very demanding and involved parents.
19 National College for School Leadership (2009) "The National Standards for School Leadsership". http://www.ncsl.org.uk/publications-index/publications-nationalstandards.htm, 28 June 2009.

20 Office for Standards in Education, Children's Services and Skills (2009) *Framework for the inspection of Maintained Schools in England from September 2009.* London: OFSTED.

21 Organization for Economic Cooperation and Development.

22 Bolivar, A. and Moreno, J.M. (2006) "Between transaction and transformation: the role of school principals as education leaders in Spain", *Journal of Educational Change*, 7 (1–2): 19.

23 Ibid., pp. 19–31.

24 Ibid., p. 23.

25 Myers, J. (2007) 'Democraticizing school authority: Brazilian teachers' perceptions of the election of principals", *Teacher and Teacher Education*. www.sciencedirect.com, September 2008, pp. 1–15.

26 Ibid., p. 13.

27 Ibid., p. 13.

28 Bush, T. and Oduro, G. (2006) "New principals in Africa: preparation, induction and practice", *Journal of Educational Administration*, 44 (4): 359–75.

29 http://www.humanrights.ge/rss/index.php?a=more&r=analytical&id=2589&lang=en, 27 May 2009.

30 Aho, E., Pitkanen, K. and Sahlberg, P. (2006) *Policy Development and Reform Principles of Basic and Secondary Education in Finland Since 1968.* Washington, DC: World Bank.

31 Porter, M., Schwab, K., Sala-i-Martin, X. and Lopez-Claros, A. (eds) (2004) *The Global Competitiveness Report.* New York: Oxford University Press.

32 OECD (2004) *Learning for Tomorrow's World: First Results from PISA 2003.* Paris: OECD.

33 Ibid.

34 Hargreaves, A., Halász, G. and Pont, B. (2007) *Finland: A Systemic Approach to School Leadership.* Case Study Report for the OECD Activity "Improving School Leadership", p. 21.

35 Ibid., p. 16.

36 I have based much of this description on Hargreaves et al., ibid., with help from Pasi Sahlsberg, personal communication.

8

Succeeding Leaders

If you have arrived at this point looking for *the* answer to the succession challenge, I'm afraid you will be bitterly disappointed. I learned very early in my consulting career, after some rather humbling experiences, that my answers to the problems of others usually failed to account for the unique contexts in which they worked. As the different settings of my *Three Countries* study illustrate very well, "one size fits all" solutions don't lend themselves to distinctive situations. To survive in the competitive consulting field, I quickly realized that the most helpful support that an outsider like me can provide to others is to assist them to ask better questions of their contexts, to problem seek, to look at things from different perspectives. I'm convinced that the only people who have the answers to the problems of a particular context are the people who work in that situation, and have to live with the consequences of the decisions they make. Rather than pull together a list of best practices or try to outline a foolproof step-by-step approach to the succession challenge (which doesn't exist), in this final chapter I have tried to provide a summary of the previous seven chapters by using a number of policy options as an organizer that I believe politicians, education officials, and school leaders must address if they intend to understand and resolve the succession challenge in a meaningful way in their context.

Images of Leadership: Leaders of Learning or Managers of Things

As successive generations evolve and then slowly disappear, so do their ideas of organizations and leadership. The "greatest" generation and us "silents" brought "the first wave" of organizations built along militaristic and corporate lines, within which leadership was structured into chains of command designed to ensure predictability of results, control of variables, and compliance to the dictates of superiors in the hierarchy. These models were heavy on design and stifling for individual and group emergence. Vestiges of this model still exist in state and provincial departments of education, in many districts and local authorities, and in most secondary schools. The highly competitive, boundlessly optimistic "boomers" in their turn attempted to undermine these structures by elevating the market from a useful economic device for the distribution of goods and services to an ideology that has infused Second and Third Way thinking in the past 20 years, and in its purest forms opened the public sector to private and individualistic forms of competition to motivate the good and drive out the bad. We see manifestation of this kind of thinking in league tables, adequate yearly progress, school takeovers by senior levels of government, charter schools, and vouchers. Leaders are seen as entrepreneurial and heroic, ceaselessly marketing their schools, pressuring all and sundry to raise test scores, accommodating customers, and outsmarting the school down the road to attract the best students and most supportive parents. In more recent years, these boomer values have conflicted with the younger, more diverse generations over such issues as the war in Iraq, gay marriage, government supported health care, and immigration policies. Raised on information technology and more recently social networking, "generation X" and particularly "millennials" are comfortable with the Fourth Way thinking that views schools and other organizations as living systems, interconnected in spheres of mutual influence, each one a network of strong cells organized through cohesive diversity.[1]

Leadership within living systems operates on a different logic from traditional images. As noted management guru Henry Mintzberg explains:

> management has to be *everywhere*. It has to flow with the activity, which itself can not be predicted or *formalized* ... Management also has to be potentially everyone. In a network, responsibility for making decisions and developing strategic initiatives has to be distributed, so that responsibility can flow to whoever is best able to deal with the issue at hand.[2]

In webs or networks, control has to give way to collaboration. They have no center or apex, just a multiplicity of connections and threads that link various communities that leaders must try to understand and influence to achieve organizational goals. Mintzberg adds that "bosses and subordinates running up and down the hierarchy have to give way to the shifting back and forth between 'colleagues' on the inside and 'partners' on the outside." Webs need designated leaders to connect and contribute, not command and control. "And that means that managers have to get inside those networks. Not be parachuted in, without knowledge, yet intent on leading the team. No, they must be deeply involved, to *earn* any leadership they can provide."[3] He contends that leadership within the organizational logic of a web is

> not about taking clever decisions and making bigger deals, least of all for personal gains. It is about energizing other people to make better decisions and do better things ... it is about releasing the positive energy that exists naturally within people. Effective leadership inspires more than empowers; it connects more than it controls; it demonstrates more than it decides. It does all this by *engaging* – itself above all, and consequently others.[4]

A first step in addressing the succession challenge is to determine what kind of leadership will move our schools and will enhance deep learning for all students. Do we want an image of leadership built upon the values of fading generations, or should we shift our vision to capture and engage newer, younger generations? Refocusing leadership on learning, and finding the balance between design and emergence that allows schools and school systems to reach their potential as living systems, will necessitate a radically different approach to ensuring a well-prepared and sufficient supply of leaders; it also requires a significant rethinking of the demands that are presently placed on leaders. Rather than looking at school leaders as just individuals, we need to look at school leadership as a pervasive force across schools and school districts. If schools and districts are to continue to improve they must observe Packard's law. Named after the co-founder of Hewlett Packard, Bill Packard's law states: "no company can consistently grow revenues faster than its ability to get enough of the right people to implement that growth and still become a great company."[5] If we replace "company" with school or school district, and "revenue" with student learning, then we have a formula for continuing and sustained school improvement.

We need also to examine how dedicated "mortals" can work together to shape school and district leadership in ways that ensure challenging, creative learning experiences for all students. In thinking about developing and sustaining leadership that real people can accomplish, there are certain aspects of leadership that must never change, and other aspects that must change as circumstances dictate. I would argue that absolute *commitment* to student learning, and a set

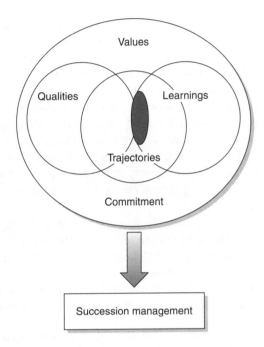

Figure 8.1   *Leadership components*
Fink, D. *Leadership for Mortals: Developing and Sustaining Leaders of Learning* © 2005.

of life-affirming *values* that sustain leaders through good times and bad, are aspects of leadership that should remain constant. I would also suggest that the *learnings* required to be leaders of learning, and the intellectual and emotional *qualities* that all potential leaders possess, must always be in a continuous state of development, as leaders at all levels move through their career *trajectories*. Elsewhere I have put these pieces into the image of leadership shown in Figure 8.1, which I believe develops and sustains leaders of learning.[6]

Hiring for Potential or Proficiencies

The most successful organizations hire and promote people based on their leadership potential rather than on the degree to which they are capable of handling the proficiencies required of existing leaders. These organizations look for people who have the intellect and drive to learn the important learnings that will sustain the organization not only in the present but in the future. These leading edge organizations develop a pool of aspirant leaders; they challenge them, and when openings occur, promote them. Around the world, educational jurisdictions are madly at work designing leadership models, articulating leadership behaviors, and codifying leadership standards based largely on what leaders do now. In my view, these often complicated models or exhaustive lists of expectations and standards are relatively useless, because by the time their designers have completed and disseminated them, the world of education and educational leadership will have moved on. I would suggest that they do more harm than good because they intimidate potential leadership aspirants, create guilt among incumbent leaders who know they cannot meet all the expectations, and trigger martyrdom among a few who try, fail, and burn out and in the process create unfortunate role models for potential leaders.

Succession management for future leaders of learning will need to be based on a coherent and connected set of learnings that are consistent across time and space and to target student learning as opposed to laundry lists of best practices that intimidate and demotivate and include everything that can possibly happen in a school. As my colleagues Louise and Lorna and I have written elsewhere:

> Leadership for learning is not a destination with fixed co-ordinates on a compass, but a journey with plenty of detours and even some dead ends. Effective educational leaders are continuously open to new learning because the journey keeps changing. Their maps are complex and can be confusing. What leaders require for this journey is a set of interrelated learnings looking at school leadership in a holistic rather than reductionist way. These learnings can be deepened, elaborated, nurtured, abandoned, and connected and related to other learnings as the journey progresses.[7]

We identified seven sets of learning that we suggest provide a useful organizer for redefining leadership:

- *Understanding learning.* If our business is learning then all educational leaders need to have a deep, current, and critical understanding of the learning process to promote learning and support others' learning. Not only do they need to have insight into "deep" learning for all students; they must also have a "deep" understanding of how adults learn if they are to support teachers' learning and to mobilize the school's human and material resources to this purpose.
- *Contextual knowledge.* Successful leaders make connections by developing firm knowledge and understanding of their contexts. Context relates to the particular situation, background, or environment in which something is happening. Internal context includes the students, subjects, and departments, and the school itself; external context encompasses, among other influences, the district or local education authority of which the school is a part, the school's parent and

neighboring community, the relevant employee unions, and the appropriate government(s) of the day. The research evidence is clear: schools can only be understood in their context.[8]

- *Political acumen.* Political acumen is a key learning for leaders. At micro-levels, schools are filled with groups and individuals with different interests and varying degrees of power that occasionally lead to conflict. Leaders use political methods such as negotiation and coalition building to move schools toward agreed goals. School leaders also must represent the interests of their school with their governing bodies, communities, and government agencies. Politics is about power and influence, and to ignore political issues or consider that political activity is unworthy of a leader is to leave the school and its staff, students, and parents vulnerable to competing social forces.

- *Emotional understanding.* Leaders of learning learn to read the emotional responses of those around them and create emotional bonds with and among those with whom they interact. Andy Hargreaves explains that the emotions of educational change most commonly addressed are those helping to defuse so-called resistance to change like trust, support, involvement, commitment to teamwork, and willingness to experiment.[9] Leaders with emotional understanding do, however, lead their colleagues into uncharted territory on the change journey through the "impassioned and critical engagement or critique" of ideas, purposes, and practices.

- *Critical thinking.* What tends to differentiate effective and ineffective leaders is the quality of their judgments – whether their decisions work for the students in the long term. Knowing and remembering to ask the right questions depend on both wisdom and judgment. A significant part of a formal leader's job is to act as a gatekeeper, to ask the right questions, to know what initiatives to support, what to oppose, and what to subvert. This questions-asking facility is a necessary learning to enable leaders to help to develop a school's capacity to deal with change. They need to develop good "crap detectors". When policy makers base their arguments on phrases such as "the research says", leaders need to ask questions like: whose research? Who is paying for the research? Who benefits from its results? Who is damaged by the results? Does the research meet the criteria of scholarly adjudication? When best practices are advocated, leaders need to ask: best practice in what context? What is the evidence? Who has determined it to be best practice? What is there in this practice that is useful in my context? Innovation and creativity, which are the lifeblood of leadership for learning, require the ability to ask better questions, not recycle old answers.

- *Making connections.* It is also a leader's role to see the entire organization and help stakeholders to view the school in a holistic way. Leaders provide coherence and make connections so others can see the interrelationships and interconnections of the many things happening in a school. The development of a school-wide perspective is an important learning to promote positive change. Leaders of learning not only make connections in space, they make connections over time.

- *Futures thinking*. Successful leaders must learn how to connect the past, the present, and the future. Leaders' awareness and understanding of forces influencing the life of a school are crucial to shaping a school community's shared sense of vision in productive and inspiring ways. Leaders are also aware of shifting currents of local political, social, and economic forces and help staff to understand the connections between and among global, national, and local forces. Anticipating the future enables leaders to help colleagues act strategically rather than randomly as they journey into the future.[10]

Taken together, these learnings provide the framework, the curriculum, for a succession management program that can provide a pool of qualified leaders of learning.

I reiterate: great organizations look for people with the potential to develop the learnings necessary to provide creative leadership well into the future, rather than the common practice in many public service organizations, such as schools, of hiring people who possess a set of proficiencies required at the moment to do the job. For example, if one were to ask Bill Gates what the software business will look like in 15 years, he could speculate but not be very precise. If you asked him the kind of learnings a successful leader in his industry must possess in 15 years to be successful, I suspect he could arrive at a fairly comprehensive list that goes across time and space. What will education look like in 15 years? Who knows? But, I would argue, people who have the potential to learn how to analyze contexts, understand learning, think politically and critically, possess emotional understanding, think imaginatively about the future, and make connections, can within a well-developed succession management program become leaders of learning who will make a difference to the learning of all students, in ways that top-down policy initiatives never have and never will.

Virtually every principal who completed my questionnaire or that I interviewed said that they wished they had more time to be leaders of learning. While their image of what this meant differed, they all saw the same impediment: paper, or the electronic equivalent. Sheryl Boris-Schacter explains the situation this way:

> I would argue that the struggle to find adequate time to be an instructional leader is no less than a struggle with professional identity and purpose. The challenge is to manage the cognitive dissonance between what principals

imagined they would be doing before assuming the principalship and how they actually spend their time when they are in the job.[11]

A first step to making leaders' jobs more doable and potentially attractive to new applicants is to cut back on top-down communications and mandates. Since most school leaders work in First Way, balkanized bureaucracies in which one department seldom knows what another is doing, there seem to be few controls on the memos, mandates, and e-mails that place demands on schools and their leaders. Even efforts to use social networking sites tend to result in more information distribution rather than feedback loops. As an experienced female principal in Ontario explained:

> There are too many days when I get an e-mail saying I need this report and I need it yesterday, I need this information two days ago. I can't do that and run a school of 800 kids. I can't do it. It is not possible. Those are the things that drive me and other administrators crazy. Wherever the source of the pressure, and I think it is the Ministry of Education, we need to have a better sense of timing. Don't send me a budget on Thursday and tell me that on Monday you need to know exactly how I am going to spend all the money. I have a good sense of where it's going to go but when you want to know the exact dollars I need to have a bit of time to put those exact dollars in place well.

A principal in the *Change Over Time?* study echoed the same frustration. She explained that when she used to go to meetings, she always figured that she had a day or two before she had to respond to the minutes of the meeting. Now, the minutes and any jobs that resulted from the meeting were waiting for her at the school. School districts, authorities, and provincial state and national governments need to create mechanisms to control and coordinate communications to schools and reporting requirements. The clear message from principals is that all levels of government need to practice "organized abandonment", to use Peter Drucker's term.

A related concern for all school leaders was the range of things for which they were directly responsible. A list of just administrative responsibilities for principals from one American state included the following tasks:

- supervision of staff
- capacity management
- resource management
- financial management
- vendor management
- operations management

- problem management
- legal and regulatory management
- parent/community relations.

While all of these are necessary, in fact crucial to the successful operation of a school, and some are clearly part of a principal's responsibility, does a principal have to be responsible for them all? Are there not other people who can attend to these better than a person trained (one would hope) to be an educational leader? Should all schools have business managers or bursars? Should their responsibilities be broadened? Perhaps small schools can band together to get this kind of help. In the Midlands Authority one principal of a small school reported that:

> In our authority there are a number of schools that have clustered together, of their own accord, without support from the LA. These schools work very well together and have developed their own learning communities. Unfortunately this is not equitable across the county and other schools are left with very little in terms of support networks or learning opportunities.

As is probably evident by now, I am not a great fan of the British local management of schools because it has turned school leaders into managers of things, and to my knowledge there is no evidence that it enhances the learning of students. From a business point of view I question its efficacy in getting economies of scale, and from a practical point of view I would suggest that bus routes, clogged urinals, and leaky roofs are better handled by experts who know what they are doing than principals and heads who are trained as educators. The principals in the American school district and the Ontario school board in my study had fewer worries about these and other business related things because they received support from central office. In both situations, judging by the amount of talk around educational topics in the interviews, they seemed to attend more to issues of teaching and learning than did their British colleagues, who have a much broader managerial and political mandate.

In his summary of leadership in the Eastern District, a senior official of the district hit on an issue that few principals addressed in the interviews:

> I honestly believe that most principals want to be educational leaders. I think that there are a couple things getting in the way. I think that the expectation of the person still doing those managerial tasks is part of the problem, but I think the other part and probably the bigger part of the problem is that I'm not so confident that we have prepared principals to

truly do the job of an educational leader. I don't think that one person can do it on his or her own. But I think that they need to understand the breadth of the job and what types of supports that they can access and what types of supports that they're expected to provide for their staff. I just think that it's much more complex than it looks on the surface.

Many if not most experienced leaders don't know how to be an instructional leader or leader of learning, and are caught in a stressful bind between what they always have done, and learning new ways to influence classroom practices. I suspect some school leaders have unintentionally communicated their anxiety to younger people on their staff. A number of senior leaders admitted that perhaps they were not the best people to persuade younger people to take on the challenges of leadership.

A soon-to-retire principal in the South Board explained, after years of focusing on running a "good" school, that the demands on school leaders have shifted significantly. Principals are obliged to be "more focused on student academic achievement as defined by EQAO."[12] There is, he explains, "tremendously greater pressure to develop capacity in old guys like me to become instructional leaders. We are getting a lot of instruction on instructional leadership that is far more focused and specific – much more prescriptive – such as best practices in classrooms, literacy blocks, creative pathways – very prescriptive in terms of research based."

Salary seems to be another major deterrent to prospective leaders who must trade off family and personal time for the pressures and extra hours of leadership jobs. The clear message passed on by principals is that many people capable of assuming leadership roles are saying – "it is just not worth it." In Ontario the differential between senior teacher and vice principal salaries after taxes is miniscule, and in some situations a person actually stands to lose money. The same appears to be true in the American context. In England, where salaries are determined by governors in individual schools within a range determined by government, there are some interesting anomalies. For example, a deputy head in a large school would lose money by becoming a head of a smaller school. A head, who might want to move to another school, might lose money if the school is no larger than the one which he or she already leads. There seems to be no financial advantage to taking on a school in trouble, especially if the salary is pegged fairly low by the school's governors. It seems obvious to me that the best principals and heads should be in schools in difficult areas, regardless of size, and should be paid substantially more than the norm because they are taking on a much greater challenge. I would make the same argument for teachers in such areas. It always amazes me that the solution to raising student achievement in deprived areas, where the majority of failing schools are located, is to put more pressure on the existing staff. Altruism just goes so far, and ultimately the best staff members move to the leafy suburbs, leaving the least successful teachers behind. If we are to flatten the educational landscape so that "No Child Left Behind" becomes more than a fervent hope, then policy makers and senior leaders must find ways to recruit, reward, and support leaders and teachers in challenging schools. At the moment there seem to be mostly disincentives. Calling people losers does not create winners.[13] It will require money, time, and above all a change in the attitudes of policy makers who demand change by turning up the heat on already overworked leaders and teachers.

Grow Your Own, or Hire and Hope

Throughout the book I have tried to make the case, especially in Chapter 5, that systems must grow their own if they are to sustain quality leadership over time. Two of the three subject school systems that I researched in some depth tended to follow a replacement planning approach in which they advertised and then "hired and hoped" for the best results. Both have arrived at the point where they recognize that this strategy is unsustainable and perhaps more importantly sends the wrong message to their own potential leaders. In both the Eastern School District in the US and the South School Board in Ontario there is a growing undercurrent of resentment within the ranks that suggests that coming from outside is a preferred route to leadership; or, to put it in negative terms, known applicants from the Eastern District or South Board find themselves at a disadvantage in competition with a largely unknown outside candidates who can do a great sales job in an interview. Leaders in both systems are aware of these feelings and are in the process of developing programs to encourage internal candidates for leadership. Conversely, the Midlands Authority with its well-established succession management programs has successfully recruited and helped many internal candidates to get leadership positions in spite of the wide-open market approach to leadership recruitment in the UK.

   Interestingly, principals in all three countries felt it was healthy for the system to recruit from outside their school system, but recognized that hiring from outside is more risky than selecting from internal candidates who are known. Two of my Ontario respondents hired from outside the board had originally applied to become principals but were hired as vice principals and placed in schools where the principal was retiring within a year with the promise that they would then move up.

Both suggested that this was a marvellous way to learn the system, learn the school, and get up to speed on working in the new situation without the immediate pressure of being the final arbiter in a school.

Identification of Potential Leaders

What should be reassuring to senior leaders is the unanimous commitment of existing school leaders to encouraging potential candidates to come forward. I asked interview participants what criteria they looked for to identify leadership aspirants. They all recognized that identification of potential leaders is an inexact science. However, based on interviews with school and district leaders and my own years of experience trying (sometimes not successfully) to identify potential leaders, I offer the following questions about potential leadership candidates as an initial guide to determining who should be recruited for leadership roles:

- Does this person genuinely like and respect the students?
- Is this person a dedicated and proficient teacher?
- Is this person committed to learning for *all* students?
- Does this person operate from a life affirming set of values and have the courage of his or her convictions?
- Has this person initiated professional growth activities to enhance his or her personal abilities – reason, ethics, imagination, intuition, memory, and common sense?
- Has this person the intellectual and relational potential to master the meta-learnings for leadership such as "understanding learning", "critical thinking", "futures thinking", "contextual knowledge", "political acumen", "emotional understanding", and "making connections"?
- Does this person have the organizational skills to manage a school or a department?
- Does this person relate well to colleagues? To parents? To superiors in the organization?
- Does this person have a tolerance for ambiguity?
- Does this person have a strong work ethic and a well-developed "crap detector"?

The Hay Group in England, a private consulting firm, in its very useful publication concerning leadership identification in the public sector, offered these "early warning signs" of leadership potential derived from discussions with senior system leaders:

- confidence and credibility
- the ability to see the big picture, to make connections and think of the whole organization

- mastering the basics of their role quickly and looking for more
- getting involved (doesn't look the other way or walk past incidents)
- initiative and self-motivation (the sort of people you can't stop from leading)
- intellectual curiosity and capacity (sees the common threads)
- resilience and empathy (to survive the pace of acceleration and learn from others).[14]

A National College for School Leadership publication entitled *Identify and Grow Your Own Leaders: A Practical Guide and Case Studies* suggests the following criteria:[15]

- seeks opportunities to learn
- acts with integrity
- adapts to cultural differences
- is committed to making a difference
- seeks broad business knowledge
- brings out the best in people
- is insightful – sees things from new angles
- has the courage to take risks
- seeks and uses feedback
- learns from mistakes
- is open to criticism.

One of the secondary principals I interviewed in Ontario asked her leadership team members to outline leadership qualities they would look for in aspirants. While the school's insights dovetail well with the other lists that are derived from existing leaders, they provide followers' perspectives on what should be expected of leaders:

Attitudes

- Have an understanding of the diversity in our schools and in the ways that families are raised these days. Students will start from a variety of different "places" in their learning.
- Be open to using all of the available resources.
- Be willing to share the leadership.
- Be flexible and willing to try new strategies.
- Be open to (and not threatened by) suggestions and recommendations from staff members.

Skills

- Demonstrate strong communication skills with families and support staff.
- Show an ability to turn theory into practice and motivate people into action.

- Be able to organize and multi-task.
- Have an ability to prioritize.
- Listen to and hear what is said.

Qualities

- Show fairness: fair is not equal.
- Be adaptable: change happens quickly.
- Persevere and see tasks through to the end.
- Be objective: see the larger picture and the greater needs.
- Remain calm and non-judgmental until all information is in.
- Always remember that we are dealing with human beings in our schools; don't lose sight of the human perspective.
- Remember that "everything" is your job.

While these four approaches have many overlaps and common themes, a close reading suggests a tension between a focus on students and learning, and possession of the managerial skills to attend to an imposed agenda. It seems rather obvious that schools and systems leaders need to arrive at a consensus on the purposes of leadership and the qualities and skills they need to move forward. Identification, recruitment, and even development will be undermined, however, if leadership selection processes are not sensitive to the long-term needs of the school, the system, and prospective leaders.

Selection

Selection processes can sometimes act as a deterrent to leadership aspirants seeking a leadership role. It is a risk for them to put themselves forward to pursue a position of leadership in any organization. Selection processes must be thorough and rigorous without being intimidating, inclusive without being tokenism, and fair, and perceived to be fair. They can, if handled correctly and in timely fashion, become a useful learning process. While each of the three school jurisdictions I studied made the final decision on a leader or leaders through interviews, my research indicated that respondents considered the selection processes that hired leaders directly to a school to be fairer, and provided more useful feedback to both successful and unsuccessful candidates. The organizers of school-based selections had the advantage of providing specific information on the school and its requirements, as opposed to the system-based hiring in which requirements of necessity were generic. Some districts and authorities have tried to make the process smoother by providing tutoring or, in some cases, courses on how to prepare for and succeed in an interview process.

Rotating Leaders or Jobs for Life

One of the thorniest questions related to succession is the moving of school leaders from school to school. As we have seen, businesses have always moved people to make certain that they have the right experiences for future promotion, or to ensure that they don't get stale in their job. The argument for this approach in education is that it enables the system to place the right person in the right place at the right time and hopefully for the right reasons. For example, some principals do better in some settings than in others. In a crisis, the system can move a principal with a strong track record to a school that is experiencing difficulties. In my own experience, I have observed principals who excelled in rural settings, yet had great difficulty in more urban schools, and vice versa. Some principals functioned very well in more affluent communities and not so well in high-needs communities. Some form of mobility can renew a principal, a school, and a staff. In my first year as a family of schools superintendent, I kept receiving phone calls from concerned parents about the lack of energy and direction in one of my schools. The principal was a year away from retirement and was burned out after a long and meritorious career. Because I had the ability as a system leader to make changes, I was able to place a bright and dynamic assistant principal with him to get him through the year, let him retire with dignity, and replace him with an outstanding principal. My phone calls from upset parents dried up, the staff regained their vigor, and the school became an exciting learning place for children. The downside, as mentioned previously, is that staff members can avoid new initiatives by waiting till the activist principal or vice principal moves on.

The practice of moving principals and vice principals such as operates in the South Board in Ontario can be either good or poor practice depending on timing, and on the sensitivity of the process to the needs of schools and the leaders involved. Certainly rapid cyclical rotation of school leaders, as we found in the *Change Over Time?* study, can be counter-productive. Chris James and Una Connolly have made a cogent case for ensuring stability in leadership in schools,[16] especially during periods of significant turbulence. The challenge for policy makers is to find the balance between stability and immobility, incremental change and frenetic change, and a useful timely infusion of new energy and a continuous leadership carousel. As one who experienced internal transfers and participated in the process of transferring leaders and supervising the aftermath, I suggest school districts take a long look at their practices and consider some form of mobility. I'm convinced that it can, if done with wisdom and discretion, revive or prolong careers, energize schools, and help to address the succession challenge. Perhaps the solution is to move assistant (vice) principals and deputy and assistant heads in the British system to provide growth experiences.[17] This suggestion in turn raises another policy issue: are those people who are second in command (or in the British system second and third) principals in training or in career positions?

Deputies and Assistant Principals: Career Office Holders or Principals in Training

Whether a policy of rotating school assistant principals or deputy and assistant heads through a number of schools makes any sense in an educational jurisdiction really depends on whether policy makers consider that these positions are preparatory roles for the next generation of principals and heads, or career positions to be occupied by the same person for long periods of time. Ontario principals strongly supported the idea of vice (assistant) principals as principals in training; British heads had very mixed feelings and pointed out the difficulties within their system. As one generation X British head explained:

> I think it can be both. I read an interesting piece. It's the *Times Ed.*[18] a few weeks ago. A professor was saying that the deputy should be a temporary position and that they should be appointed for three to five years and then after that they should have to reapply for the job or move into headship. I thought that was really interesting because that'll stop those career deputies. I do think it depends on the individual and the school. I think it's really hard to be able to say it should be one model or another model because I think different things will work in different schools and different sizes of school. It depends on the turnaround of staff. I think it will be dangerous if you had a head and a deputy who both started out in one school together and both of them just carried on because there wouldn't be that need for change.

Her colleague who was principal of quite a large elementary school found the idea intriguing but was also of two minds on the idea:

> I have split views on that. With my senior management team, the sort of four of us, I have a deputy and two assistant heads. Because my deputy head, I'm being very selfish, because my deputy head is absolutely wonderful and I couldn't do my work for the local authority without her, I've actually virtually priced her out of going for headship because financially it wouldn't be worth her while. So whereas I don't want her to move on, my assistant heads I do want to move on to either deputy

headship or headship. One of them will but one of them is not interested. And they frustrate me to hell because I don't think they should be assistant heads. So can you see I'm confused really? Because for my own selfish needs I don't want the deputy to move on but I do actually believe that deputies should be heads in waiting. So I do that through my assistant heads because I'm in such a big school I can do.

My own view, for what it is worth, is that instead of looking to move principals and heads on a cyclical basis, school systems should view all other leadership posts as training grounds for future promotion. From my observations of the three national situations, it would appear that career assistants have plugged the normal training pipeline. It may sound hard-hearted, but career assistants should move either up or out. Both directions may be difficult. With political will and determination, however, policy makers in all three countries can unblock the pipeline by accelerating incumbents' preparation for promotion such as has happened in Scotland, or finding a way for them to step down with dignity into alternative roles within the system. One starting point is to make all new appointments to assistant-type positions "acting," so that after three or four years a determination can be made by the person and the system whether he or she will move forward or return to a previous position with no penalty.

Succession Planning: Planned or Unplanned, Continuous or Discontinuous

In Chapter 4 I reported on four succession planning scenarios derived from our *Change Over Time?* study based on two dimensions of the leadership transition processes: were the changes planned or unplanned; and was the new leader expected to maintain continuity with the previous leader's directions or promote discontinuity by developing new objectives? In both the British and American cases, the school focus of selection and placement allowed for a clearly planned process and at least some notion of where the superintendent in the American case, and school governors in the British situation, wanted the school to go. In Ontario, most principals and vice principals had little or no idea why the board officials assigned them to a particular school, or if they had a mandate for change or were merely expected to build on their predecessor's record. The degree of planning and direction depended solely on the family of schools superintendent and how well he or she was tuned into the school.

What all three did share however was a serendipitous approach to the actual transition from one leader to another. It seems obvious to me that school districts need to articulate an entry process protocol that advises new leaders on who to talk to, what documents to review, and any other pertinent information that would help them learn their new context quickly. At the same time school authorities need to develop procedures that direct departing heads on what kinds of information they should make available to their successor. A pile of keys and some security codes does not a transition make. In addition, school jurisdictions should articulate some requirements for both the departing and arriving leaders to spend meaningful time together reviewing all aspects of the school. A group of principals and assistants (heads and deputies) could develop these approaches in very short order and make leadership succession a great deal more professional and seamless.

Timing of transitions is always a problem, and one that really must be addressed if departing and arriving leaders are to have the time to effect a smooth and inclusive transition. A practice of some schools and school jurisdictions is to hire new leaders a few months in advance of the departure of the old leader, and have the new person act as an assistant for a few months. This enables the staff to adjust to the new person and allows the arriving leader to get a good idea of what the school is about and some possible new directions to explore.

Timing is always important in a change process, and equally important is determining when to bring closure. Many years ago a group of my principal colleagues attended a conference workshop that was scheduled for an hour and a half. After 30 minutes the presenter folded up his materials and announced to his audience, "well I'm out of stuff," and walked out of the room. Ever after that in my old school board, my colleagues would often terminate a presentation with the infamous words, "I'm out of stuff." Well I'm out of stuff. The truth is that the topic is so broad and the literature on it seems to grow exponentially that there seems to be more and more stuff on leadership succession every day. I've included my e-mail in case you want to let me know about your stuff and critique my stuff.[19] You never know, I may get sufficiently inspired to do a second edition. Thanks for joining me on this journey and staying to the end.

Notes

1 Hargreaves, A. and Shirley, D. (2009) *The Fourth Way: The Inspiring Future for Educational Change*. Thousand Oaks, CA: Corwin.
2 Mintzberg, H. (2004) *Manager Not MBAs: A Hard Look at the Soft Practice of Managing and Management Development*. San Francisco, CA: Berrett-Koehler, p. 141.
3 Ibid., p. 141.

4   Ibid., p. 143.
5   Collins, J. (2009) *How the Mighty Fall: and Why Some Companies Never Give In*. New York: HarperCollins, p. 56.
6   For purposes of this book I have merely summarized what the reader can find in detail in Fink, D. (2005) op. cit.
7   Stoll, L., Fink, D. and Earl, L. (2003) op. cit., p. 103.
8   Hallinger, P. and Murphy, J. (1986) "The social context of effective schools", *American Journal of Education*, 94 (3): 328–55; Teddlie, C. and Stringfield, S. (1993) *Schools Make a Difference: Lessons Learned from a 10-year Study of School Effects*. New York: Teachers' College Press; Tyack, D. and Tobin, W. (1994) "The grammar of schooling: why has it been so hard to change?", *American Educational Research Journal*, 31 (3): 453–79; Fink, D. (2000) op. cit.
9   Hargreaves, A. (1998) "The emotional politics of teaching and teacher development: with implications for educational leadership", *International Journal for Leadership in Education*, 1 (4): 316–36.
10 Davies, B. and Ellison, L. (1999) *Strategic Development and Direction of the School*. London: Routledge.
11 Boris-Schacter, Sheryl (2007) "Got a minute? Can instructional leadership exist despite the reactive nature of the principalship?" http://www.acer.edu.au/ documents/RC2007_Boris-Schater-GotAMinutepdf, 3 August 2009, p. 25.
12 The Ontario testing scheme.
13 Williams, P. (2002) *Paradox of Power: A Transforming View of Leadership*. New York: Warner/Faith.
14 Hay Group (2007) *Rush to the Top: Accelerating the Development of Leaders in Public Services*. www.haygroup.co.uk, p. 3.
15 National College for School Leadership (2009) *Identify and Grow your Own Leaders: a Practical Guide and Case Studies*. http://www.ncsl.org.uk/identify-and-grow-your-own-leaders.pdf, 15 July 2009.
16 James, C. and Connolly, U. (2000) *Effective Change in Schools*. London: Routledge/ Falmer.
17 In many large British schools, the administrative team is often composed of a head and a deputy who have usually been chosen by the school governors, and one or more assistant heads, chosen by the head, who look after large administrative units and report to the head. Only the deputy can replace the head when the head is absent. In this system assistant heads would be easier to move than deputies.
18 *The Times Educational Supplement*.
19 My email is – deanfink@cogeco.ca.

Index

Leadership for Mortals
Developing and Sustaining Leaders of Learning

Dean Fink, *Educational Development Consultant, Ontario*

'It is a 'must read' for those in educational leadership roles in schools, both to gain invaluable insights and to draw on a framework for individual reflection' - *Professor Brent Davies, University of Hull*

`This book is a welcome antidote to the notion of school leaders as heroic figures. Dean Fink's commitment to enhancing the life chances of young people shines through the pages' - *Kate Myers, Times Educational Supplement*

This resource for prospective and practising school leaders:

- addresses the challenges of contemporary school leadership
- presents a model for leadership development, selection and succession
- challenges existing and prospective leaders to develop and live by a set of core values based on students' learning
- describes the intellectual 'tool kit' that leaders can develop
- describes the trajectories through which leaders proceed, and the 'learnings' required at each stage of the leaders evolution.

Contents:

Challenge / Commitment / Values / Qualities / Learnings / Trajectories / Succession

2005 · 192 pages
Paperback: 978-1-4129-0054-6
Hardback: 978-1-4129-0053-9

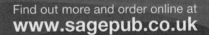

CORWIN
A SAGE Company

The Corwin logo – a raven striding across an open book – represents the union of courage and learning. Corwin is committed to improving education for all learners by publishing books and other professional development resources for those serving the field of PreK–12 education. By providing practical, hands-on materials, Corwin continues to carry out the promise of its motto: **"Helping Educators Do Their Work Better."**

O N T A R I O
P R I N C I P A L S'
C O U N C I L
Exemplary Leadership
in Public Education

The Ontario Principals' Council (OPC) is a voluntary professional association for principals and vice-principals in Ontario's public school system. We believe that exemplary leadership results in outstanding schools and improved student achievement. To this end, we foster quality leadership through world-class professional services and supports. As an ISO 9001 registered organization, we are committed to **"quality leadership – our principal product."**